THE SOCIAL PSYCHOLOGY OF TIME

SOME OTHER VOLUMES IN THE SAGE FOCUS EDITIONS

8. **Controversy (Second Edition)**
Dorothy Nelkin
21. **The Black Woman**
La Frances Rodgers-Rose
31. **Black Men**
Lawrence E. Gary
32. **Major Criminal Justice Systems (Second Edition)**
George F. Cole, Stanislaw J. Frankowski, and Marc G. Gertz
41. **Black Families**
Harriette Pipes McAdoo
50. **Cuba**
Jorge I. Dominguez
51. **Social Control**
Jack P. Gibbs
54. **Job Stress and Burnout**
Whiton Stewart Paine
57. **Social Structure and Network Analysis**
Peter V. Marsden and Nan Lin
58. **Socialist States in the World-System**
Christopher K. Chase-Dunn
59. **Age or Need?**
Bernice L. Neugarten
60. **The Costs of Evaluation**
Marvin C. Alkin and Lewis C. Solmon
63. **Organizational Theory and Public Policy**
Richard H. Hall and Robert E. Quinn
64. **Family Relationships in Later Life**
Timothy H. Brubaker
65. **Communication and Organizations**
Linda L. Putnam and Michael E. Pacanowsky
66. **Competence in Communication**
Robert N. Bostrom
67. **Avoiding Communication**
John A. Daly and James C. McCroskey
68. **Ethnography in Educational Evaluation**
David M. Fetterman
69. **Group Decision Making**
Walter C. Swap and Associates
70. **Children and Microcomputers**
Milton Chen and William Paisley
71. **The Language of Risk**
Dorothy Nelkin
72. **Black Children**
Harriette Pipes McAdoo and John Lewis McAdoo
73. **Industrial Democracy**
Warner Woodworth, Christopher Meek, and William Foote Whyte
74. **Grandparenthood**
Vern L. Bengtson and Joan F. Robertson
75. **Organizational Theory and Inquiry**
Yvonna S. Lincoln
76. **Men in Families**
Robert A. Lewis and Robert E. Salt
77. **Communication and Group Decision-Making**
Randy Y. Hirokawa and Marshall Scott Poole
78. **The Organization of Mental Health Services**
W. Richard Scott and Bruce L. Black
79. **Community Power**
Robert J. Waste
80. **Intimate Relationships**
Daniel Perlman and Steve Duck
81. **Children's Ethnic Socialization**
Jean S. Phinney and Mary Jane Rotheram
82. **Power Elites and Organizations**
G. William Domhoff and Thomas R. Dye
83. **Responsible Journalism**
Deni Elliott
84. **Ethnic Conflict**
Jerry Boucher, Dan Landis, and Karen Arnold Clark
85. **Aging, Health, and Family**
Timothy H. Brubaker
86. **Critical Issues in Aging Policy**
Edgar F. Borgatta and Rhonda J.V. Montgomery
87. **The Homeless in Contemporary Society**
Richard D. Bingham, Roy E. Green, and Sammis B. White
88. **Changing Men**
Michael S. Kimmel
89. **Popular Music and Communication**
James Lull
90. **Life Events and Psychological Functioning**
Lawrence H. Cohen
91. **The Social Psychology of Time**
Joseph E. McGrath
92. **Measurement of Intergenerational Relations**
David J. Mangen, Vern L. Bengtson, and Pierre H. Landry, Jr.
93. **Feminist Perspectives on Wife Abuse**
Kersti Yllö and Michele Bograd
94. **Common Problems/Proper Solutions**
J. Scott Long
95. **Falling from the Faith**
David G. Bromley
96. **Biosocial Perspectives on the Family**
Eric E. Filsinger
97. **Measuring the Information Society**
Frederick Williams
98. **Behavior Therapy and Religion**
William R. Miller and John E. Martin

THE SOCIAL PSYCHOLOGY OF TIME

New Perspectives

Edited by

Joseph E. McGrath

SAGE PUBLICATIONS
The Publishers of Professional Social Science
Newbury Park Beverly Hills London New Delhi

For information address:

SAGE Publications, Inc.
2111 West Hillcrest Drive
Newbury Park, California 91320

SAGE Publications Inc.
275 South Beverly Drive
Beverly Hills
California 90212

SAGE Publications Ltd.
28 Banner Street
London EC1Y 8QE
England

SAGE PUBLICATIONS India Pvt. Ltd.
M-32 Market
Greater Kailash I
New Delhi 110 048 India

Printed in the United States of America

Library of Congress Cataloging-in-Publication Data

Main entry under title:

The Social psychology of time.

(A Sage focus edition)
Bibliography: p.
1. Time—Social aspects. 2. Time—Psychological aspects. 3. Time perception. I. McGrath, Joseph Edward, 1927-
HM299.S585 1988 302 87-37700
ISBN 0-8039-2766-5
ISBN 0-8039-2767-3 (pbk.)

Contents

1

Introduction

The Place of Time in Social Psychology

JOSEPH E. McGRATH

Human lives unfold in time. All human activity has a temporal dimension, and all of it takes place in a temporal as well as a spatial context. Time, therefore, would seem to be a fundamental dimension of every field of the social and behavioral sciences, as it has been for most of the physical and biological sciences. But, in fact, time has been given remarkably little attention in social psychology, far less attention than its key role in human lives would seem to warrant.

The Neglect of Time in Social Psychological Research

There are some strong reasons for this neglect, some practical, some methodological, and some strategic. Time can enter social psychological research activities in several capacities: as a dimension of the behavior being studied, as a crucial feature of the study context, and as a basic parameter of the study design itself. On the practical side, it is difficult

AUTHOR'S NOTE: Research underlying this chapter was supported in part under National Science Foundation Grant BNS-06805 (J. E. McGrath, Principal Investigator).

and expensive to conduct studies that properly reckon with time in any of these capacities, let alone in all of them. Perhaps in part because of these practical considerations, we have failed to commit very much effort toward developing and using methods of study that would give adequate attention to time.

These practical and methodological problems, in turn, are related to (and some might say, derive from) some paradigmatic assumptions that underlie modern social psychology. By and large, social science, in general, and psychology and social psychology, in particular, have worked from an equilibrium-based research paradigm. That paradigm treats variation, conflict, and change as unintended and undesired perturbations in what are looked upon as essentially stable, harmonious, and equilibrium-seeking adaptive systems. This static orientation virtually *trivializes* the temporal features of the system under study, thereby eliminating any need to resolve the practical and methodological barriers to the study of time. It has proven to be much easier to define time out of our problems than to study the myriad temporal features of those problems.

The Many Functional Roles of Time in Research

Yet, in spite of our neglect of time, temporal matters permeate the phenomena of our field. Time plays several important roles in social psychological phenomena. There are important temporal aspects of our theoretical concepts and relations. There are crucial temporal issues in our methodology. And above all, there are many critical temporal features of the substantive phenomena in our field.

Matters of time enter social psychological research in at least three functional capacities. Time can play the role of independent variable. This function can be expressed as the role of temporal factors in various social psychological phenomena. Time can also be the dependent variable of interest. This function can be expressed as the effect of various social psychological factors on the perception, experience, and use of time. Furthermore, time enters all research as a key methodological factor. There are important temporal features of research strategies, study designs, threats to validity, and measurement techniques; and time plays a crucial conceptual role in the causal logic of our research paradigm.

Modern social psychology operates at each of several system levels, and temporal factors play an important part at each of those levels. At the level of the individual, human life is played out on a temporal as well as a spatial stage. There are important cultural, subcultural, and individual differences in temporal orientations and perceptions, in the experience of time, in the tempo or pace of life, and in the allocation and use of time across multiple potential activities. At the interpersonal level, many aspects of social interactions are marked by interpersonal synchronization of rhythms of behavior and recurrent cycles of development and socialization. At more macro-system levels—formal organizations, complex behavior settings, and sociocultural level systems—many critical problems center on key temporal issues such as temporal uncertainty, temporal conflict, and the inherent scarcity of time.

This book is about time in all of those capacities.

Some Treatments of Time

A focus on the overall neglect of temporal matters in our field ought not blind us to the areas in which temporal factors have been given considerable attention. For one thing, although there has been extreme neglect of temporal factors in social psychology, some related fields have done much better in that regard. There is a considerable literature on time in the life sciences (see Moore-Ede, Sulzman, & Fuller, 1982, for a good review of the material dealing with circadian rhythms). Time is a matter of long-standing concern in philosophy (see Heath, 1956), and a set of unresolved issues in that field can be a focus for analysis in social psychology as well (see McGrath & Kelly, 1986). There is some literature on time in other social sciences, especially sociology and anthropology. Furthermore, there is a substantial body of research on time in several very specific areas of psychology. In biological psychology, temporal factors have been studied in relation to circadian rhythms, hormonal excretions, temperature regulation, and other processes (see Brown & Graeber, 1982; Satinoff, 1978). In experimental psychology, there has been a vast literature throughout this century on judgments of the passage of time. (For relatively recent integrations of that work, see Ornstein, 1969; Fraisse, 1963, 1984; and especially Doob, 1971.) More recently, there is a growing literature on temporal perspective and related concepts. (See, for example, the work of Cottle, 1967, and the excellent recent work of Nuttin, 1985, and colleagues.) In the area of human factors, temporal matters have been of importance in studies of attention, distraction, and other threats to effective individual task performance. (See, for example, Folkard, 1982; Wever, 1982; Wilkinson, 1982.) In clinical psychology, time has been the focus of study most notably in regard to the psychopathology of time perception (see Doob, 1971, for an interesting review of much of that work as well). More recently, temporal factors have played a major part in psychopathological research on such topics as circadian rhythms, the sleep-wake cycle, depression and mania, and the time-urgency aspect of stress-related type A syndrome. (See, for example, Burnam, Pennebaker, & Glass, 1975; Cohen, 1978; Friedman & Rosenman, 1974; Gastorf, 1980; Poirel, 1982; Wehr, 1982.)

With such attention to temporal factors in so many surrounding areas, the stark absence of research on time within mainstream social psychology is all the more remarkable. This glaring discrepancy—between how important and ubiquitous temporal factors appear to be in social psychological phenomena, on the one hand, and on the other hand, how little research and discussion of temporal matters there has been within social psychology—has not gone entirely unnoticed. There have been at least two very recent treatments of time and social psychology that should be noted here. One is a contributed volume edited by Gergen and Gergen (1984) which offers sharp criticism of the currently dominant research paradigm in social psychology. The editors and contributors to that volume urge the development of a "historical social psychology" that is attuned to the temporal or historical context of behavior. They make some beginning contributions to such a scholarly attainment, and, above all, point up the importance of giving attention, within social psychology, to the dynamics of change over time.

The other is a recent monograph by McGrath and Kelly (1986) that argues for development of a full-fledged social psychology of time. Those authors draw on the literature of the philosophy of time to present an analysis of a variety of cultural and subcultural conceptions of time. They then examine how such conflicting conceptions of time play into day-to-day living, and how some of the evidence in the time research area can be accounted for by such conflicting conceptions. McGrath and Kelly also present evidence of social entrainment effects (analogous to the biological entrainment effects found in research on circadian and other rhythms). These social entrainment effects operate at individual and interpersonal levels, as well as for more macro focal units. McGrath

& Kelly also examine a number of the temporal issues that are embedded in the research methodology of our field.

This volume aims to add to those two major critiques and, especially, to build on the latter in its attempt to show the scope and shape of a full-fledged social psychology of time.

An Organizing Schema

The main body of this book is organized in a complex pattern that reflects at least four features of the material. That pattern of organization is shown in Table 1.1. It involves (a) which (of five) temporal facets is emphasized, (b) what size social unit is emphasized, (c) at what temporal scale the phenomena involved are, and (d) whether the material emphasizes a perspective that is "internal" or "external" with respect to the focal social unit.

Regarding the first of these: The ten main chapters of this book are presented in pairs. Each pair addresses one of five temporal facets, in the following order: the *pace* of behavior in everyday life; the coordination of *rhythms* of behavior in interaction; the *allocation*, use, and enjoyment of time; *developmental cycles* in social systems; and *continuity and change* processes in complex social systems. As Table 1.1 shows, each pair of chapters deals with one of those five temporal facets, in the order listed above.

Those pairs of chapters are ordered in a sequence that generally reflects a progression in the size or scope of the social units involved, from micro to macro level. The focal social unit emphasized in those five pairs of chapters range, respectively, from a concern with individual behavior in a cultural context (in the pace section), to a focus on interaction of dyads in performance settings (in the section on rhythms), to evaluating behavioral preferences in social settings (in the section on time allocation), to analyzing the life cycles of small social systems (in the section on developmental cycles), to the description of continuity and change processes in complex social systems (in the section on continuity and change).

The material included under each of these five temporal facets, dealing with five progressively larger sized social units, at the same time emphasizes phenomena at progressively larger levels of *temporal scale*. This is, in effect, a sixth temporal facet (one stressed in the Werner et al. chapter). The chapters dealing with pace are dealing in temporal patterns at the level of subseconds and seconds. The material on

TABLE 1.1
Multifacet Organization of the Book

Temporal Facet	*Level of Social Unit*	**Perspective* Internal	External	*Scale*
Pace of life	Individual in a cultural context	Jones	R. Levine	subseconds/ seconds
Rhythms of behavior	Dyadic and small group	Warner	Kelly	seconds/ minutes
Allocation and enjoyment	Individual in social setting	Freedman/ Edwards	Robinson	minutes/ hours
Developmental cycles	Small social systems	Moreland/ J. Levine	Wicker/ King	hours/days/ weeks
Continuity and change processes	Larger social systems	Werner et al.	Stokols	weeks/ months/ years

*An *internal perspective* means that the chapter gives primary attention to processes internal to the unit that is being focused upon (e.g., individual, dyads, and so on). An *external perspective* means that the chapter gives primary attention to relations between the focal unit and its embedding context (e.g., dyad in a task performance context, small group in an organizational context, and so on).

rhythms is concerned with patterns involving seconds and minutes. The allocation emphasis is concerned with activities lasting minutes and hours. The chapters on developmental cycles are concerned with behavior phenomena that involve temporal scales of hours, days, and weeks. Finally, the chapters dealing with continuity and change processes involve temporal periods of weeks, months, and years.

Aside from these features distinguishing the five pairs of chapters from one another (a given temporal facet, social unit, and temporal scale), the two chapters within each pair differ from each other in the perspective taken. The first chapter in each pair takes as its perspective (more or less) an experiential view from a point of reference internal to the social unit involved—an individual, a dyad, a small or large social system. The second chapter in each pair takes as its perspective (more or less) an external view of the behavior of that social unit in relation to its context—the individual behaving in a cultural setting; a dyad performing an assigned task; and so on.

The Five Temporal Facets

The five temporal facets are distinct enough so that they can be used to organize the sequence of chapters in this book, and they could also be used to organize a lot of material in the literature on the social psychology of time. Yet there are many interconnections among them, both at the general conceptual level and in the concrete instances of the chapters in this volume. Some of those distinctions and connections are noted in the rest of this section.

The Pace of Everyday Life

In the section on pace, James Jones argues that certain subcultures—specifically, Afro-Americans—may move to a different temporal beat in many ways, and that these play intimately into everyday life. Specifically, Jones argues that differences in temporal perceptions and experience are crucial aspects of what differentiates the life experiences of Afro-Americans from those of "mainstream" White Americans. Robert Levine documents the different paces at which the lives of people in different cultures unfold, and traces some of the concomitants of those tempo differences. Pace is dealt with in other sections as well. Werner, Haggard, Altman, and Oxley incorporate aspects of pace within their transactional comparison of two traditions. Pace is at least implicit in many parts of R. Moreland and J. Levine's analysis of group development and member socialization, as well as in the task performance of individuals and groups as studied by Freedman and Edwards and by Kelly.

Rhythms in Behavior

In the section on rhythms, Rebecca Warner and Janice Kelly both deal with the synchronization of behavior across individuals. Warner presents strong evidence for synchronization (i.e., the coordination of phase and periodicity) of the speech behavior of the members of interacting dyads. Kelly deals with patterns of entrainment—that is, synchronization of phase and periodicity—in the rate and quality of individual and group task performance, and in the patterning of their interactions. She presents evidence that the work rates, work quality, and interpersonal interaction patterns of individuals and small groups become entrained to outside pacers such as time limits. Rhythm is important in the chapters of other sections too. Rhythms are an important issue in the Werner, Haggard, Altman, and Oxley analysis of traditions. They are a part of Wicker and King's conception of the life cycles of behavior settings. Rhythms are also involved in R. Levine's as well as Jones's treatments of the flow of everyday life in different cultures and subcultures.

Time Allocation and Enjoyment

The third section, on allocation, use, and enjoyment of time, is not as integrated a section as the others. Both chapters of that section deal with how individuals distribute time among activities under conditions of time scarcity, and with the levels of satisfaction or enjoyment that they derive from those activities. In the first of that pair of chapters, Jonathan Freedman and Donald Edwards report studies in which tasks were done under time pressure, and examine the levels of both task performance and psychological reactions (e.g., boredom, enjoyment, and so on) that resulted from those activities. Freedman and Edwards interpret those studies within a broad conceptualization that emphasizes both the positive and the negative aspects of time pressure or time scarcity on individual performance and psychological experiences. In the second chapter of that section, John Robinson reviews a number of large sample surveys that have used "time diary" methods to explore how people allocate their time across activities and the consequent involvement with and enjoyment of those activities. Robinson examines how social scientists can measure such allocations, and summarizes some of the major findings of that work. The two chapters complement each other nicely. Robinson deals with how people allocate their time across activities, and how much they enjoy those activities, when they are acting in everyday circumstances and are therefore more or less free to choose how to use their time (or at least are not constrained by an arbitrary experimenter). Freedman and Edwards deal not with how people allocate their own time when they are free to choose, but rather with how people react to having arbitrary task performance time limits imposed on them from external sources. The question of allocation of time arises in other sections as well. Allocation is an important issue underlying the ideas of Wicker and King about behavior settings, and of Moreland and Levine about development of and socialization within groups. Issues involving time scarcity are important in Jones's treatment of the subcultural group on which he focuses, and in Kelly's consideration of rate and quality of task performance.

Developmental Cycles

The fourth section is on *cycles* that mark stages of development in groups and in behavior settings. In the first chapter of that pair, Richard Moreland and John Levine provide a systematic formulation of a temporally ordered set of stages of group development, and a parallel set of stages of the socialization of individual members within the group. They then draw out some of the implications of those two conceptualizations when the development and socialization processes are considered together. In the second chapter of this pair, Allan Wicker and Jeanne King present a detailed analysis of the life cycles of behavior settings. They trace the temporal phases in the development, operation, and demise of behavior settings. Cycles of development are dealt with in other sections too. The analysis of tradition by Werner et al. incorporates a number of cyclical processes, as does Stokols's transformational perspective and Jones's TRIOS concept.

Continuity and Change

The fifth section contains two chapters that deal with *continuity and change* processes in complex social systems. In the first chapter of that pair, Carol Werner, Lois Haggard, Irwin Altman, and Diana Oxley provide an analysis of cultural ritual and celebration from a transactional perspective. In the second chapter of the pair, Daniel Stokols explores transformational processes by which person-environment relations change. Both the Werner et al. chapter and the Stokols chapter emphasize that continuity and change processes are fundamental, not epiphenomenal, in human life. And both focus on the dynamic nature of the person-environment relations that are at the heart of a social psychology of everyday life. Change and continuity is dealt with in other sections as well. Change processes are implicit in the idea of synchronization or entrainment in the work of Warner and of Kelly. The study of change over time is central to Robinson's review of time diary evidence. The twin ideas of continuity and change are vital to the developmental ideas of Moreland and Levine as well as to the stages of Wicker and King's model of behavior settings. Cultural change and conflict underlie the conceptions of both R. Levine and Jones about the pace of everyday life.

Conclusion

The book ends with a final chapter in which McGrath tries to draw out some of the integrative themes of the main chapters of the book, and to set an agenda for future research that will build toward a social psychology of time.

REFERENCES

Brown, F. M., & Graeber, R. C. (Eds.). (1982). *Rhythmic aspects of behavior.* Hillsdale, NJ: Lawrence Erlbaum.

Burnam, M., Pennebaker, J., & Glass, D. (1975). Time-consciousness, achievement striving and the type A coronary-prone behavior pattern. *Journal of Abnormal Psychology, 84*, 76-79.

Cohen, J. B. (1978). The influence of culture on coronary-prone behavior. In T. Denbroski, S. Weis, J. Shields, S. Haynes, & M. Feinleib (Eds.), *Coronary prone behavior.* New York: Springer-Verlag.

Cottle, T. J. (1967). The circles test: An investigation of temporal relatedness and dominance. *Journal of Projective Techniques and Personality Assessment, 31*, 58-71.

Doob, L. W. (1971). *Patterning of time.* New Haven, CT: Yale University Press.

Folkard, S. (1982). Circadian rhythms and human memory. In F. M. Brown & R. C. Graeber (Eds.), *Rhythmic aspects of behavior.* Hillsdale, NJ: Lawrence Erlbaum.

Fraisse, P. (1963). *The psychology of time.* New York: Harper & Row.

Fraisse, P. (1984). Perceptions and estimation of time. *Annual Review of Psychology, 35*, 1-36.

Friedman, A. P., & Rosenman, R. H. (1974). *Type A behavior and your heart.* New York: Knopf.

Gastorf, J. W. (1980). Time urgency of the type A behavior pattern. *Journal of Consulting & Clinical Psychology, 48*, 299.

Gergen, K., & Gergen, M. (Eds.). (1984). *Historical social psychology.* Hillsdale, NJ: Lawrence Erlbaum.

Heath, L. R. (1956). *The concept of time.* Chicago: University of Chicago Press.

McGrath, J. E., & Kelly, J. R. (1986). *Time and human interaction: Toward a social psychology of time.* New York: Guilford.

Moore-Ede, M. C., Sulzman, F. M., & Fuller, C. A. (1982). *The clocks that time us.* Cambridge, MA: Harvard University Press.

Nuttin, J. (1985). *Future time perspective and motivation: Theory and research method.* Hillsdale, NJ: Leuven University Press and Lawrence Erlbaum.

Ornstein, R. E. (1969). *On the experience of time.* Middlesex, England: Penguin.

Poirel, C. (1982). Circadian rhythms in behavior and experimental psychopathology. In F. M. Brown & R. C. Graeber (Eds.), *Rhythmic aspects of behavior.* Hillsdale, NJ: Lawrence Erlbaum.

Satinoff, E. (1978). Neural organization and evolution of thermal regulation in mammals. *Science, 201*, 16-22.

Wehr, T. A:. (1982). Circadian rhythm disturbances in depression and mania. In F. M. Brown & R. C. Graeber (Eds.), *Rhythmic aspects of behavior*. Hillsdale, NJ: Lawrence Erlbaum.

Wever, R. A. (1982). Behavioral aspects of circadian rhythmicity. In F. M. Brown & R. C. Graeber (Eds.), *Rhythmic aspects of behavior*. Hillsdale, NJ: Lawrence Erlbaum.

Wilkinson, R. T. (1982) The relationship between body temperature and performance across circadian phase shifts. In F. M. Brown & R. C. Graeber (Eds.), *Rhythmic aspects of behavior*. Hillsdale, NJ: Lawrence Erlbaum.

PART I

Pace

2

Cultural Differences in Temporal Perspectives

Instrumental and Expressive Behaviors in Time

JAMES M. JONES

All human events occur *in time*. But the character of those events and the time in which they occur vary widely from person to person, from culture to culture. While most social scientists who consider time in relation to culture see it as an aspect of culture, Hall (1983) goes further to assert that time is culture. On this grand note, one might revise the Cartesian criterion for being thus: *Tempus Fugit, ergo, sum!*

It is always provocative to discuss ways in which different cultures approach time. While a temporal unit may be as precise as chronometric capability allows in one culture, in another culture, it may be as general, but nevertheless practical, as "the time it takes a pot of water to boil." Studies of cultural differences in pace of life (Levine & Bartlett, 1984) present interesting data on the speed with which life is transacted, as well as how time is reckoned and time-relevant behaviors judged. For example, in Brazil, in contrast to the United States, one has to arrive significantly later than the appointed hour in order to consider oneself late (Levine, West, & Reis, 1980; see also Chapter 3, this volume).

In views like those of Hall, Levine, and colleagues, to talk about differences in time perspective is more fundamental than talking about cultural or individual idiosyncrasies. It may well be that differences in time perspective are the essence of individual and cultural differences. In the present chapter, I take the view that time perspective is an essential characteristic of culture, and that relevant cultural comparisons follow from it, rather than precede it.

Furthermore, I am going to focus attention on one aspect of culture that bears an important relationship to temporal perspective—*goal-directed behavior*. In keeping with the preceding viewpoint, I will assume that goal-directed behavior *follows from* temporal perspective, rather than vice versa.

Problems of racial/cultural differences in the United States can be seen from this time/culture/goal-direction perspective. In earlier work (Jones, 1972), I introduced the notion of cultural racism to account for a situation in which mutual interdependence between people from substantially different cultural backgrounds led to behavioral outcomes that were heavily influenced by a power asymmetry favoring Whites of European descent over Blacks of African descent. I here assert that the central feature around which these cultural differences are organized is the underlying time perspectives (Jones, in press).

Finally, I will argue that the rapprochement of these cultural divergences is the rapprochement of temporal perspectives. Over time, the symbiotic interaction of Blacks and Whites, as well as other ethnic/racial groups in this increasingly multiethnic society, results in a widening of the time perspective that influences members of each group. The widening of temporal perspective is a pragmatic consequence of population diversity and, in extended form, is represented by the concepts of *biculturalism* (Jones, 1985) or, more broadly, *multiculturalism* (Triandis, 1976).

Cultural Differences in Time Perspective

Achievement Orientation: Goal Setting and the Future

There are a variety of legacies that have driven the development of the United States, but the one perhaps most widely acknowledged is the rugged individualism associated with the Protestant ethic of the pioneer immigrants from Western Europe. It is this ethic that gives rise to the most characteristic quality of this country, its high level of achievement (McClelland, 1961).

Achievement is defined generally in terms of successful goal-directed behavior. People set goals, then adopt strategies and behaviors intended to attain those goals. Goals typically are to be met at some point in the future, and behaviors carried out in the present are *expected* to increase the probability of reaching the goals. Thus achievement is related to goal setting and attainment, both of which are set in future time. Viewed in these terms, future time perspective is a cognitive process that is a necessary condition for achievement (Nuttin, 1985).

To sustain this future time perspective over extended periods of time, one must believe that there is in fact a high probability that present actions increase the probability of reaching future goals. DeVolder and Lens (1982) found that high school boys in Belgium who had higher GPAs believed in a stronger relation between present actions and future outcomes that did students with lower GPAs. Moreover, these same (high GPA) students articulated goals that could be located in the more distant future, compared to the goals articulated by students with lower GPAs.

Similar results have been obtained when comparing students who vary in need achievement and the perceived instrumentality of college academic performance for future career success (Nisan, 1972; Raynor, 1970; Raynor & Entin, 1982). In another study (Raynor & Rubin, 1971), college students were given a series of tests under two conditions: (a) contingent performance—where success on a test was a precondition for continuing with subsequent tests; and (b) noncontingent performance—where working on any test was independent of prior success or failure.

All students were led to expect a .5 likelihood of success on the tests. Raynor and Rubin found that students high in achievement motivation performed worse under the contingent instructions, compared to the noncontingent instructions.

A future time perspective, therefore, seems to be a function of two things:

(1) strength of the belief in the conditional probability that if a specific act (say, studying hard) is performed in the present, the probability of some future goal state (say, getting a good job and having a successful career) will be greater; and
(2) strength of the tendency to value goals whose attainment can only occur in the future.

If these two tendencies are critical to future time perspective, and if future time perspective is critical to success in this achieving society, it is important to consider the experiences that are likely to produce these tendencies.

Consider the first of these two tendencies. Historically, growing up Black in the United States has meant receiving a lot of disconfirming evidence about the conditional probability that present action will alter future outcomes. For Blacks in America, getting good grades by studying hard has often not been reinforced with the prospect of thereafter getting better jobs. Institutional racism severs this connection and reduces the extent to which it is practical for Black Americans to believe in the present action-future outcome contingency that underlies a future time perspective. This is not to imply that Blacks have no sense of control over their lives. Rather, the reality of institutional racism requires a more complicated set of strategies for gaining a measure of control when routine correlations between effort and outcome do not obtain. One way in which control is obtained is via the creative use of available economic, political, and social systems—or improvisation (Jones, 1979). While the outcome of improvising connections between present behaviors and future outcomes may be successful, it also has the feature of focusing attention on the present. This tendency further enhances the present orientation of many Black Americans.

The second tendency implies that an emphasis on, and greater value of, *distal* goals is a characteristic of future time perspective. In support of this implication, I would argue that during cultural evolution, different ecological requirements placed specific demands on temporal perspective. Those cultures that evolved in mild climates in general were not required to consider future goals in the formulation of present activities. The year-round availability of sustaining goods, and the general absence of threatening environmental changes, permitted a focus on *proximal* goals that could be satisfied in the present or relatively near future. In contrast, inclement climates placed future considerations at the forefront of adaptability and survival. It would not be surprising, therefore, that successfully surviving in such circumstances would lead to placing a high value on successful planning that takes the future into account.

The second tendency, therefore, distinguishes between the distal goals of a future time perspective (FTP) and the proximal goals of an alternative present time perspective (PTP). To the extent that U.S. society has evolved in a cultural legacy in which distal goal attainment is at the forefront of achievement, and achievement is at the forefront of its dominant ethic (i.e., a future time perspective), descendants of any culture with a present time perspective, with its focus on proximal goals, are at a marked disadvantage in adapting to the dominant culture's interpretation and utilization of time.

Any Time is Trinidad Time

In the early 1970s, while I was conducting field research on the humor of calypso and carnival in Trinidad (Jones & Liverpool, 1976), I learned of the expression "any time is Trinidad time." It is apropos of this discussion that the original work on delay of gratification (Mischel, 1958) was conducted in Trinidad. That work, as is well known, showed that Trinidadians of African descent, compared to Trinidadians of East Indian descent, were significantly more likely to accept a small reward when offered than a larger reward promised for a week later. Researchers sought to explain this general finding in terms of what was conceived as an *inability* of these Black Trinidadians to delay gratification.

This "inability" was associated with higher instances of social deviance and lower levels of achievement motivation (Mischel, 1961a, 1961b). In contrast, results of my research suggested that the so-called inability to delay gratification was based on a present time perspective that rejected both of the premises of the future time perspective that were discussed above. That present time perspective, instead, suggested two different premises:

(1) The present time perspective supports the idea that the probability of achieving a distal goal is no greater as a result of present behaviors than it would be as a result of future behaviors initiated when the goal becomes more proximal. This might be recognized as characteristic of the *mañana* cultures. Never do today what you can put off until tomorrow. If putting off until tomorrow does not materially alter the probability of successful goal attainment, there is little reinforcement for anticipatory goal behavior.

(2) In the present time perspective, it was quite clear that proximal goals were more important than distal ones. In some cultures it is a generally held value that enjoying today is more important than worrying about enjoying tomorrow. Thus the larger candy bar that is available next week is *not* more desirable because value is attached to those real events that occur now.

These ideas and arguments suggest the possibility that cultural/racial differences in social behavior derive in part from different perspectives on goal behavior, which in turn derive from different temporal perspectives. I am here arguing that *temporal perspective drives goal setting and the values placed thereon, not the other way around.* To make more sense of this claim, we need to look in more depth at the basic concept of temporal perspective.

Comparison of Temporal Perspectives: Future and Present

We can distinguish between time as a structured, unitized measure of the sequence of unfolding events, *compelled toward some distant outcome*, and time as the backdrop for behaviors, thoughts, and feelings. The former is a conception of action that occurs within a time that flows linearly, inexorably, and necessarily forward. It is a perspective that is strongly guided by the future. The latter is a feeling of behavior that occurs *in-time*, where time consciousness is suspended and action occurs in the infinite present (Ornstein, 1977).

I believe that these extremely different ways of perceiving, coping, feeling, and behaving can be conceptualized within a scale of future time perspective and present time perspective. I further argue that the phenomenal worlds that correspond to these different perspectives are different in significant ways, and that individuals may themselves move back and forth between these worlds. What may distinguish among individuals and among groups is the value placed on each of these two "modes of being," and the relative amount of time spent in each world.

Many scholars have proposed conceptions of time that include a similar opposition. Hall (1983) distinguished monochronic (M-time) from polychronic (P-time) time. M-time is a pattern of sequential behavior governed by schedules, against which success and failure are measured. P-time is a pattern of simultaneity, a moment-in-time that stresses involvement with people and completion of transactions. For Hall, M-time requires sequential processing of one thing at a time, whereas P-time often involves simultaneous processing of several things at once.

Ornstein (1977) distinguishes between linear time characterized by sequentiality and casual inference, and nonlinear time, characterized by simultaneity and patterned wholes. The former is monitored by clocks and involves cognitive constructions of temporal intervals and cause-effect sequences. The latter is a form of timelessness that is centered in the present and is relatively unresponsive to the future.

Melges (1982) makes a basic distinction (in a Freudian vein) between the time-bound sequentiality of consciousness and the timelessness of unconscious processes. He further argues that "disorders of psychological time, such as disturbances in rate, sequence, and temporal perspective, may be involved in the disorganized thinking and misconstrued expectations of a variety of psychiatric syndromes" (pp. 3-4). Melges suggests that timelessness is characteristic of the unconscious, involves "primary process," and is characterized by dreams or dreamlike states. "Normal" time is characterized by sequential relations of past, present, and future and involves prediction, reasoned logic, and "secondary process." Melges considers a third form of temporal experience, similar to Ornstein's nonlinear form, that involves "tertiary processing" of simultaneous holistic patterns, and that is characteristic of metaphorical thinking. For Melges, it is the imposition of a timelessness mode characteristic of the unconscious on a ("normal") sequential-linear world that is associated with several varieties of psychopathology.

Lauer (1981) distinguished "social time" from "clock time." Clock time is an objective, external nonsocial referent for the unfolding of behavior. In its extreme use, it defines linear time as a succession of seconds, where a second is measured by 1,192,631,700 cycles of the frequency associated with the transition between two energy levels of the isotope cesium 133. By contrast, social time "refers to the patterns and orientations that relate to social processes and to the conceptualization of the ordering of social life" (p. 21). Social time grows out of social relations and behavior and is influenced by the histories, feelings, beliefs, and desires of people. Social time, like P-time and nonlinear time, is functional, nondirectional, and present oriented. Societies in which social time is based on the ordering of clock time will be characterized by linear, structural features, whereas societies in which social time is based on the interpersonal, social psychological orderings of its inhabitants will be characterized by its polychronic, nonlinear features.

Thus a number of scholars have argued that people and groups differ in real and meaningful ways with respect to their time perspectives. Furthermore, when people or groups with different perspectives interact, conflicts often arise. Misunderstandings occur when intention and action are judged, by different participants, on different temporal scales. Values are attached to these scales. The differences in temporal perspective often go unrecognized by the participants. But the differing temporal scales have values associated with them nonetheless, and the temporally divergent actions lead to value inferences by the participants about each other. For example, a person who is late (lateness being a clock time or linear time construal of events) is judged to be indifferent, unreliable, lazy, or stupid.

A future time perspective is the basic formulation for construal of events in what Hall (1983) calls AE (i.e., American-European) culture. And it seems, in general, that judgments of character based on time-relevant behaviors are more common to persons who hold a future time perspective. That is, people who see time as units of value seem to be offended by people whom they perceive to waste it or be indifferent to it. People who see the extended present as the unit of personal expression, however, seem less concerned with people who are influenced by future time considerations.

It is important to note, however, that the positivity associated with features of both future time perspective and present time perspective are relative to the cultures and subcultures within which those perspectives are found, and the valence associated with particular behaviors can be reversed when those behaviors are viewed from a different perspective. Behavior that fits a future time perspective is generally regarded as uptight and misplaced in Trinidad and Micronesia. Behavior that fits a present time perspective is regarded as unproductive and indulgent in the United States. Moreover, there are negative as well as positive features associated with each perspective even when viewed within its own "natural" cultural locus. A future time perspective not only can produce type A behaviors with associated health risks for the individual, but also extreme individualistic (hence antisocial) patterns of behavior as well. People who are centered in a present time perspective may lack ambition and feel apathetic about the future, not only for themselves but for other people as well. Thus both perspectives harbor potentially negative and even destructive possibilities.

But in our AE culture, the portrayal of time perspectives within the literature of both our scientific and our lay culture has been one-sided. The positive attributes and overtones of the FTP have been paired with the negative attributes and overtones of the PTP. The present time perspective is portrayed as a deficiency of character and/or capacity, whereas the future time perspective has been presented simply as the "right" way to view the world. In fact, what people need to function well in our complex world is a blend of the best characteristics of each perspective within an integrated functional whole.

Time Perspectives as Complementary

We all move in and out of present and future time perspective. For most people, workdays involve linear sequences of goal setting and attainment. Evenings and weekends may also involve some degree of goal setting, goal attainment, and future time perspective, but generally they permit more engagement of a present time perspective and more enacting of behaviors that are themselves "goals." Individuals who are rigidly locked into one or the other perspective will encounter difficulties.

Our worlds are complex. Achievement is often a prerequisite for enjoyment. One strong cultural norm states that people should work first and then play ("business before pleasure"). *Work* might be defined as actions that lead to goal attainment. *Play*, then, can be viewed as actions that are themselves goals. That is, play is doing what you *want to do* (Lepper, Greene, & Nisbett, 1973). If the reward is in the goal, then work presupposes the belief that rewards come later, whereas play presupposes the belief that rewards are to be reaped now.

But future and present goal attainment, work and play, are not mutually exclusive. Future goals may be the cumulative results of a series of actions driven by a present time perspective. For example, daily running may be both immediately rewarding and cumulatively health-promoting. Conversely, people often enjoy the concentrated efforts that lead to goal attainment. That is, one's work can come to have intrinsic value, even though it is goal directed. Such efforts and enjoyment occur as though they were a part of a present time perspective.

The point is that, even in a society dominated by a future time perspective with a Protestant work ethic, the future and present time perspectives merge, overlap, and are functionally intertwined, rather than being mutually exclusive opposites. We have studied one of them, the future time perspective, much more than we have the other, however, and we yet know little about the other, the present time perspective.

Of course, all behaviors take place in the present. But, as Nuttin (1985) has pointed out, cognitions about the future (and about the past) can play a major role in determining which behaviors will be performed and how. "Time perspective is the temporal zone to which one's mental view virtually extends itself when considering the objects and conscious determinants of behavior" (Nuttin, 1985, p. 21). Objects and outcomes are "located" in temporal zones via cognitive representations. The FTP reflects localization of objects and goals in the extended or distant future. The PTP, by contrast, reflects localization of objects and goals in the present. For Nuttin, goals localized in the distant future can affect present behavior only if there is a *temporal integration* that makes the future continuous with the present, and *internal causal attributions* that recognize personal control in achieving outcomes. Such integration and attributions are therefore necessary conditions for sustaining an FTP.

Most research on time perspective has sought (a) to measure individual's perspectives by locating self-referent cognitions in the past, present, or future, and (b) to identify those behaviors, attitudes, and feelings associated with past, present, and future perspectives. Such research has generally shown that more future-oriented perspectives are associated with more positive or desirable behavioral outcomes. For example, as previously discussed, Dutch-speaking Belgian boys aged 17 and 18, who believed that studying hard was instrumental for reaching goals in the distant future, who placed greater value on studying hard, and who did in fact have more persistent study habits (in short, boys that had a FTP), also had higher GPAs (DeVolder & Lens, 1982). In a somewhat different line of inquiry, Rappaport, Enrich, and Wilson (1985) explored ego identity and personal crisis in relation to time perspective. They divided a population of male undergraduates into four categories: those who had made a commitment to a given ego identity, some of whom did so while responding to a crisis (identity achievement category) and some of whom did so without a crisis (foreclosure category); and those who had yet to become committed to an ego identity, either in relation to a crisis (moratorium category) or without a crisis (identity diffusion category). They found that the boys who were committed to an ego identity, with or without a crisis, were significantly more future time oriented than boys who were not yet committed to an ego identity with or without a crisis. Thus, it seems, commitment to a personal future not only guides the nature of present behavior, but is linked to an overall future time orientation.

Research, however, has also found that, when ecological circumstances make an FTP inappropriate, results are reversed in that positive outcomes are associated with a PTP. For example, Bochner and David (1967) found that Aboriginal Australian children who were present oriented (by delay of gratification type measures) had higher IQs than did those children who showed a future orientation. One interpretation of those results is that the uncertainty of the future was *correctly* viewed with distrust by the more intelligent children. In another vein, Zimbardo, Marshall, and Maslach (1971) used hypnosis to induce a present time perspective. Control subjects included those with normal time perspectives, and those who were instructed to role-play being in an expanded-present time frame. Subjects operating in an induced "expanded present," compared to the control subjects, showed more intense affective reactions to obscene humorous material, a more intense and focused involvement with a creative clay sculpting task, and more indifference to the messiness of the clay and the experimenter's instructions to stop playing. This focus on the present seems to heighten affective reactions to ongoing activities, in part by reducing attention to abstractions (values, norms, and so on) whose meaning is salient beyond the immediate experiential context.

Thus both within the same culture and between cultures and subcultures, people vary in the extent to which the cognitions they hold about activities, goals, and outcomes that guide their ongoing behavior are localized in the distant future or in the present. Furthermore, ecological and cultural conditions vary such that either a future time perspective or a present time perspective can be associated with the major positive outcomes available in that setting. Finally, cultures, subcultures, and particular groups differ in their fundamental temporal perspectives, hence in their attitudes, values, and associated behaviors. It is to these latter subcultural differences, especially in regard to the role of temporal perspective in Black culture, to which I now turn.

TRIOS: The Role of Time in Black Culture

TRIOS is an acronym standing for five dimensions of human experience: time, rhythm, improvisation, oral expression, and spirituality. I developed the concepts in relation to an analysis of racial differences in sports performance (Jones & Hochner, 1973), African religion and philosophy (Jones, 1972; Mbiti, 1970), Trinidadian culture (Jones & Liverpool, 1976), and psychotherapy with Black clients (Jones & Block, 1984). For a detailed review of the development of the TRIOS ideas, see Jones (1979, 1985).

These five dimensions reflect basic ways in which individuals and cultures orient themselves to living. They refer to how we experience and organize life, make decisions and arrive at beliefs, and how we derive meaning. TRIOS is important in the present context because there are sharp differences on these dimensions between Euro-American and Afro-American perspectives, and because temporal perspective underlies the TRIOS schema.

The pattern resulting from the "high" ends of all five TRIOS dimensions organizes experience and behavior into a characteristic constellation of attitudes, abilities, beliefs, and values. Time perspective is the overarching aspect of each dimension, in the following ways:

Time

High TRIOS features a present time orientation. In general, a present orientation is characterized by nonlinear, patterned, simultaneous, polychronic, social time perspective. The other four dimensions of TRIOS derive their characteristic expressions from that pattern.

Rhythm

Rhythms are recurring patterns of behavior within a given time frame. Once that frame is defined, the rhythms associated with it govern the expression of energy, feeling, and social relations in given contexts. Hall (1983) has made the strongest claim for the importance of rhythm in *The Dance of Life*:

> It can now be said with assurance that individuals are dominated in their behavior by complex hierarchies of interlocking rhythms . . . every facet of human behavior is involved in the rhythmic process. . . . Rhythm is, of course, the very essence of time. (p. 140)

Rhythms refer to the characteristic patterns of recurring behavior; they represent a flow of energy in time, and in relation to the environment both social and nonsocial. It is assumed that when rhythms are in synchrony, energy flows more effortlessly, and relations, performances, and feelings are enhanced. The force that rhythm brings to human behavior is described with eloquence by the late President of Senegal, Leopold Senghor:

> Rhythm is the architecture of being, the inner dynamic that gives it form, the pure expression of the life force. Rhythm is the vibratory shock, the force which, through our sense, grips us at the root of our being. It is expressed through corporeal and sensual means; through lines, surfaces, colours, and volumes in architecture, sculpture or painting; through accents in poetry and music; through movements in the dance. But doing this, rhythm turns all these concrete things toward the light of the spirit. In the degree to which rhythm is sensuously embodied, it illuminates the spirit. (1956, p. 60)

Improvisation

This dimension refers to creative, expressive goal attainment under immediate time pressures. The "high" end of the improvisation dimension refers to conditions in which a goal is suddenly presented. Such goals are always proximal. They may be either self-generated or imposed by the environment. The jazz musician improvises by choice, whereas response to an unexpected crisis requires improvisation on demand. In either case, the improviser draws on a store of ideas, abilities, and feelings, and implements and organizes them—on-line—to reach an immediate goal. Where improvisation is self-generated, it often bears the signature of its creator. Style is an important feature of improvisation. And the ability to improvise is an important feature of a PTP.

Oral Expression

This term refers to the characteristic medium of information exchange. Oral communication occurs in the present and is thus a feature of PTP. Oral communication is an important feature of social organization and interaction. In contrast to written material, with oral communication, information is contextualized and can be influenced by feelings. Furthermore, in oral communication, the relationship between speaker and audience is crucial; hence, successful oral communication is influenced by rhythms, improvisations, and social relations as they converge within the communication setting.

Spirituality

This term is defined as a belief in nonmaterial causation. Such a belief renders the usual cause-effect relations framed in space-time inoperative. More important, it suggests that present behaviors *may not* bear a specific relation to future outcomes. The ideas about personal control that are prevalent in our culture and implied by FTP are replaced by ideas about cosmic/spiritual forms that exert influence on the course of events. Such ideas are compatible with, if not implied by, a PTP.

These TRIOS concepts provide a context within which the major features of FTP and PTP can be contrasted. The PTP end of the time, rhythm, improvisation, and oral expression dimensions result in a pattern in which the individual formulates, values, and strives to attain goals that are to be realized primarily in the present or very near future.

Spirituality rejects the conditional probability that ties present behaviors to future outcomes. Thus the "high" end of the five TRIOS dimensions epitomizes the expression of a "pure" PTP, whereas the opposite end of those TRIOS dimensions (a linear view of time, asynchronous rhythms, inability to improvise, emphasis on written communication, and time-space anchored cause-effect interpretation of events) is for the most part an expression of a "pure" FTP. But, as already noted, human behavior is never a "pure" expression of any one particular temporal perspective, but rather a mixture of present, future, and perhaps other temporal perspectives. I will now turn to an exploration of how such mixtures or integrations come about.

Toward a Temporal Integration of Future and Present Perspectives

Earlier, I claimed that time perspective is a basis of culture, that it guides the development and implementation of goal behavior, and that it is a central feature of bicultural adaptation. I am thus suggesting that we can view a multicultural society, in part, as consisting of subcultural groups with different time perspectives, and that those different time perspectives influence formulation, valuing, and attainment of goals. Some behaviors (of any subcultural group) support goal achievement, and are thereby *instrumental.* These are often based on time perspectives that are at variance with—indeed, often, in sharp conflict with—traditional cultural patterns of *expressive* behaviors.

Figure 2.1 offers a schematic representation of the relations among time perspective, goal-directed behavior, cognitive representations of that behavior, and values attached to those representations. That presentation is based on the following assumptions:

(1) All behavior occurs in the present, hence can be reduced to the proximal goals it serves. Thus, for both PTP and FTP, behavior is instrumental to achieving these proximal goals.

(2) Present behaviors that follow from FTP are also assumed to have instrumental value as a means of achieving desired future goals.

(3) Present behaviors that follow from PTP are assumed to be expressive of feelings at that time.

(4) Both present and future time perspectives are influenced by both affective and cognitive processes. Affective processes, however, play a more dominant role in present-oriented behavior, while cognitive processes play a major role in future-oriented behavior.

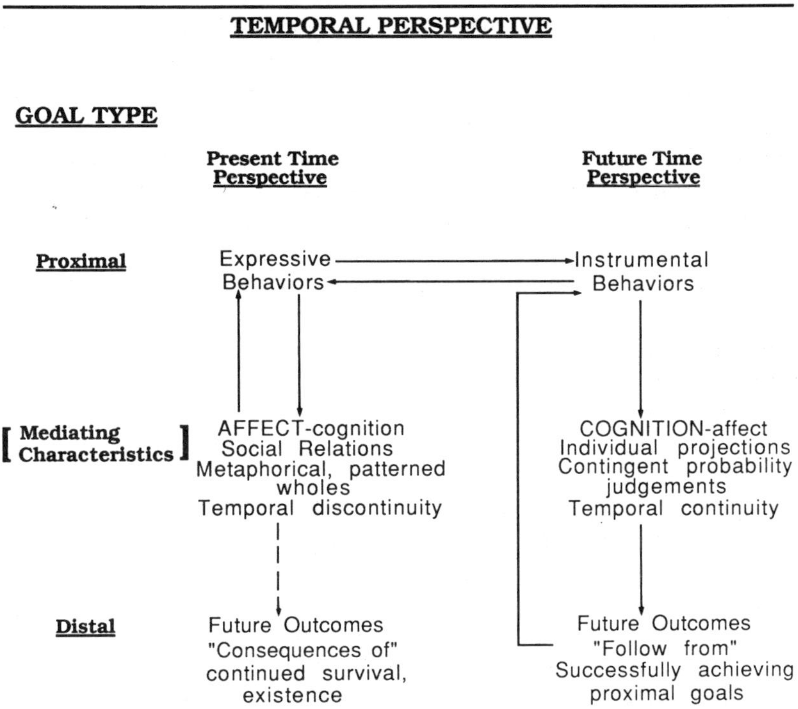

Figure 2.1. A Model of Temporal Integration of Future and Present Perspective

(5) For persons responsive to a present time perspective, the future is a consequence of continued survival or existence. Therefore, to secure a positive future, one need only maintain positive outcomes in the present. In this view, the value or valence of the future is equal to the valence of the present. For persons following a future time perspective, the future "follows from" successfully attaining proximal goals that have been judged to bear definable relations to the future. Thus it is the valence of the future goals that drives present behavior. Said differently, *the present drives the future for PTP, while the future drives the present for FTP.*

(6) Both perspectives involve feedback. It occurs, however, at different places in each perspective. FTP requires feedback relative to the present-future contingencies and the "follow from" relationship. PTP requires feedback from the immediate social environment regarding the status of survival and the conditions supporting positive affect.

In terms of this presentation, all behaviors have instrumental properties. A macro-level characterization of time perspective—FTP or

PTP—fails to capture the similarities. *What differs between the two perspectives is not the instrumentality of behavior, but the location of the goals in temporal extension.* Moreover, the dichotomy between instrumental and expressive behaviors is not nearly so sharp as has been implied. Even within FTP, behavior assumed to be instrumental in relation to a goal, near or far in the future, can acquire secondary reinforcing properties and become enjoyable and desirable in its own right. For example, jogging, done for weight loss and improved health, can become a dominant, present-oriented behavior valued for its direct consummatory payoff. If expressive behaviors are reinforcing in their own right, and if instrumental behaviors can become expressive behaviors, then the differences between PTP and FTP are further blurred.

The critical factors differentiating the two time perspectives are the perceived relations between present behaviors and cognized future goals, and the value placed upon those future goals relative to potential alternative proximal goals.

It is possible to persist in future-driven behavior when present circumstances are themselves unrewarding or not enjoyable. It is also possible to persist in surviving in intolerable circumstances because cognizing a different more desirable future is not possible. It is also the case that reaching for a dream can give meaning to the present as can maximizing the positive outcomes and experiences on a daily basis. To return to an earlier theme, racism in this society has tended to subvert the positive qualities associated with a present time perspective by undermining the development of a future perspective and by narrowly focusing many victims of racism on survival. Similarly, a narrow version of the achievement ethic subverts the dreams of accomplishment and growth by excessive striving that deprive too many people of the positive potentials of every day.

In the best of worlds, the expression of the human spirit and the instrumentalities of human capability combine in a temporal balance. That balance might metaphorically be seen as the balance of cultural orientations driven by temporal perspectives.

REFERENCES

Bochner, S., & David, K. H. (1967). Delay of gratification, age and intelligence in an Aboriginal culture. *International Journal of Psychology, 31,* 169-174.

DeVolder, M., & Lens, W. (1982). Academic achievement and future time perspective as a cognitive motivational concept. *Journal of Personality and Social Psychology, 42,* 566-571.

Hall, E. T. (1983). *The dance of life: The other dimension of time.* Garden City, NY: Anchor Press/Doubleday.

Jones, J. M. (1972). *Prejudice and racism.* Reading, MA: Addison-Wesley.

Jones, J. M. (1979). Conceptual and strategic issues in the relationship of Black psychology to American social science. In A. W. Boykin, A. J. Franklin, & J. F. Yates (Eds.), *Research directions of Black psychologists* (pp. 390-432). New York: Russell Sage.

Jones, J. M. (1985). TRIOS: An approach to biculturality in Black Americans. *First International Conference on Cultural Values and Collective Action.* Nags Head Conference Center, NC.

Jones, J. M. (in press). Racism: A cultural analysis of the problem. In J. F. Dovidio & S. L. Gaertner (Eds.), *Prejudice and discrimination and racism: Theory and research.* New York: Academic Press.

Jones, J. M., & Block, C. B. (1984). Black cultural perspectives. *Clinical Psychologist, 37,* 58-62.

Jones, J. M., & Hochner, A. R. (1973). Racial differences in sports activities: A look at the self-paced versus reactive hypothesis. *Journal of Personality and Social Psychology, 27,* 86-95.

Jones, J. M., & Liverpool, H. (1976). Calypso humour in Trinidad. In A. Chapman & H. C. Foot (Eds.), *Humour: Theory and research* (pp. 259-286). London: John Wiley.

Lauer, R. H. (1981). *Temporal man: The meaning and uses of social time.* New York: Praeger.

Lepper, M. R., Greene, D., & Nisbett, R. E. (1973). Undermining children's intrinsic interest with extrinsic reward: A test of the "overjustification" hypothesis. *Journal of Personality and Social Psychology, 28,* 129-137.

Levine, R. V., & Bartlett, K. (1984). Pace of life, punctuality, and coronary heart disease in six countries. *Journal of Cross-Cultural Psychology, 15,* 233-255.

Levine, R. V., West, L., & Reis, H. (1980). Perceptions of time and punctuality in the United States and Brazil. *Journal of Personality and Social Psychology, 38,* 541-550.

Mbiti, J. S. (1970). *African religion and philosophy.* New York: Doubleday.

McClelland, D. C. (1961). *The achieving society.* Princeton, NJ: Van Nostrand.

Melges, F. T. (1982). *Time and the inner future: A temporal approach to psychiatric disorders.* New York: John Wiley.

Mischel, W. (1958). Preference for delayed reinforcement: An experimental study of a cultural observation. *Journal of Abnormal and Social Psychology, 56,* 57-61.

Mischel, W. (1961a). Preference for delayed reinforcement and social responsibility. *Journal of Abnormal and Social Psychology, 62,* 1-7.

Mischel, W. (1961b). Delay of gratification, need for achievement, and acquiescence in another culture. *Journal of Abnormal and Social Psychology, 62,* 543-552.

Nisan, M. (1972). Dimension of time in relation to choice behavior and achievement orientation. *Journal of Personality and Social Psychology, 21,* 175-182.

Nuttin, J. (1985). *Future time perspective and motivation: Theory and research method.* Leuven Belgium: Leuven University Press/Lawrence Erlbaum.

Ornstein, R. E. (1977). *The psychology of consciousness.* New York: Harcourt Brace Jovanovich.

Rappaport, H., Enrich, K., & Wilson, A. (1985). Relation between ego identity and temporal perspective. *Journal of Personality and Social Psychology, 48,* 1609-1620.

Raynor, J. O. (1970). Relationships between achievement-related motives, future orientation, and academic performance. *Journal of Personality and Social Psychology, 15,* 28-33.

Raynor, J. O., & Entin, E. E. (Eds.). (1982). *Motivation, career striving, and aging.* Washington, DC: Hemisphere.

Raynor, J. O., & Rubin, I. S. (1971). Effects of achievement motivation and future orientation on level of performance. *Journal of Personality and Social Psychology, 17,* 36-41.

Senghor, L. E. (1956). *Ethiopiques.* Paris: Editions du Seuil.

Triandis, H. C. (1976). The future of pluralism. *Journal of Social Issues, 32,* 179-208.

Zimbardo, P. G., Marshall, G., & Maslach, C. (1971). Liberating behavior from time-bound control: Expanding the present through hypnosis. *Journal of Applied Social Psychology, 1,* 305-323.

3

The Pace of Life Across Cultures

ROBERT V. LEVINE

"If a man does not keep pace with his companions, perhaps it is because he hears a different drummer." Thoreau's thought strikes a chord in so many people that is has become part of our language. We use the phrase "the beat of a different drummer" to explain any pace of life unlike our own.

Adjusting to an alien pace of life can pose as many difficulties as learning the foreign language itself. In an investigation into the roots of culture shock, Spradley and Phillips (1972) asked 83 returning Peace Corps volunteers to rank order 33 items as to how much difficulty they posed for cultural readjustment. Their list included issues ranging from "the type of food eaten" to the "personal cleanliness of most people," "the number of people of your own race," and "the general standard of living." But, after "the language spoken," the stressors that posed the greatest adjustment difficulties to the volunteers both related to temporal matters: "the general pace of life" followed by "how punctual most people are." Howard (1980) reported that overseas business managers and their families experienced similar problems when returning home from slower paced cultures.

Why such difficulties? For one thing, from a developmental point of view, ideas of pace and tempo are the last and most difficult to be mastered. According to Piaget (1966) Western children learn about time in four successive stages. They first learn temporal succession, or the idea that one thing happens, and then another thing happens. This is followed by temporal order, the idea that one specific occurrence is always followed by another, and the two are not always reversible. Third is temporal duration, understanding that some events take longer than others. Only after these concepts are mastered does the child learn about temporal velocity, the idea that some people are faster than others and that actions can be speeded up or slowed down.

Furthermore, cultural norms for appropriate tempos in work, in play, in what constitutes punctuality and lateness, and in the meaning of "now" and "later" are all aspects of what Hall (1959) describes as the "silent language." There are no dictionaries to translate a culture's temporal rules formally. These informal patterns of time "are seldom, if ever, made explicit. They exist in the air around us. They are either familiar and comfortable, or unfamiliar and wrong" (Hall, 1959, p. 156). With no formal definitions to help us along, it is little wonder that this silent language can pose as many difficulties for cultural adaptation as differences in formal spoken language itself.

The concept of pace or tempo of life has been variously defined as the rate (Lauer, 1981), speed (Amato, 1983), or "relative rapidity or density of experiences, meanings, perceptions and activities" (Werner, Altman, & Oxley, 1985, p. 14). It is the velocity element of the temporal rhythms that Rebecca Warner addresses in Chapter 4, and Janice Kelly addresses in Chapter 5.

Operationally, pace of life has been most often measured by walking speed (e.g., Amato, 1983; Bornstein, 1979; Bornstein & Bornstein, 1976). Some studies have also included measures of work pace, such as the speed of post office transactions (Levine & Bartlett, 1984; Levine & Wolff, 1985; Lowin, Hottes, Sander, & Bornstein, 1971), gas station transactions (Lowin et al., 1971), currency exchanges (Amato, 1983; Lowin et al., 1971), cigarette purchases (Lowin et al., 1971; Lucia, 1985), and betel nut purchases (in New Guinea; Amato, 1983). Others have measured the speed of lunch consumption (Lucia, 1985), the speed with which children proceed down the aisles in grocery stores (Wright, 1961), sensitivity to clock time and punctuality (Levine & Bartlett, 1984; Levine, West, & Reis, 1980; Lowin et al., 1971) and talking speed (Levine & Lynch, 1985).

This chapter will focus on cross-cultural differences in the pace of life and their implications for well-being. First it reviews the major research findings on the pace of life, with an emphasis on urban-rural differences and cross-cultural differences. It then reviews our own studies on punctuality and the pace of life around the world. Finally, it examines the relationship of pace to psychological and physical well-being.

Previous Research

A number of studies, from a variety of perspectives and disciplines, have investigated the pace of life both across and within cultures. The issue that has probably generated the most attention is the influence of urban versus rural environment.

Urban Versus Rural Differences

The pace of life has been a central issue in studies of the effects of urbanization on the quality of our lives. A number of aspects of urban living that require faster tempos have been identified and often used to demonstrate the costs of city life.

Wright (1961), for example, in his large-scale "City-Town" project, observed the speed and behavior of children in typical city supermarkets and town grocery stores. The average city child walked nearly twice as fast through the supermarket as did the town child through the smaller grocery. Conversely, the town child spent three times as much time with clerks and other shoppers and spent significantly more time physically touching objects.

Milgram (1970) similarly found faster mean walking speeds in Boston as compared to the less populous town of Concord, Massachusetts. Berkowitz (in Milgram, 1970) also reported slightly faster walking speeds in Philadelphia, Boston, and New York than in a matched sample of small and moderate-sized towns.

The most precise description of the relationship between walking speed and population size has been provided by Bornstein and his colleagues. In their first studies, Bornstein and Bornstein (1976) observed walking speeds in main downtown locations in a total of 25 cities spread across Czechoslovakia, France, Germany, Greece, Israel, and the United States. They found a very high correlation between population size and walking speed ($r = .91$) across this heterogeneous sample. Further, they found that this relationship could be described by the formula: $V = 0.86 \log P + 0.05$ (where V = velocity and P = population size).

In a second series of studies, Bornstein (1979) replicated the conditions of his earlier investigation in a sample of cities and towns in Ireland, Scotland, and the United States. He again found a very strong positive correlation between population size and walking speed (r = .88). He also found that once again the formula V = 0.86 log P + 0.05 successfully described the relationship between the two variables. It is difficult to argue with his conclusion that "a highly predictable relationship seems to exist between the pace of life that characterizes a locale and the size of its population" (p. 85).

One limitation of the above studies is their reliance on walking speed as a lone indicator of pace of life. Walking speed is a behavior that may be affected by within city factors ranging from location to temperature to time of day (Fischer, 1976). This consideration has led several investigators to sample a wider variety of behaviors reflecting the pace of life.

In one of the earliest studies of this type, Lowin, Hottes, Sander, and Bornstein (1971) looked at five aspects of tempo in a sample of eight cities and towns across the United States. Along with pedestrian walking speed, they observed work speed at standard tasks for postal clerks, gas station attendants, bank clerks, and store clerks. Significantly faster times were found in the urban settings for all measures except bank clerk speed.

Two studies have examined multiple indicators of urban versus rural pace of life cross-culturally. Amato (1983) looked at pedestrian walking speed, the speed at which change was given in shops, and the time of betel nut transactions in open marketplaces in a large city and two rural towns in New Guinea. He found faster urban speeds for walking pace and the betel nut transactions. There were no urban-rural differences on the change measure, which he attributed to a lack of sensitivity to this type of activity in these samples.

Finally, my own colleagues and I (Levine & Bartlett, 1984) observed average walking speed, the speed of postal transactions, and the accuracy of bank clocks in the largest and one medium-sized city in Japan, Taiwan, Indonesia, Italy, England, and the United States. We found a tendency for faster walking speeds and more accurate clocks in the larger cities of most of these countries. This study will be described more fully later.

In summary then, there is evidence that population size is positively related to a number of behaviors associated with the pace of life. This relationship is especially strong for walking speed.

Why the Urban-Rural Differences?

Bornstein (1979) has hypothesized four potential classes of mechanisms that may be responsible for the "highly predictable" relationship that exists between pace of life and population size.

(1) Ergonomical or energy factors. Ambulation, like other physical activities, expends energy. Although Bornstein admits that the specific ergonomical dynamics are somewhat obscure, he hypothesizes that urban-rural tempo differences may reflect some heretofore unidentified adaptation to the requirements and resources typically provided by urban environments.

(2) Social facilitation. In 1898, Triplett (1897-1898) made the observation that bicyclists rode faster when they raced in head-to-head competition than when they rode alone. Since then it has been observed that the presence of others facilitates the performance of behaviors ranging from the running of simple mazes by cockroaches to complex, learned behaviors in humans (Zajonc, Heigartner, & Herman, 1969). It has been argued that this "social facilitation effect" is strongest for simple, well-learned motor responses, a class of behavior into which walking certainly falls. Social facilitation might therefore help to explain the increased velocities or performances of individuals in more populated areas.

(3) Economic factors. Hoch (1976) has presented a simple economic explanation for population size effects: "As a city grows larger, the value of its inhabitants' time increases with the city's increasing wage rate and cost of living, so that economizing on time becomes more urgent, and life becomes more hurried and harried" (p. 857).

(4) Cognitive factors. The explanation for urban-rural differences that has received the most attention is the late Stanley Milgram's (1970) system overload theory. Milgram proposed that today's urban dweller is bombarded with more stimulation than can be effectively processed. He or she adapts to this overload through a number of cognitive withdrawal responses by which all but those stimuli that require responses for survival are filtered out. These adaptive mechanisms eventually evolve into behavioral norms that streamline interactions. The result, according to Milgram, is that the psychological and social norm in urban environments is to focus on one's goal and literally walk toward it as rapidly as possible.

The precise explanation for the more rapid pace of urban life has not yet been determined. Bornstein merely offers these four as possible candidates. Perhaps all are operating independently and in interaction with each other and with other variables (such as the pace of development of a city or its incidence of crime).

Cross-Cultural Differences

Some of the most dramatic differences in pace of life occur between people from different cultures. Most of this research has taken the anthropological, case study approach to compile broad, often subjective, descriptions of specific behaviors and norms in the given culture. The pace of life has frequently been part of these descriptions.

Anthropologists have distinguished between "fast" and "slow" cultures. Bohannan (1980), for example, has looked at greeting style among the Tiv, a primitive people in Nigeria, versus the Hausa people, their neighbors. The Tiv, he concludes, are fast people. They spend little time with the perfunctory nonsense of rituals such as greetings. They like to get their hellos out of the way quickly and get immediately down to business.

The Hausas, on the other hand, are described as a slow people. Bohannan tells of having once observed an English anthropologist and a Hausa string out their hellos for 20 minutes. They both apparently enjoyed the ritual, each having had long practice and conditioning in its intricacies.

As one might expect, the more highly industrialized North American and Northern European nations are described as prototypically "fast" cultures. The value of promptness, the sense that time is a commodity not to be wasted, and the need to make every minute count have been seen as particularly characteristic of people from the United States, Germany, and Switzerland (Hall, 1959). People from urban centers in economically developed Eastern countries, such as Japan, are also often described as having fast paces of life. As will be discussed later, however, the motivating values, and subsequent physical consequences, behind the rapid tempo of the Japanese worker are different from those in the Western industrialized nations (Dressler, 1984).

Descriptions of slow people can often be dramatic. Hall (1959) relates the story of an Afghani man in Kabul who could not locate a brother with whom he had an appointment. Investigation by a member of the American embassy eventually revealed the root of the problem: The two brothers had agreed to meet in Kabul, but had neglected to specify what year. Hall portrays a similar lack of concern with exactness in time and the neglect for making every minute count among such diverse groups as the Navajo Indians, traditional Mediterranean Arabs, and Latin Americans.

Perhaps the prototype of the slow-paced culture has been described in the *manana* philosophy of the Mexican people. This term, meaning "tomorrow" or, literally, the "morning," stereotypes the Latin American as one who, whenever it is possible, will put off today's work until tomorrow. Calvert (1975), for example, writes how Mexicans can typically expect lateness for appointments of up to 30 minutes unless the time has been specified as *hora ingles* (English time). Later I will discuss how these norms have frequently resulted in intercultural misunderstandings.

Some anthropological-type studies have focused on the social time structure of subcultures within countries. Henry (1965) has written of "colored people's time," (CPT) as contrasted to the prevailing majority "white people's time" in the United States. Similarly, Horton (1972) writes of "cool people" time among the "sporadically unemployed young Black street corner population" in the United States. People in these groups are slow-paced most of the time, but speed up their tempos when they want to. According to Horton, a street dude is on time by the standard clock whenever he cares to be and is not on time when he doesn't want to be. The latter case most often prevails. Time for the cool person is "dead" when resources are low—when money is tight, when he is in jail, and so forth. But time is "alive" when there is "action."

In summary, these anthropological studies have contributed invaluable case-by-case profiles of the pace of life and overall social time structures of people from a great many cultures. Like most research taking an idiographic approach, they present a depth and richness of description unobtainable by more broad-based nomothetic methods. Their shortcoming, however, is that they do not present quantitative data for a sufficient number of subjects to allow systematic nomothetic cross-cultural comparisons. Without suitable comparison groups, it is difficult to gauge the meaning of *fast* or *slow* or to grasp the implications of one people's time constructions for another's. With the exception of a very few studies on urban-rural differences, such as those described earlier by Bornstein and Bornstein (1976), Bornstein (1979), and Amato (1983), little research has taken this more broad-based social psychological approach. With this consideration in mind, my colleagues and I have carried out a series of cross-cultural comparisons in countries on four continents over the last several years.

Our Studies

Study 1: Punctuality in Brazil and the United States

Our first series of studies focused on conceptions of time and punctuality in Brazil and in the United States (Levine, West, & Reis, 1980). We began with the Latin American view of time articulated in the concept of *manana* in Spanish and *amanha* in Portuguese, which is so deeply rooted in the Anglo-American stereotype of the South American. Travel guides warn that in Latin America, "whenever it is conceivably possible, the business of today is put off until tomorrow" (Epstein, 1977, p. 52). This lack of concern with punctuality is often used as evidence of a passive, fatalistic, apathetic, and generally irresponsible Latin temperament, a stereotype that is responsible for damaging racial prejudice on many levels (Hernandez, 1970).

As a starting point, we assumed that Brazilians are, in fact, more frequently late for appointments than are people from the United States—an assumption that our data later proved to be correct. But we questioned whether it was necessary to attribute this behavior to such broad personality dispositions as laziness and irresponsibility.

While serving as a visiting professor in Brazil, I had observed a number of behaviors that indicated that the explanation might not be all that simple. For example, although the students in my Brazilian classes did tend to be more casual about arriving late than I am used to here in the United States, they were also more causal about staying late. In my classes in the United States, I don't need to wear a watch to know when the session is over. My students gather their books at two minutes before the hour and show all signs of a serious anxiety attack if I do not dismiss them on time. At the end of each class in Brazil, however, some students would slowly drift out, more would stay around to ask questions for a while, and some would stay and chat for a very long time.

I could not, in all honesty, attribute their lingering to my superb teaching style. I had just spent two hours lecturing on statistics in broken Portuguese. Apparently, for many of my students, staying late was simply of no more importance than arriving late in the first place. As I observed this casual approach in infinite variations during the year, I learned that the *amanha* stereotype oversimplified more fundamental Anglo-Brazilian differences in conceptions of time (Levine & Wolff, 1985).

With the assistance of colleagues Laurie West and Harry Reis, I designed a series of field and questionnaire studies to investigate the various meanings and conceptions of punctuality in Brazil and in the United States. These studies were conducted in Niteroi, Brazil, and Fresno, California, each of which is a secondary metropolitan center with a population of about 350,000.

In one of our questionnaire studies, we asked some students from comparable universities in Niteroi and Fresno what they would consider early or late in five different situations, ranging from a meeting with a government official to a hypothetical lunch appointment with a friend. In all five situations, Brazilians were more flexible in their definitions of both early and late. For the lunch appointment with a friend, for example, the average Brazilian student defined lateness for lunch as 33 minutes after the scheduled time, compared to only 19 minutes for the Fresno students. But Brazilians also allowed an average of about 54 minutes before they would consider someone early, while the Fresno students drew the line at 24.

It appears from this and a great deal of other data we gathered that Brazilians are simply more flexible in general in their concepts of time and punctuality. How do we explain this? One explanation relies on the potentially destructive stereotype of the apathetic, fatalistic, and irresponsible Latin temperament. But when we asked a sample of students why they and their fellow countrypeople are usually late for appointments, Brazilians were actually less likely than North Americans to attribute their lateness to their own lack of caring. They were more likely to point to external situational causes.

And, we found some evidence to support their argument. Transportation, for example, is less reliable and punctual in Brazil. We also found fewer public clocks and watches there, and those that did exist were less accurate than ours (see below). If it is not unusual for Brazilian watches and clocks to be off, say, by five minutes, then a ten-minute difference between any two watches would not be uncommon. What meaning, then, is there in being ten minutes late for an appointment? All cultures have accepted errors of punctuality for different situations. In a typical classroom in the United States, for example, few instructors would object if a student were a minute late. The case in Brazil may be no more than an extension of this allowance.

Data from several of our studies were consistent with this idea. In one study, we found that bank clocks, which we reasoned would represent an accurate time measure to passersby, were significantly less accurate in Brazil than in the United States. Similarly, the time on pedestrians' watches in busy downtown areas were less accurate in Brazil. Further, when we checked the differences in the time reported by subjects after looking at their watches versus the exact time that actually appeared on their watches, we found that Brazilians were again less accurate. (These data were gathered before digital watches became the norm in the United States. The other day I asked a student what time it was, he looked at his watch and answered "Three-twelve and eighteen seconds.")

Why are Brazilian timepieces less accurate? Certainly it is likely that at least to some extent this reflects less concern with punctuality. But, once again, there are alternative explanations that do not require attributions to personality dispositions. At the time these data were gathered, for example, watches and clocks typically cost five or six times what they did in the United States, reflecting steep Brazilian import duties. This resulted in fewer and poorer quality watches and clocks. Perhaps most striking to a visitor to Brazil was the lack of any public clocks (there was none in the classrooms of my university, for example). And there was an almost total lack of electric clocks, which we usually turn to for accurate time readings. Furthermore, frequent power blackouts made it difficult to trust those few electric clocks that did exist. Whereas in the United States I am constantly reminded of the exact time of day (recently by symphonies of little beeps emanating from people's watches every hour on the hour), in Brazil it was difficult to locate the correct time ever. Under these conditions, I quickly found it necessary to be more flexible in my definition of punctuality.

We do not know, of course, whether these unreliable time reminders are the cause or are the result of greater flexibility in time intervals in Brazil. But even if inaccurate timepieces are the result of less concern with punctuality, the lack of accurate clocks and watches would make tighter time concerns difficult for people. In other words, the initial norm may sustain itself in the manner of a self-fulfilling prophecy by making compliance unavoidable.

Concepts of punctuality are also reflected in a culture's written language. We learned this when we translated our questionnaires into Portuguese. Several of our questions were concerned with how long the respondent would *wait* for someone to arrive versus when they *hoped* the person would arrive versus when they actually *expected* the person would come. Unfortunately for us, it turns out that the terms *to wait*, *to hope*, and *to expect* are all typically translated as the single verb *esperar* in Portuguese. In many ways our translation difficulties taught us more about Brazilian-Anglo differences in time conception than did the subjects' answers to the questions.

The point is that peoples' notions of time and punctuality are complex phenomena. Attributing Brazilians' lateness to their simply not caring will just not suffice. Certainly, we found that Brazilians don't see it that way. Rules of punctuality and tempo are closely intertwined with the more fundamental beliefs and values of a culture.

We saw this clearly in another study in which we asked people their thoughts about the relation between success and punctuality for appointments. Those we questioned in the United States tended to rate people who are never late for appointments as more successful than those who are either occasionally or always late. But Brazilians rated the person who is *always* late for appointments as most successful.

Now, even in the land of *amanha,* from people who are not very concerned with punctuality, this was surprising. It is one thing to be flexible and another thing to believe that not getting there on time actually pays. I was hoping to break through the simple *amanha* stereotype and, instead, now found myself in the middle of a Latin joke.

But I soon learned that I was missing the point. It turns out that success and lack of punctuality do, in fact, tend to go together in Brazil. It is assumed that those with high status and control will arrive late for appointments and that those of less importance will arrive on time. Lack of punctuality is more than merely acceptable in people with high status in Brazil. It is a badge of success. Successful people are expected to be unpunctual. In the United States we resent it when powerful people, such as doctors, keep us waiting. But Brazilians of lower status do not appear to resent having to wait on high status people any more than they resent earning less money than their superiors. They are envious. Someday they, too, hoped to be successful enough to wear expensive shoes and keep people waiting.

In other words, the reason that our Brazilian subjects rated unpunctual people as most successful was because it was a fact. But it turns out that this was not so much because they believed that lack of punctuality causes success but because they saw it to be a result of success.

The main lesson from these Brazil studies is the importance of evaluating social behavior within its overall cultural context. Attributing the Brazilians' relative lack of punctuality to an apathetic and irresponsible temperament is both damaging and misses the larger meaning. Brazilians are more flexible than people from the United States in their attitudes toward time, and this norm is a result of a complex of social, psychological, environmental, and economic factors. As J. T. Frazer wrote, "Tell me what to think of time, and I shall know what to think of you." (For a complete description of the methods and results of the Brazilian studies, see Levine, West, & Reis, 1980.)

Study 2: The Pace of Life in Six Countries

The Brazil studies addressed a single aspect of social tempo—punctuality. Our next series of studies (Levine & Bartlett, 1984) attempted to extend and refine these investigations in several ways.

First, rather than focus only on conceptions of punctuality, we examined the more general issue of pace of life by adding measures of walking speed and work pace. Second, these studies were extended to a number of European and Asian countries: Japan, Taiwan, Indonesia, Italy, England, and the United States. This allowed for comparisons between Eastern and Western cultures varying in degree of economic development. Third, in order to sample each country in a more representative manner, data were gathered in more than one area in each country. Although it would have been impractical to conduct these investigations in rural areas, we did collect data both in the largest city and in one medium-sized city (population between 415,000-615,000) in each country. Finally, in these studies we examined some of the consequences of pace of life for psychological and physical well-being.

Data were collected in 12 cities in six countries: Taipei and Tainan (Taiwan), Tokyo and Sendai (Japan), Jakarta and Solo (Indonesia), Rome and Florence (Italy), London and Bristol (England), and New York City and Rochester, New York (United States). We examined three indicators of tempo in each city. First, as in the Brazilian studies, we measured the accuracy of a sample of bank clocks in main downtown areas.

Second, we measured the average walking speed of randomly chosen pedestrians over a distance of 100 feet. All of these measurements were taken during main business hours on clear days in at least two locations on main downtown streets. Locations were chosen that allowed pedestrians to move at potentially maximum speeds. In order to control for the effects of socializing, only pedestrians walking alone were used. Neither subjects with clear physical handicaps nor those who appeared to be window-shopping were timed.

Third, as a measure of work pace, we measured the speed with which postal clerks fulfilled a standard request for stamps. In each city, including those in the United States, we presented clerks with a note in the native language requesting a common-priced stamp—the then standard 20-center in the United States, for example. They were also handed paper money—the equivalent of a $5 bill. We measured the elapsed time between the passing of the note and the completion of the request.

Our results indicated a number of consistent cross- and within-national differences. There were significant main effects for country on all three measures. As seen in Figure 3.1, the Japanese were highest on all measures: They had the most accurate clocks, the fastest walking speeds, and the fastest postal clerks. The United States was second on the bank clock and post office measure and slightly but significantly slower than Japan on walking speed (22.5 seconds versus 20.7 seconds).

On the other end, Indonesia had far and away the least accurate clocks and the slowest walking speeds. When it came to efficiency of postal service, however, the Indonesians were not the least efficient (although they did place far behind the Japanese postal clerks). That distinction went to the Italians, whose infamous postal service took 47 seconds on the average (compared to Japan's average of 25 seconds).

There also were a number of within-country differences, including a country × city size interaction for walking speed. As expected, we found here that people in the larger cities walked faster than those in the smaller cities. But the interaction indicated that this difference was greatest in the least developed countries in our sample—Indonesia followed by Taiwan. Perhaps, we hypothesized, this reflects the persistence of a traditional village life style among people in the smaller cities in Indonesia and, to a lesser extent, Taiwan. The traces of a traditionally rural slow pace of life may be less evident, or never existed in some cases, in the smaller cities of the more industrialized nations.

One of the strongest findings to come out of these studies was the consistency of the three pace of life measures across the 12 cities in our sample. Accuracy of clocks was positively related to faster walking speeds ($r = .82$) and to faster completion of postal requests ($r = .71$). Walking speed was positively correlated with postal efficiency ($r = .56$).

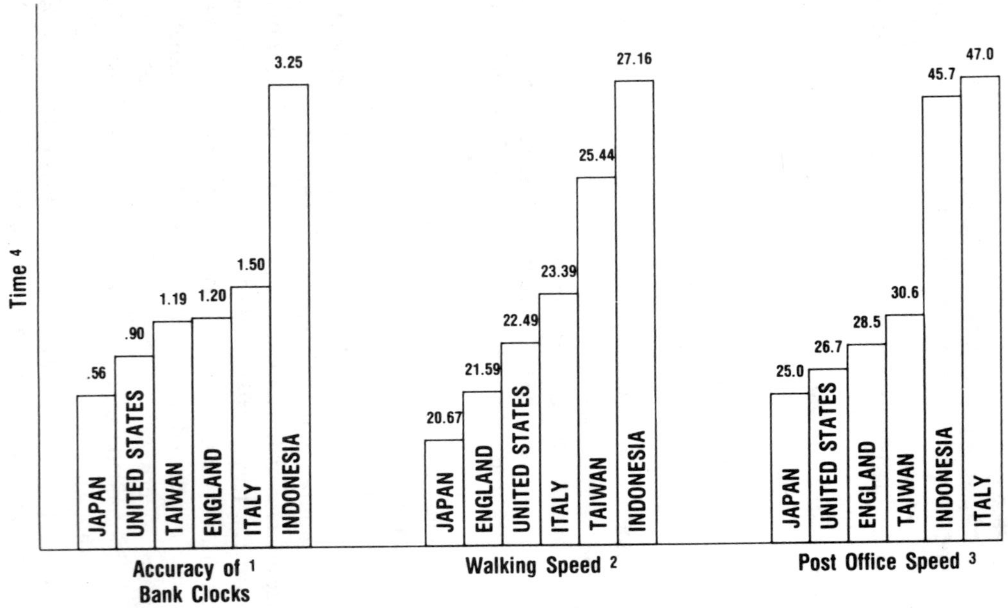

1 Deviations are reported in minutes
2,3 Speeds are in seconds
4 Smaller numbers indicate more accurate clocks, faster walking speeds and faster office speeds respectively

SOURCE: From Levine and Wolff (1985).

Figure 3.1. The Pace of Life in Six Countries

These data provided strong evidence for the stability and generality of the pace of life concept. It appears reasonable, at least on the level of the city, to speak of an overall pace of life that is evidenced by a number of distinct behaviors.

In summary, these results demonstrate that there are strong and consistent differences among nations in their paces of life, and that these differences are relatively stable across measures. It appears reasonable to speak of a characteristic pace of life of a particular people and to distinguish between cultures on the basis of this characteristic.

Pace of Life and Well-Being

Our next question focused on the significance of these cultural differences for the quality of life of its members. Is there a relationship between the tempo of a city or country and the psychological and physical health of its people?

There is tangential evidence from a number of sources that implies that the pace of life is important for psychological and physical well-being. Feeling rushed, in particular, appears to have a number of negative consequences. Witmer, Rich, Barcikowski, and Mague (1983), for example, found that the rate of life pace, as defined mostly by how rushed people reported their lives to be, was negatively related to their ability to cope with stress. Robinson and Converse (1972), in a national survey, similarly found that self-reported life satisfaction was negatively related to how rushed respondents felt their lives to be.

How rushed one feels also appears to have consequences for physical health, as evidenced by data on the type A (coronary-prone) behavior pattern (Friedman & Rosenman, 1974). A defining component of the type A pattern is a sense of time urgency—a continual struggle to achieve a great many goals in a short period of time. Gastorf (1980), for example, found that type A individuals arrived earlier for appointments than did non-coronary-prone Type Bs. Burnam, Pennebaker, and Glass (1975) found that type As judged the lapse of one minute sooner than did type Bs. These findings were viewed as indicators of the impatient tendencies of type As.

We reasoned from these findings that the average pace of life of a country should be related to the incidence of coronary (ischemic) heart disease in its population. Specifically, we attempted to correlate countries' relative rankings on our three pace of life measures with their rates of death from ischemic heart disease (World Health Organization, 1980).

A thorough search, though, revealed no available statistics for the rate of heart disease or related illness for either Taiwan or Indonesia (see Levine, 1985). (It may not be a coincidence that these were the two slowest countries in our sample.) Because statistics were available for only four countries in our sample, no statistical analyses were performed. We did, however, observe some interesting trends.

For the three Western nations, the data generally confirmed our predictions. Italy, which had the least accurate clocks, the slowest walking speed, and the slowest postal speed, had the lowest rate of death due to coronary heart disease of the three Western countries. There was very little difference in the overall pace of life between the United States and England and, again as predicted, virtually no difference in their coronary death rates.

But the data for Japan were diametrically opposed to our hypothesis. The Japanese had the smallest clock deviations, fastest walking speeds, and fastest postal performances but the lowest incidence of death from coronary heart disease.

One should be cautious, of course, in generalizing from a relation based on only four data points. The relatively low rate of coronary heart disease for Japan might be due to any of a number of factors, ranging from the effect of dietary differences (Switzer, 1963) to the problem of inaccuracy in international disease statistics (Reid, 1975). But data from other sources indicate that our Japanese data may reflect more fundamental cross-cultural limitations in the hypothesized relation between pace of life and well-being in general, and in the concept of the type A behavior pattern in particular.

Winkelstein (1975) has conducted a series of studies on the relation between acculturation and coronary heart disease among Japanese-Americans living in California and Hawaii. He found that mortality from coronary heart disease increased with greater exposure to Western life-styles—it was highest in California, intermediate in Hawaii, and lowest in Japan. Marmot and Syme (1976) conducted a retrospective study of Japanese Americans in California that provided even stronger evidence for the effect of acculturation on coronary heart disease. Acculturation, or "culture of upbringing," was measured by items such as years spent in Japan, time spent studying the Japanese language, religion while growing up, years spent with parents, and others items. They found that men with a nontraditional upbringing were 2 to 2.7

times more likely to have coronary heart disease than men with more traditional backgrounds. Further, these results held even when smoking, dietary preference, cholesterol, blood pressure, triglycerides, obesity, glucose, and age were controlled. These findings have also been replicated in studies of men of Japanese descent living in Hawaii (Yano, Blackwelder, Kagan et al., 1979), and in people from other non-Western cultures (see Dressler, 1984, for a complete review of studies on this issue).

It appears, then, that Japanese people who are more exposed to Western life-styles are at a greater risk of developing CHD, and that cultural factors play at least some role in this relation. The question, now, is just what cultural differences might account for these findings? What characteristics of Japanese culture explain why the nation with the fastest pace of life in our study has lower rates of coronary heart disease than slower Western nations?

Perhaps one explanation is the greater emphasis on cooperation and group achievement among the Japanese, as opposed to the more competitive, individual emphasis common to Western workers. Nakane (1970) argues that the typical Japanese worker is most strongly motivated by a desire to see his or her work group, his or her company, and his or her nation succeed. It is possible that this approach to production and success does not carry with it the stress seen in Western nations.

Data from a factor analysis of the type A scale for Japanese subjects are consistent with this hypothesis (Cohen, Syme Jenkins, Kagan, & Zyzanski, 1975). The scale contained two independent factors for the Japanese sample. The two factors, which had been in a single factor in the original U.S. sample, separated questions about being hard driving and competitive from those about being hardworking. Coronary heart disease was related to the hard-driving and competitive aspects but not to the hardworking aspects of the behavior pattern for the Japanese. As Cohen (1978) points out, much of the type A behavior pattern may not have the same relationship to coronary heart disease in all cultures.

In summary, the relation of pace of life, and the extreme case of type A behavior, to coronary heart disease is not as yet clear. In our own research, Karen Lynch and I are presently investigating the correlation of pace to a number of general indicators of psychological and physical well-being in cities across the United States. More specifically, we are collecting field data reflecting work speed, walking speed, talking speed, and time sensitivity in a sample of 36 small and large cities. This pace of life data will be correlated to statistics concerning the rates of suicide, coronary heart disease, drug abuse, alcoholism, divorce, and other indicators of the well-being of the populations of each city.

Whatever the exact relation turns out to be between pace and health in Western nations, the data from Japan indicate that the relation will probably not be universal, and will probably be mediated by other factors. If this turns out to be the case, it becomes critical to identify the nature and role of these mediating factors in other cultures. Let us look at the value of such research more closely.

Discussion

Systematic cross-cultural study of the pace of life and its implications for well-being is important for at least two reasons. First, in a world where communications put more and more people into daily contact, the "silent" language of time takes on increasingly greater significance. A lack of understanding of other cultures' norms and rules of tempo may have unfortunate consequences. Watzlawick (1976) has pointed out that members of Arab and Latin American cultures tend to stand closer when speaking to another person than do people from the United States. This difference has frequently been misinterpreted by Westerners as reflecting aggressive and disrespectful qualities in these strangers. Similarly, Americans tend to attribute the lack of punctuality of Brazilians to deep-seated personality dispositions, the irresponsible, apathetic, and fatalistic Latin temperament, and to a lack of appropriate motivation. In reality, however, the differences reflect a misunderstanding about prevailing norms and available information about time.

In some cases, intercultural misunderstandings about rules of pace and tempo have literally threatened international relations. When Queen Elizabeth recently visited Morocco, King Hassan, who is a notorious late arriver, kept her waiting for 15 minutes before receiving her. The Queen apparently was not amused. When it came time for the Charles-Diana nuptials, the King (because of his eminence) had to be asked. But the invitation was hedged by statements alluding to the high value that Anglo-Saxons place on promptness and the "hope" that His Majesty could manage to be on time for the ceremony. The King responded in due course that certain pressing affairs would, unfortunately, preclude his personal appearance. He sent the Crown Prince in his place. Some believe that relations between Morocco and England never totally recovered.

But perhaps what is most interesting is that Moroccans still can't understand why the British were so concerned about the King's lack of promptness. "The King could never have kept the Queen or anyone else waiting," one of them later said, "because the King cannot be late" ("King Hassan of Morocco," 1984, p. 47).

International misunderstandings have even resulted from divergent interpretations of tempo-related words. In 1985, for example, a group of Shiite Muslim terrorists hijacked a TWA jetliner, holding 40 Americans hostage with the demand that Israel release 764 Lebanese Shiite prisoners being held in their prisons. Shortly after taking the Americans prisoner, the terrorists handed the hostages over to Shiite Muslim leaders who assured that nothing would happen to the prisoners if all demands were met.

At one point during the delicate negotiations, Ghassan Sablini, the number-three man in the Shiite militia Amal, said that the hostages would be handed back to the hijackers in two days if there were no movement toward their demand that Israel release its Shiite prisoners. This created a very dangerous situation. The U.S. negotiators knew that neither they nor the Israelis could yield to these terrorist demands without striking some face-saving compromise. By setting a limit of "two days," the Shiite leader made a compromise unlikely and elevated the crisis to a very dangerous level. Everyone held their breath. But when Sablini realized how his statement was being interpreted, he quickly backed off: "We said a couple of days but we were not necessarily specifying 48 hours" ("Ships with 1800 Marines," 1985). Forty deaths and a possible war were nearly caused by a miscommunication over the meaning of the word *day*. But this misunderstanding was hardly surprising between people for whom ideas like "fast" and "slow" are as far apart as the countries themselves.

At this point, it is easy to understand why Spradley and Phillips's Peace Corps volunteers, who were mentioned at the beginning of this chapter, experienced so much difficulty with the pace of life and rules of punctuality when they crossed into foreign cultures. Not only are our rules of tempo literally worlds apart, but there are no dictionaries or formal definitions to help us along. Cross-cultural research on the pace of life can provide those coming in contact with other cultures with some formal guidance. It is at least a beginning toward reducing temporal misunderstandings at both interpersonal and international levels.

The second reason that cross-cultural study of the pace of life is important is that it gives us needed perspective on our own way of living. We saw earlier, most clearly in the case of Japan, that the relation between pace of life and physical and psychological health may be mediated by other factors that are particular to a given culture. In the United States, the urgency of using time efficiently and the need to make every minute count is often seen as a prerequisite to success. We have come to view the choice between rushing and leisurely activity as a tradeoff between accomplishment on the one hand and peace of mind on the other. But pace of life and time urgency may not be as directly related to psychological stress and the coronary-prone personality pattern in other societies as they are in the United States. Learning how to be hardworking without being hard driving and competitive is an admirable goal; studying the habits of other cultures may help us come closer to achieving it. We may learn that self-destructiveness is not a necessary by-product of productivity.

REFERENCES

Amato, P. R. (1983). The effects of urbanization on interpersonal behavior. *Journal of Cross-Cultural Psychology, 14,* 353-367.

Bohannan, P. (1980). Time, rhythm, and pace. *Science, 80*(1), 18-20.

Bornstein, M. H. (1979). The pace of life: Revisited. *International Journal of Psychology, 14,* 83-90.

Bornstein, M. H., & Bornstein, H. (1976). The pace of life. *Nature, 259,* 557-559.

Burnam, M., Pennebaker, J., & Glass, D. (1975). Time-consciousness, achievement striving and the type A coronary-prone behavior pattern. *Journal of Abnormal Psychology, 84,* 76-79.

Calvert, P. (1975). *The Mexicans: How they live and work.* New York: Praeger.

Cohen, J. B. (1978). The influence of culture on coronary-prone behavior. In T. Denbroski, S. Weis, J. Shields, S. Haynes, & M. Feinleib (Eds.), *Coronary-prone behavior.* New York: Springer-Verlag.

Cohen, J. B., Syme, S. L., Jenkins, C. D., Kagan, A., & Zyzanski, S. J. (1975). The cultural context of type A behavior and the risk of CHD. *American Journal of Epidemiology, 102,* 434.

Dressler, W. W. (1984). Social and cultural influences in cardiovascular diseases: A review. *Transcultural Psychiatric Research Review, 21,* 5-42.

Epstein, J. (1977). *Along the gringo trail.* Berkeley, CA: And/Or Press.

Fischer, C. S. (1976). *The urban experience.* New York: Harcourt Brace Jovanovich.

Friedman, A. P., & Rosenman, R. H. (1974). *Type A behavior and your heart.* New York: Knopf.

Gastorf, J. W. (1980). Time urgency of the type A behavior pattern. *Journal of Consulting & Clinical Psychology, 48,* 299.

Hall, E. T. (1959). *The silent language.* New York: Doubleday.

Henry, J. (1965). White people's time-colored people's time. *Trans-Action, 2,* 31-34.

Hernandez, D. (1970). *Mexican American challenge to a sacred cow.* Los Angeles: University of California Chicano Studies Center.

Hoch, I. (1976). City size effects, trends and policies. *Science, 193,* 856-863.

Horton, J. (1972). Time and cool people. In T. Kochman (Ed.), *Rappin and stylin' out* (pp. 19-31). Urbana: University of Illinois Press.

Howard, C. G. (1980). The expatriate manager and the role of the MNC. *So Personnel Journal, 59,* 838-844.

King Hassan of Morocco. (1984, July 9). *New Yorker,* pp. 46-48.

Lauer, R. H. (1981). *Temporal man: The meaning and uses of social time.* New York: Praeger.

Levine, R. (1985, December). It wasn't the time of my life. *Discover,* pp. 66-71.

Levine, R., & Bartlett, K. (1984). Pace of life, punctuality and coronary heart disease in six countries. *Journal of Cross-Cultural Psychology, 15,* 233-255.

Levine, R., & Lynch, K. (1985). [The pace of life across the United States]. Unpublished raw data.

Levine, R., West, L., & Reis, H. (1980). Perceptions of time and punctuality in the United States and Brazil. *Journal of Personality & Social Psychology, 38,* 541-550.

Levine, R., & Wolff, E. (1985, March). Social time: The heartbeat of culture. *Psychology Today,* pp. 28-35.

Lowin, A., Hottes, J., Sander, B., & Bornstein, M. (1971). The pace of life and sensitivity to time in urban and rural settings: A preliminary study. *Journal of Social Psychology, 83,* 247-253.

Lucia, M. (1985). *Effect of season, day of week, and the degree of urbanization on pace of life.* Unpublished master's thesis, California State University, Fresno.

Marmot, M. G., & Syme, S. L. (1976). Acculturation and coronary heart disease in Japanese-Americans. *American Journal of Epidemiology, 104,* 225-247.

Milgram, S. (1970). The experience of living in cities. *Science, 167,* 1461-1468.

Nakane, C. (1970). *Japanese society.* Berkeley: University of California Press.

Piaget, J. (1966). Time perception in children. In J. T. Fraser (Ed.), *The voices of time* (pp. 202-216). New York: Braziller.

Reid, D. D. (1975). International studies in epidemiology. *American Journal of Epidemiology, 102,* 469-476.

Robinson, J. P., & Converse, P. E. (1972). Social change reflected in the use of time. In A. Campbell, & P. E. Converse (Eds.), *The human meaning of social change.* New York: Russell Sage.

Ships with 1800 Marines off Lebanon. (1985, June 23). *Fresno Bee,* p. 1.

Spradley, J. P., & Phillips, M. (1972). Culture and stress: A quantitative analysis. *American Anthropologist, 74,* 518-529.

Switzer, S. (1963). Hypertension and ischemic heart disease in Hiroshima, Japan. *Circulation, 28,* 368-380.

Triplett, N. (1897-1898). The dynamogenic factors in pacemaking and competition. *American Journal of Psychology, 9,* 503-533.

Watzlawick, P. (1976). *How real is real.* New York: Random House.

Werner, C. M., Altman, I., & Oxley, D. (1985). Temporal aspects of homes: A transactional perspective. In I. Altman & C. M. Werner (Eds.), *Home environments: Vol. 8. Human behavior and environment: Advances in theory and research* (pp. 1-32). New York: Plenum.

Winkelstein, W. (1975). Cooperative studies of blood pressure in Japanese in Japan, Hawaii, and the United States. In O. Paul (Ed.), *Epidemiology and control of hypertension.* Miami: Symposia Specialists.

Witmer, J. M., Rich, C., Barcikowski, R. S., & Mague, J. C. (1983). Psychosocial characteristics mediating the stress response: An exploratory study. *Personnel & Guidance Journal,* pp. 73-77.

World Health Organization. (1980). *World health statistics annual, 1980: Vital statistics and causes of death.* Geneva: Author.

Wright, H. F. (1961). *The city-town project: A study of children in communities differing in size.* Unpublished grant report.

Yano, K., Blackwelder, W. C., Kagan, A. et. al. (1979). Childhood cultural experience and the incidence of coronary heart disease in Hawaii Japanese men. *American Journal of Epidemiology, 109,* 440-450.

Zajonc, R., Heigartner, A., & Herman, E. (1969). Social enhancement and impairment of performance in the cockroach. *Journal of Personality & Social Psychology, 13,* 83-92.

PART II

Rhythm

4

Rhythm in Social Interaction

REBECCA WARNER

There has been a substantial amount of research on rhythms in social interaction (Davis, 1982) and partner influence in adult-adult and adult-infant interactions (Cappella, 1981). Most of this research has been concerned with merely documenting the existence of rhythms, however, and there has been little theoretical background for many of the studies (McGrath & Kravitz, 1982). The most ambitious theoretical work on interaction rhythms is by a behavioral anthropologist, Chapple (1970a, 1971, 1982). The aim of this chapter is to review the major elements of Chapple's theory, evaluate them in light of recent research and ideas of other social interaction researchers, and propose a research agenda based on a modified version of Chapple's theory. This research agenda deals with issues such as temperament, interpersonal attraction, dominance, social conflict, and stress.

Basic Issues in Research on Rhythm in Social Interaction

Definitional Issues

The term *rhythm* has been used to refer to many different types of patterns. For instance, Jaffe and Feldstein (1970) used the term *rhythm* to refer to any pattern of serial dependence in on-off vocal activity data, such that the probability that an individual will speak at time t is different depending upon whether the individual was speaking or silent during the previous time interval, t-1. When the term *rhythm* is used in this broadest possible sense, it can refer to any predictable pattern in behavior over time.

In this chapter, the term *rhythm* will be used in a much narrower sense, to refer to recurrent cycles in behavior. But cycles can also have many different shapes or waveforms, for instance, the spiked profile of the cardiac cycle. The particular cycle shape, or waveform, that will be used here to define rhythm is a sinusoid (see Figure 4.1). This smooth curve provides a fairly good description of many well-documented physiological and behavioral rhythms; for instance, body temperature has a circadian rhythm (a cycle length of about 24 hours) that is approximately sinusoidal. This cycle shape has four parameters: M, the overall mean activity level; T, the length of the cycle, or the time from peak to peak; R, the amplitude; and P, the phase, or location of the first peak relative to the time origin or any other arbitrarily designated reference point in time. The set of all possible sinusoids can be obtained by choosing different values of M, T, R, and P. It is fairly simple to fit a sinusoidal curve to time-series data; in fact, given a particular value of T (cycle length or period), the other parameters M, R, and P can be estimated using ordinary least squares methods (Bloomfield, 1976). When T is not known a priori, exploratory data analysis is necessary to judge what value(s) of T or what cycle lengths provide a good fit to observed activity patterns; these methods include periodogram analysis, Fourier transforms, and spectral analysis. The reasons for preferring a sinusoidal waveform to represent rhythm will be developed in more detail in a later section. The primary justifications are the reasonably good fit of sinusoidal cycles to social interaction data in a number of studies, reviewed below; and the mathematical convenience of using such a smooth and symmetrical function. Many other cycle shapes that might seem like reasonable candidates (for instance, box-shaped or saw-toothed waveforms) do not lend themselves well to exploratory analysis or statistical significance testing.

Thus, in this chapter, *rhythm* is defined as the presence of sinusoidal cycles in amount or intensity of activity. For instance, several studies of amount of vocal activity have reported fairly regular alternations between periods of high vocal activity (long or frequent vocalizations) and periods of low vocal activity (brief or infrequent vocalizations) (Cobb, 1973; Dabbs, 1983; Hayes & Cobb, 1979; Warner, 1979). Dabbs (1983) referred to these cycles in amount of activity as "megaturns" to distinguish them from the "turns" reported by other investigators (e.g., Duncan & Fiske, 1977).

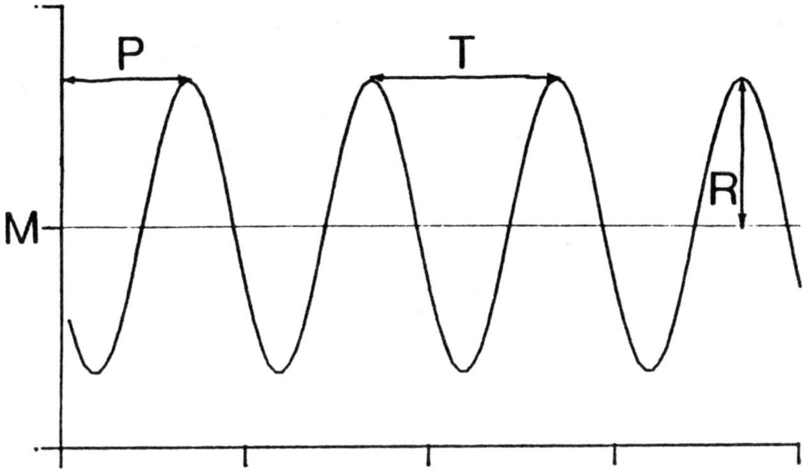

Figure 4.1. Parameters of a Sinusoidal Waveform

Other investigators have defined rhythm quite differently. For instance, some have used models of serial dependence such as first-order Markov process models (Jaffe & Feldstein, 1970); others have used the patterning of movement boundaries observed by human coders (Condon & Sander, 1974). A narrower definition of rhythm has been adopted here to keep the literature review manageable and to avoid vagueness or imprecision. The theory of interaction rhythm that is developed here poses its questions in terms of cycles, but many of the same questions about the relationship between activity pattern parameters and person perceptions, temperament, interpersonal attraction, and so forth, may be applicable to research on other kinds of temporal patterns that are not cyclical. It is important to note that while amount of activity tends to vary cyclically, cycles are not perfectly regular. Many other factors potentially influence amount of social activity, such as mood, interpersonal distance, visual or auditory events that attract the attention of speakers, and so forth.

Data Issues: Basic Features of Social Interaction Data

There are many choices that investigators make in designing time-series observational studies. These include (a) the behaviors to be observed (vocal activity, gaze direction, body movements, and so on);

(b) categorical versus continuous measurements; (c) time-based versus event-based recording; (d) sampling frequency; (e) data record length; and (f) methods of data aggregation and analysis. In many studies, vocal activity has been coded as present or absent by having an analogue-to-digital converter compare voice loudness to a preset threshold value, several hundred times per second. The percentage of time spent speaking during some longer time interval (such as one-third second or five seconds or five minutes) is then obtained by aggregating these decisions. This yields a continuous variable that is observed at equally spaced points in time. Generally, categorical time-series data are analyzed using information theory or lagged conditional probabilities (Gottman & Bakeman, 1978); whereas continuous time-series data can be analyzed using lagged autocorrelations, Box-Jenkins time series models, and spectral analysis (Gottman, 1981). This wider range of analytic methods makes it advantageous to work with continuous data, where possible.

It should be noted that the decisions that a computer makes about variations in amount of talking over time, and the decisions that a human coder makes about the boundaries of turns or other units, do not yield identical information. In fact, they are related to each other in much the same way that a topographical map (showing details of the terrain) is related to a political map (showing boundaries between nations) (Warner, 1979). While the political boundaries often follow geographic features, they do not always do so. Analysis of units such as turns is also very valuable; but we learn something different, and equally valuable, from simply looking at the amount of activity without trying to break it up into units such as turns.

Another important point is that basic design decisions about the sampling frequency and data record length determine the order of magnitude of structures that can be seen in time-series data, much like levels of magnification in a microscope (Hayes, Meltzer, & Wolf, 1970). The shortest cycle that can be observed is equal to two observations, and the longest complete cycle that can be observed is equal to the length of the data record. For vocal activity, cyclic patterns have been reported at many orders of temporal magnitude. Cycles on the order of kilohertz (thousands of cycles per second) provide the spectral identity of speech sounds and also voice pitch. Cycles on the order of 40 to 1200 seconds have been reported in the amount of talk during conversations (Cobb, 1973; Dabbs, 1983; Warner, 1979). Cycles on the order of 90 to 100 minutes have been reported in amount of conversational activity (Hayes

& Cobb, 1979). Some a priori notion of the cycle lengths that are being looked for is necessary in order to make appropriate decisions about sampling frequency.

Conceptual Issues: Why Study Rhythm?

Three important theoretical issues underlie research on rhythms:

How pervasive are rhythmic processes in human behavior?
Why are social systems organized rhythmically?
What testable hypotheses can we derive from the assumption that rhythm is a fundamental organizing principle of social interaction?

One major reason for studying rhythm is because it's there! In a later section I review the substantial research literature showing the pervasiveness of rhythmic processes in social systems. Furthermore, the data needed to study rhythms—observations about amounts of time spent in given activities (or inactivity)—can be gathered reliably using either human coders or automated systems. As Fiske (1979) pointed out in his discussion of the observation versus interpretation of behavior, many of the variables used in social psychology are interpretive judgments about behavior made by trained observers, and thus they have theoretical assumptions already built into them. On-off activity data involve simpler observations that can be made with minimal previous assumptions. Neither of these justifications, however, is likely to satisfy critics who see this form of data collection as rather sterile. A more compelling reason for studying social interaction rhythm is that this research may provide answers to two types of questions: Why are so many social interactions rhythmically organized, and what factors influence rhythm? And what consequences does social interaction rhythm have for the perceptions and feelings of social interaction partners?

Why should social systems be organized rhythmically? One argument for the pervasiveness of rhythms is borrowed from theories in biology. When biological rhythms were first observed, they were viewed as a mere curiosity. In recent years, however, many eminent biologists and physiologists have come to view rhythm as a fundamental organizing principle of living systems (Bunning, 1973; Goodwin, 1970; Iberall & McCulloch, 1969; Pittendrigh, 1975; Yates, 1974). Two crucial advantages of rhythmic organization are, first, that rhythm is a form of dynamic equilibrium that makes it possible for an organism to vary its metabolic, reproductive, and other activities over time while still keeping system parameters within limits; and second, that rhythm facilitates the coordination of many physiological processes within an organism, and also helps the organism coordinate its activities with a periodically varying environment (Goodwin, 1970).

The notion of dynamic equilibrium can be explained quite simply by contrasting it with static equilibrium. For instance, if body temperature exhibited static equilibrium, homeostatic regulatory mechanisms would always tend to restore body temperature to a constant level of 98.6 degrees Fahrenheit. In fact, that is not what happens; in the absence of disruptive environmental influences, body temperature tends toward a circadian (approximately 24-hour) cycle, and when temperature is perturbed, the homeostatic mechanisms tend to *restore it to this cycle, not to a constant level.* The equilibrium level varies cyclically. Many biologists now believe that most, if not all, physiological processes show dynamic equilibrium (cyclic variation) rather than static equilibrium (Yates, 1974). Many social psychological theories use the idea of equilibrium (e.g., Cappella & Greene, 1982; Patterson, 1976) to describe the regulation of intimacy and arousal during social interaction; however, most theories implicitly assume a static equilibrium. Iberall and McCulloch (1969) argue that social as well as physiological processes are rhythmically organized. This idea merits at least some attention; by continuing to rely on static equilibrium models, we are using an outdated version of physiology. The substantial within-individual variability over time that occurs due to cycles is ignored in many studies of physiological "arousal" or activity level. Depending upon the design of the study, variance due to rhythmic organization may be a substantial part of what we have usually treated as error variance, or may be confounded with other factors in the designs.

The second function of rhythm in physiological systems is to facilitate coordination among many physiological events (e.g., timing of DNA replication and cell wall division, Goodwin, 1970). Gradually, it is becoming apparent that many rhythmic physiological processes are coupled to each other; for instance, heart rate varies as a function of the respiratory cycle (Porges, Bohrer, Cheung, Drasgow, McCabe, & Keren, 1980). Many of the linkages among internal physiological rhythms may be weak, or complex and nonlinear. Pittendrigh (1975) has proposed, however, that an organism can be viewed as a (loosely) coupled "population of oscillators." An oscillator here refers to a rhythmic or cyclic physiological process. A certain amount of temporal order among these oscillators is important to the physical well-being of the organism.

If we borrow this idea and apply it to the social system, a social system can also be viewed as a "population of oscillators" (see Chapple, 1970a), in that each member's activity varies rhythmically and the behaviors of members become coordinated during joint activities such as conversation, team work, walking or marching, dancing or singing, and so forth. Rhythm could conceivably serve the same function in social systems that it has been claimed to serve in physiological systems: facilitating coordination of activities.

This argument by analogy merely indicates that rhythm might play a similar role in all complex living systems whether they are examined at the physiological or the social level of analysis. Of course, the details of rhythmic organization at each level would need to be worked out empirically. The arguments above are not testable hypotheses; they are conjectures about why rhythm might have evolved or why it might be characteristic of many different kinds of systems.

Statistical Issues

One basic question that haunts research on rhythms is the problem of statistical artifact. Could the rhythms reported in social interaction data in fact be statistical artifacts or mistaken subjective impressions of observers? There is a very real danger involved in any definition of rhythm that relies on subjective visual examination of data and post hoc identification of boundaries. Jaffe, Breskin, and Gerstman (1972) demonstrated that one type of cyclicity reported in on-off vocal activity data could in fact be generated by a random process. The famous case of "Biological rhythms in the unicorn" (Cole, 1957) illustrates how apparent cyclicity can be introduced into data by commonly used data manipulations.

One reason for adopting the sinusoidal cycle as a definition of rhythm (see Figure 4.1 above) is that this definition makes it possible to test goodness of fit. It is possible to estimate the percentage of variance that is accounted for by fitting one or more periodic components to time-series data. Also, we can do statistical significance tests of the null hypothesis that the time series data represent a random process. This model may not ultimately be the best description of the waveform, but at least it puts the analysis of rhythm into the form of potentially falsifiable hypotheses. There is still a great deal of subjective judgment and interpretation that goes into the design and interpretation of data analyses that examine cyclicity, but it is possible in principle to describe the decision process clearly enough so that it can be replicated by others.

There are many potential sources of artifact in statistical rhythm analysis; these include the effects of nonstationarity, leakage, and aliasing, among other problems (Bloomfield, 1976). As investigators become more sophisticated and more careful about these problems, however, such artifacts should become less worrisome. To summarize: The danger that some reported rhythms represent statistical artifact or mistaken subjective impressions is very real. It is extremely important that investigators evaluate the potential violations of assumptions before beginning data analysis.

Summary

The idea that the temporal organization of social interaction is an important focus for study is not entirely new to social psychology. Parsons (1951) pointed out that there can be conflict over time allocation in social systems, just as there is conflict over other scarce resources; and control of time, like control of other resources, is a basis of power. Strauss (1965), in an introduction to collected works of G. H. Mead, noted that Mead's work points toward a view of "negotiated temporal order" in social systems. Each member brings preferences about the timing of activities to any organizational setting, and the activities of members of social organizations need to be coordinated for the organization to function smoothly. Strauss suggested that we need to work out the empirical details of negotiation over time allocation; this issue applies to all social systems ranging from dyadic conversations to large organizations.

The most important reason for doing research on social interaction rhythm is that a fairly simple model of social interaction (social system as a "population of oscillators") generates a very extensive set of testable hypotheses and may provide a unified framework for the description of individual differences (temperament), person perception, interpersonal attraction, dominance, attachment, the effects of bereavement, and many other facets of social interaction. The most extensive theory proposed to date (Chapple, 1970a) is reviewed and evaluated in subsequent sections.

A Theory of Rhythm in Social Interaction

Basically, Chapple's theory, as outlined here, represents a social interaction as a "population of oscillators." Each participant has one or more rhythms in activity and, during the social interaction, the participants' interaction rhythms may become mutually entrained (that is, the cycle lengths become equal). From this simple model, it is possible to derive predictions about temperament, interpersonal attraction, and dominance. There are a number of problems with Chapple's argument. What I propose to do is to retain the basic idea of a social interaction as a population of oscillators and modify several of the specific elements of this theory to clarify them in relation to psychological theories or to make them more easily testable.

Chapple's Social Interaction Theory

Chapple's theory of social interaction rhythm has been most extensively presented in his book (1970a) and in later articles and chapters (1971, 1982). The major elements of this theory are briefly outlined here, and are discussed critically and modified in a later section.

(1) Most physiological processes are rhythmically organized.

(2) The probability of initiating and maintaining activity varies as a function of (rhythmically varying) physiological states.

(3) It follows that, if one could observe interaction tempo under "free-running" conditions (that is, with no environmental influences that would disrupt the individual's activity pattern), the social interaction tempo would be influenced by physiological rhythms.

(4) This interaction tempo can be described by a box-shaped waveform that consists of an action followed by an inaction. A human coder determines when actions begin and end; an action includes not only vocal activity but any other activity such as body movement. A is the duration of an action; S is the duration of the silence or inaction. Chapple suggested that these durations tend to be constant for an individual. The cycle length T is the sum of A + S. The percentage of time spent active is simply A/ (A + S).

(5) There are consistent individual differences in these interaction tempo parameters A and S (or equivalently, T and percentage of time spent active). These are based upon individual differences in physiological rhythms.

(6) Temperament and emotional reactions to social situations can be described by examining the individual's reaction to interruptions or nonresponses of partners that interfere with or disrupt the interaction tempo.

(7) An individual may have multiple interaction tempos (e.g., shorter cycles superimposed on longer cycles). Chapple believed that these would be harmonics of some fundamental frequency or period.

(8) When two people engage in a social interaction, they must adjust their interaction tempos in order to achieve reasonably smooth turn-taking. Interruptions and nonresponses serve to shape behavior of partners toward complementarity. Complementarity occurs when the periods of the interaction tempos of persons A and B are equal (Ta = Tb) and their activity levels are compatible (percentage of time that A is active added to percentage of time that B is active is approximately equal to 100%).

(9) There may be limits to the flexibility of interaction tempo. Some persons may be more flexible than others.

(10) If two people A and B have baseline interaction tempos that are naturally complementary, then neither partner has to make much adjustment in interaction tempo in order to coordinate activities. Chapple proposed that, other things being equal, people find it much easier and more pleasant to interact with a partner whose interaction tempo is complementary.

(11) If two people A and B have baseline interaction tempos that are very far from complementarity (either because their cycle lengths Ta and Tb are very different or because their percentage of time spent active sums to much more or much less than 100%), they will find it difficult or perhaps even impossible to coordinate their activities. Frequent interruptions and/or nonresponses will result. Interruptions may be interpreted as attempts to dominate, and nonresponses may be embarrassing or awkward. Thus they will tend to find the interaction difficult or unpleasant.

(12) Dominance can be defined as the ability to impose one's own preferred tempo on a social interaction.

The Causal Priority Issue

The first problematic part of Chapple's reasoning is the proposal that interaction tempo is somehow determined by physiological rhythms. It is quite possible that behavioral and physiological rhythms may be related but there is no a priori reason to assign causal priority to the physiological level. It is equally possible that social cues serve to synchronize or disrupt physiological rhythms. There is some evidence for synchronization of the circadian body temperature cycle (Aschoff, Fatranska, Giedke, Doerr, Stamm, & Wisser, 1971) and the menstrual cycle (McClintock, 1971) to social cues, and Bunning (1973) suggested that for humans, social cues may be among the most important synchronizers of physiological rhythms. It is also possible that there is mutual influence or feedback between physiological and behavioral rhythms. For example, Lenneberg (1967) pointed out that prolonged vocalization leads to hyperventilation, which depletes arterial CO_2 levels. Arterial CO_2 is the primary internal stimulus for (respiratory) inspiration; and it is conceivable that low levels of arterial CO_2 tend to inhibit (i.e., lower the probability of) both respiratory inspiration and vocalization until the gas blood level has risen. Warner, Waggener, and Kronauer (1983) found synchronized cycles in ventilation and vocal activity for some speakers that could possibly be due to such a feedback loop in which ventilation and vocalization influence each other; however, this study was only correlational and there was no direct test of the proposed mechanisms.

There has been considerable interest recently in examining physiological changes that occur during social interaction or in response to social cues (Caccioppo & Petty, 1983; Lynch, 1985; Waid, 1984). Most investigators look for a change in the *level* or mean of some physiological process in response to a social cue. For example, Dabbs and Moorer (1975) found that core body temperature increases during social interaction. Because both behavior and physiological processes are rhythmically organized, however, it may be more appropriate to ask how changes in social psychological variables correspond with physiological rhythms. Social psychological events might produce a change in the period (T) or amplitude (R) or phase (P), as well as a change in the mean (M). Social situations could either make physiological processes more rhythmic or disrupt rhythm. For example, Lynch, Thomas, Mills, Malinow, and Katcher (1974) have shown that routine pulse-taking interactions with patients in a CCU (coronary care unit) can either increase or decrease heart rate and increase or decrease the amount of cardiac arrhythmia, depending upon whether the touch is perceived as threatening. When we look for relationships between physiological and behavioral changes during social interactions, perhaps we should think about changes in rhythm as well as changes in mean activity levels.

One type of research that could be done to examine covariation of rhythmic behavioral and physiological processes is fairly simple: There are statistics such as the cross spectrum (Gottman, 1981) and the weighted coherence (Porges et al., 1980) that examine co-occurrence or statistical dependence in the frequency domain. Simple observational studies would answer the question: Is there any evidence that there are synchronized rhythms in the behavior and the physiological processes of an individual? The study of synchronized cycles in ventilation and vocal activity by Warner, Waggener, and Kronauer (1983) illustrates one possible approach. Observational studies cannot answer questions about causal priority or the mechanisms through which the coupling or synchronization occurs, however.

It is possible that co-occurrence of rhythmic changes in behavior (such as vocal activity) and physiology (such as ventilation) could be due to some other variable (such as emotional arousal) that affects both processes and leads to a spurious correlation. Both the behavioral and the physiological rhythm could be influenced by the same environmental cues that would again lead to a spurious correlation. Some reported instances of synchronization of physiological rhythms to social cues, such as social synchrony of menstrual cycles (McClintock, 1971) could be due to the fact that roommates and friends share similar environments and light/dark cycles, or they could be mediated by other influences such as olfactory communication. Most biological rhythms research is conducted under "free-running" conditions (that is, all environmental cues that are known to affect the physiological rhythms are held constant). Separating social influences from environmental influences is very difficult even under free-running conditions. It should be fairly easy to evaluate whether physiological rhythms are correlated with social interaction rhythms, but it will be considerably more difficult to evaluate the nature of the mechanisms through which they are related.

Of course, it is possible that the social interaction rhythms that Chapple saw in his data arise out of nonbiological factors such as social norms requiring turn-taking or temporal factors in information processing (Warner, 1979). Rhythm might be a powerful organizing principle in social systems as it is in biological systems, but the two sets of rhythms might in practice be quite independent of each other. Even if Chapple's notion that interaction tempo is biologically based turns out to be untenable, the other elements of this theory are still interesting as a basis for analyzing social interaction.

The Relation of Tempo to Temperament

A second problematic element in Chapple's theory is his definition of temperament. His use of this term is quite different from the definitions used by psychologists. He defines *temperament* primarily in terms of how individuals react (behaviorally and emotionally) to disruptions of their preferred interaction tempos. He has done a little research on what he calls "transients," reactions to interruptions and nonresponses, to see how individuals react to these disruptions of their preferred interaction tempos (Chapple, 1970b). Chapple cited no psychological temperament theories in the development of his argument. There are several temperament or personality theories, however, that propose a biological basis for temperament and include activity pattern parameters such as overall amount of activity or energy, speed of response, flexibility or adaptability, and intensity or rhythmicity of behavior as part of temperament assessment (Allport, 1961; Buss & Plomin, 1975; Kagan, 1967; Thomas, Chess, & Birch, 1970; see also Diamond, 1957, for a review of the notion of activity as a personality dimension). Most of these theorists measured activity pattern parameters through ratings that are based on global impressions. Allport and Vernon (1933) did an extensive study of what they called "personal tempo" and they found very high test-retest reliabilities for a variety of rate or intensity measurements of expressive behaviors such as walking, drawing, writing, and talking.

The major problem with these theories relating activity pattern to temperament is that they are rather vague about what to look for. Furthermore, there is a problem in defining and measuring temperament: Are the ratings that people use to describe themselves on paper-and-pencil tests a measure of "real" personality or temperament, or merely an example of self-presentation strategy? This problem can be sidestepped by rephrasing the question in terms of person perception, and simply asking how personality ratings (by self, partner, outside observer, or clinician) are related to activity pattern parameters. The parameters of the sinusoidal rhythm model proposed above are M, T, R, and P. Person perception, however, may also be related to many other activity pattern parameters such as speech rate, mean length of turn, and so forth.

There is a fair amount of evidence that M (overall mean activity level) is both a reliable individual difference among persons and a good predictor of ratings of dominance and likability. Warner, Kenny, and

Stoto (1979) and Jaffe and Feldstein (1970) found that mean vocal activity level (percentage of time spent speaking) is a consistent individual difference, even though speakers do adjust their activity levels to different partners. More generally, the tendency to initiate all sorts of motor activities seems to be a reliable individual difference (Takala, 1975). McGowan and Gormly (1976) found that "energeticness" is a very reliable individual difference whether it is assessed through peer ratings or actual behavioral assessments. The relationship of vocal activity level to person perception was examined in an elegant study by Hayes and Meltzer (1972) in which an on-off light display was used to represent the on-off vocal activity patterns of participants in a panel discussion. They found that ratings of dominance based on the light display were highly correlated with judgments based on a videotape of the discussion (*r*'s ranged from .55 to .92). Furthermore, while dominance ratings increased as a linear function of amount of talk, evaluative judgments were a curvilinear function of activity (with moderately active participants rated most favorably). They argued that the on-off activity pattern and the overall mean activity level were important sources of information about these fundamental social dimensions—dominance and evaluation.

Very little research has been done so far to see whether there are consistent individual differences in other cycle parameters (the period, T; amplitude, R; and phase, P). There is some evidence of individual differences in the free-running cycle lengths of many circadian physiological rhythms (Bunning, 1973; Chapple, 1970a). Blake (1967) reported that there is a difference in the phase of the body temperature circadian rhythms of introverts and extroverts; the body temperature of introverts begins to rise earlier in the day. The only suggestion that Chapple (1970a) offered about interpretation of individual differences in tempo was his observation that, if an individual has unusually short or long cycles (T) or if the individual's percentage of time active is very far from 50%, then that individual may have difficulty finding complementary partners, and may be unpopular. It is also possible that rigidity or inflexibility of physiological rhythms may be associated with a more general personality inflexibility (e.g., Richman, Patty, & Fisher, 1976).

Another useful parameter may be degree of rhythmicity (what percentage of variance in the individual's behavior over time is accounted for by periodic or cyclic components?). This is related to R; a cyclic component that has a large amplitude is also one that accounts for a large percentage of the variance. Warner et al. (1986) found that rhythmicity of social interaction had a curvilinear relationship to observer evaluations; moderately rhythmic conversations were rated more positively. Rhythmicity was a useful predictor of observer ratings even after simpler statistics (such as percentage of time spent speaking) were partialed out.

Mapping out the kinds of behaviors that affect judgments of dominance and evaluation could be viewed as a form of social psychophysics (see Brown, Strong, & Rencher, 1974). Real or simulated activity patterns can be presented to judges to see what personality characteristics they will perceive. Of course, this assesses only judges' beliefs or stereotypes about the meanings of behavior patterns. Determining the accuracy of these beliefs is more difficult. Allport (1961) felt that personal tempo and expressive behaviors were in fact a reflection of the individual's personality. It is conceivable that something fundamental about the biological identity of the individual (sex, age, state of health, emotional arousal, and so on) is communicated through the activity pattern parameters. For instance, it is possible to guess sex and age of speaker from fundamental frequency or voice pitch (Scherer & Giles, 1979). Of course, it is also conceivable that people learn self-presentation styles that modify their activity patterns, and this might make expressive behaviors less reliable as sources of information about identity.

The Choice of Cyclical Waveform

A third element of Chapple's theory that needs modification is his definition of a cycle. Chapple (1971, 1982) and Chapple and Lui (1976) suggested that a box-shaped or saw-toothed nonlinear oscillation is the best description of an individual's cycles of action and inaction. The chief problem with this definition is that the mathematics of nonlinear systems are complex and not yet fully worked out, and this definition does not lend itself to statistical evaluation (goodness of fit or significance testing). It is possible to inspect data visually and to "fit" box-shaped cycles after the fact, but there is no way to evaluate whether the cycle durations are consistent or whether the pattern over time differs from a random process.

Adopting a sinusoidal waveform as the definition of a cycle (see Figure 4.1 above) makes it possible to use statistics for exploratory data analysis. There is a whole set of techniques for analysis in the frequency domain that involve fitting sinusoids to data, including harmonic analysis, periodogram analysis, the Fourier transform, and spectral analysis (Bloomfield, 1976). Essentially, periodogram analysis works as follows. For a time series with N observations, it is possible to partition the variance into the variance that is accounted for by N/2 periodic components (each with 2 df), in a manner analogous to the analysis of variance (Box & Jenkins, 1970). The set of (orthogonal) periodic components consists of sinusoids with periods of N/1, N/2, N/3, . . . 2 (that is, the longest cycle is the same length as the data record and the shortest cycle is 2 observations long.) For instance, if the data record is 30 minutes long, the cycle lengths would be 30/1, 30/2, 30/3, . . ., 30/14, 30/15, or 30, 15, 10, . . . 2 minutes long. The null hypothesis is that the time series is "white noise" or a mixture of many sinusoidal components with equal amplitude. The periodogram yields estimates of the amplitude and phase for each of the N/2 periodic components. The amplitude for each periodic component is squared and multiplied by a constant to yield an estimate of "intensity" associated with each cycle length or period (this intensity is like a sum of squares). If the null hypothesis is true, then there should be equal intensity across all frequencies, or a flat periodogram. Of course, due to sampling error, the periodogram is typically not flat even when the data are random. If one periodic component accounts for a large share of the variance or fits the data very well, its intensity estimate will be large and it will have a peak in the otherwise flat periodogram. There are significance testing procedures to help evaluate whether a peak is likely to have arisen by chance. A simple worked example of the periodogram is presented by Box and Jenkins (1970) in a manner that makes the analogy to analysis of variance clear. In practice, the Fourier transform is generally used to decompose a time series into frequency components. The periodogram is rarely used because it is subject to large sampling error; the power spectrum is a periodogram that has been smoothed, averaged, or filtered in some way.

The major advantage of using spectral analysis is that it assists in identifying the periods of one or more cycles that may be masked by random error, and it includes estimates for cycle parameters R and P. Significance tests are available to evaluate which periodic components are unlikely to be due merely to sampling error. It is possible to obtain rough estimates of the percentage of variance accounted for by the few large or significant periodic components, although the spectrum is not a strict variance partitioning like the periodogram.

There are disadvantages associated with the use of spectral analysis. If the data contain trends, spikes, abrupt shifts in level, or other features that do not resemble sinusoids, these will create artifacts in the spectrum. Spectral analysis assumes stationarity (constancy of the mean, variance, and other process parameters over time). Violations of the stationarity assumption can often be remedied by detrending or data transformations but if these are not dealt with, the spectrum is uninterpretable. Other technical problems such as leakage and aliasing are explained by Bloomfield (1976). Violations of any of the assumptions of the analysis may either create spikes in the spectrum that do not correspond to periodic components or may mask periodic components that are present. Briefly, the assumptions that must be met for the spectral analysis to be valid include the following (see Bloomfield for further discussion): The time series must be stationary, it must be composed of sinusoidal components whose cycle lengths match the set of frequencies for which spectral estimates are calculated, and there must not be any abrupt discontinuities or sharp corners in the data record. Used alone, spectral analysis can produce misleading results; investigators should also refer back to the original time-series data before concluding that cycles are present, and band pass filtering may also be useful to examine periodic behavior at a particular frequency (Warner, Waggener, & Kronauer, 1983).

Numerous studies have found evidence of cycles in social interaction using lagged autocorrelations, Fourier transform, or spectral analysis. Kimberly (1970) found regular cycles on the order of three minutes and six minutes long in the social behavior of a mentally retarded woman. Cobb (1973) found that seven out of the nine informal conversations he analyzed using lagged autocorrelations showed significant tendencies toward regular cycles in amount of talk ($p < .001$) with estimated cycle lengths ranging from 46 to 132 seconds. Warner (1979) looked at six conversations between college students and found cycles in amount of talk that were on the order of 3 to 6 minutes and 12 to 20 minutes. Dabbs (1983) examined 24 dyadic conversations and found evidence of longer cycles in talk in "high cognitive load" conversations (32 to 128 seconds) and shorter cycles in "low cognitive load" conversations (1 to 8 seconds).

Wade, Ellis, and Bohrer (1973) looked at variations in heart rate during free play in children alone, in dyads, and in triads; they found that heart rate tended to vary cyclically with cycles on the order of 15 and 40 minutes, with the strongest periodicity in dyadic situations. A study of solitary and social oral activity in rhesus monkeys by Maxim, Bowden, and Sackett (1976) yielded cycles about 45 minutes long in both solitary and social oral (aggressive) activity. They reported that the tempo of the social oral activity was similar to the tempo of solitary oral activity for the dominant monkey.

Hayes and Cobb (1979) recorded the conversational activity of couples who lived in a laboratory apartment isolated from outside time cues for extended periods of time; they found many periodic components in amount of talk, with the most conspicuous being the 24-hour (circadian) cycle and a 90- to 100-minute cycle they theorized was related to the Basic Rest Activity Cycle.

Unfortunately, most of these studies do not report enough information to evaluate whether the reported cyclicity could be partly statistical artifact, and few studies have employed systematic statistical significance testing. Warner (1979) compared simulated on-off vocal activity data (derived from a random process) with actual vocal activity data and demonstrated that there was no evidence of periodicity in the simulated data, while there were large peaks in the averaged spectrum for the actual data. Better guidelines for the application and reporting of spectral analysis are needed in future research.

Complementarity and Interpersonal Attraction

The area where the most work has been done recently is mutual influence or contingency of behaviors. An excellent review by Cappella (1981) summarized many of the key issues in this area, although he did not deal specifically with the idea of rhythm and mutual entrainment. The modified version of Chapple's theory that is proposed here would lead to the following criteria for complementarity:

(1) Both partners should have statistically significant cyclicity with the same cycle lengths (Ta = Tb). There may be multiple shared frequencies or cycles.
(2) Cross-spectral analysis of the activity patterns of persons A and B should yield high coherence (which is like an R-squared) at the same frequencies that had significant cyclicity.
(3) There should be a consistent phase relationship between the cycles in the behavior of A and B.
(4) The percentage of time spent speaking by A and B should sum to approximately 100%.

No study has yet been done using all these components of complementarity. Hoskins (1979) looked at circadian rhythms in body temperature and predicted that conflict in married couples would be associated with desynchronized temperature cycles; she also found no significant relationship. Watts (1982) did a study of circadian rhythms of college roommates in relation to compatibility. Neither of these studies provides a very comprehensive test of Chapple's hypothesis that complementarity of interaction tempos is associated with interpersonal attraction.

Although most theorists seem to share Chapple's basic assumption that rhythmicity is associated with positive affect (e.g., Field, 1985; Hofer, 1984; Iberall & McCulloch, 1969; Warner, 1982), there are a few investigators who proceed from an opposite assumption. Gottman (1979) argued that the degree of patterning in a social interaction is an indication of the degree of social pathology. Kaplan, Burch, and Bloom (1964) found that close correlation between heart rate changes of participants in a discussion group was associated with negative affect. Levenson and Gottman (1983) found that strong serial dependence between physiological arousal changes in husband and wife dyads was associated with marital conflict. Their analysis used transfer function models, however, and did not specifically consider possible cyclicity. In any case, future researchers should not take for granted that rhythmicity is associated with either positive or negative affect. A small study by Warner, Malloy, Schneider, Knoth, and Wilder (1986) suggests that there could be a curvilinear relationship between rhythmicity of social interaction and affect, with moderately rhythmic social interactions rated most positively. This question needs further empirical work.

Of course, rhythm would not be the only factor affecting interpersonal attraction. There are many other variables including similarity of attitude, background, age, and other attributes; proximity; reward power; physical attractiveness; past interaction history; and so forth. Complementarity of rhythm might help explain why we find some available, attractive, and self-similar partners more attractive than others; or why we are sometimes attracted to persons who are not similar in attitudes and background.

Dominance and Asymmetry of Partner Influence

Gottman and Ringland (1981) proposed that one way to look for social dominance is to estimate the degree to which A's activity is predictable from partner B's past behavior, and B's activity is predictable from A's, using cross-spectral analysis and transfer function models to examine mutual influence as well as serial correlation of present actions with the actor's own past behavior. Essentially, they proposed that if B's behavior is more predictable from A's than A's behavior is predictable from B's, then A is dominant in that social situation. Although cyclicity is not one of the features of behavior included in their model, their proposed methodology might provide a useful way to test Chapple's hypothesis that dominance is the ability to influence interaction tempo and partner behavior.

It is worth noting that analysis of very simple behavioral data (such as frequency of interruption) does not by itself explain perceptions of dominance, perhaps because there are so many different kinds of interruption (Ferguson, 1977). Dominance may be a function of more subtle features of interaction tempo than simply amount of interruption.

Desynchronization and Stress

Chapple's consideration of the effects of desynchronization, or poor coordination between partner activity tempos, stopped with a consideration of immediate emotional reactions. It is conceivable that there are longer-range consequences as well.

There is considerable evidence from biological research that desynchronization among internal physiological rhythms (caused, for example, by the frequent changes in time zone experienced by airline crews or swing shift work schedules in factories) may have detrimental effects on vigilance, physical health, and mental health (Moore-Ede, Sulzman, & Fuller, 1982). Desynchronization between activity rhythms and internal physiological rhythms may be associated with neuroticism (Lund, 1974) and depression (Wehr & Goodwin, 1983), although the direction of any possible causal relationship is not clear.

It is conceivable that many social situations may either entrain or disrupt physiological rhythms. The mutual entrainment of activity rhythms may be an important element in parent-infant attachment (Field, 1985; Lester, Hoffman, & Brazelton, 1985); and one reason why isolation and bereavement are risk factors for illness may be because they deprive the individual of social cues that are essential for stimulating and synchronizing the physiological system (Hofer, 1984; Warner, 1982). Thus a long-term outcome of social stress (isolation or bereavement) may be an alteration or disruption of physiological rhythms that is detrimental to physical and mental health.

A Partial Research Agenda

It should be clear that the theory and the modifications proposed above consist mostly of untested conjectures. The primary goal of this chapter is to set up a research agenda based on this theory that provides a unified framework for analysis of social interaction rhythms. Certainly additional modifications to the theory will be necessary as empirical results come in. The theory is useful, however, even in its current primitive state, because it provides so many interesting, testable hypotheses.

Some Key Research Needs

(1) Basic descriptive work on social interaction rhythms is needed. Vocal activity is known to be cyclic—what about gaze direction and body movement? What are the typical cycle lengths?

(2) Individual differences in interaction tempo need to be examined more systematically to see how stable interaction tempo is across situations and partners.

(3) The relations between vocal activity cycle parameters (M, T, P, R) and self-ratings and observer ratings need to be examined to see whether person perceptions are affected by these activity pattern parameters.

(4) Research is needed to see what situational factors, such as task complexity, topic intimacy, interpersonal distance, and so forth, affect interaction tempo.

(5) It would be interesting to know whether there are differences in interaction tempo across languages and cultures; age, sex, and social status; and other group differences.

(6) It will be useful to see whether manipulations of physiological states (e.g., through administration of stimulant or depressant drugs) affect interaction tempo. A study by Jaffe, Dahlberg, Luria, and Chorosh (1973) found that LSD and amphetamines affected mean pause durations.

(7) It is possible to examine how manipulations of the social situation affect rhythms of physiological processes. For instance, Wade, Ellis, and Bohrer (1973) found that heart rate was more periodic for children playing in dyads than for children playing alone or in triads. Variables that might be manipulated include group size, interpersonal distance, topic intimacy, and so forth.

(8) It would be interesting to see whether interaction tempo and the degree of coordination between partners undergo changes as relationships develop over time. This would require longitudinal research.

(9) Finally, it would be interesting to see whether the detrimental effects of isolation, crowding, and many other forms of social stress or conflict on physical health are due to the disruption of interaction tempo and desynchronization of physiological rhythms from social cues.

Concluding Remarks

The research agenda for social interaction rhythms that has been proposed here has many advantages. The observations can be made simply and reliably. Most of the analysis can be done using widely available packaged computer program libraries such as BMOP (Thrall and Engleman, 1981). The methods can easily be applied to adult-adult or infant-adult interaction. Because verbal content is not needed for this type of research, cross-cultural or even cross-species comparisons of social interaction tempo can be made.

The key concepts for understanding the effects of interaction tempo are temperament, attraction, dominance, and stress. To some extent, perceptions of temperament and personality may be based upon amount and patterning of activity. Interpersonal attraction may be affected by the ease or difficulty of coordinating interaction tempos. Dominance may be defined as the ability to control or influence a partner's activity pattern, to impose one's own preferred tempo on an interaction. Stress may be the result of a breakdown in the temporal order of social systems or desynchronization of physiological rhythms as a result of bereavement, isolation, or conflict situations. All these ideas are still conjectures that have yet to be adequately tested. Studies that are designed to explore these issues, however, should yield interesting results that may help us develop a unified and consistent theory of social interaction rhythms.

REFERENCES

Allport, G. W. (1961). *Pattern and growth in personality.* New York: Holt, Rinehart & Winston.

Allport, D. W., & Vernon, P. F. (1933). *Studies in expressive movement.* New York: Macmillan.

Aschoff, J., Fatranska, M., Giedke, H., Doerr, P., Stamm, D., & Wisser, H. (1971). Human circadian rhythms in continuous darkness: Entrainment by social cues. *Science, 171*, 213-215.

Blake, M.J.F. (1967). Relationship between circadian rhythms of body temperature and introversion-extraversion. *Nature, 215*, 896-897.

Bloomfield, P. (1976). *Fourier analysis of time series: An introduction.* New York: John Wiley.

Box, G.E.P., & Jenkins, G. M. (1970). *Time series analysis: Forecasting and control.* San Francisco: Jossey-Bass.

Brown, B. L., Strong, W. L., & Rencher, A. C. (1974). Fifty-four voices from two: The effects of simultaneous manipulations of rate, mean fundamental frequency, and variance of fundamental frequency on ratings of personality from speech. *Journal of the Acoustical Society of America, 55*, 313-318.

Bunning, E. (1973). *The physiological clock.* London: English Universities Press.

Buss, A., & Plomin, R. (1975). *A temperament theory of personality development.* New York: John Wiley.

Caccioppo, J. T., & Petty, R. E. (Eds.). (1983). *Social psychophysiology: A sourcebook.* New York: Guilford.

Cappella, J. N. (1981). Mutual influence in expressive behavior: Adult-adult and infant-adult dyadic interaction. *Psychological Bulletin, 89*, 101-132.

Cappella, J. N., & Greene, J. O. (1982). A discrepancy-arousal explanation of mutual influence in expressive behavior for adult and infant-adult interaction. *Communication Monographs, 49*, 89-114.

Chapple, E. D. (1970a). *Culture and biological man: Explorations in behavioral anthropolopy.* New York: Holt, Rinehart & Winston.

Chapple, E. D. (1970b). Experimental production of transients in human interaction. *Nature, 228*, 630-633.

Chapple, E. D. (1971). Toward a mathematical model of interaction: Some preliminary considerations. In P. Kay (Ed.), *Explorations in mathematical anthropology.* Cambridge: MIT Press.

Chapple, E. D. (1982). Movement and sound: The musical language of body rhythms in interaction. In M. Davis (Ed.), *Interaction rhythms: Periodicity in communicative behavior.* New York: Human Sciences Press.

Chapple, E. D., & Lui, Y. Y. (1976). Populations of coupled non-linear oscillators in anthropological biology systems. In *Systems, man and cybernetic society conference proceedings.* Washington, DC: Institute of Electrical and Electronic Engineers, Inc.

Cobb, L. (1973). *Time series analysis of the periodicities of casual conversation.* Unpublished doctoral dissertation, Cornell University.

Cole, L. C. (1975). Biological clock in the unicorn. *Science 125*, 874-876.

Condon, W. S., & Sander, L. W. (1974). Neonate movement is synchronized with adult speech: Interactional participation and language acquisition. *Sciences 183*, 99-101.

Dabbs, J. M. (1983). *Fourier analysis of the rhythm of conversation.* (ERIC Document Reproduction Service No. ED 222 959)

Dabbs, J. M., & Moorer, J. P. (1975). Core body temperature and social arousal. *Personality and Social Psychology Bulletin, 1*, 517-520.

Davis, M. (Ed.). (1982). *Interaction rhythms: Periodicity in communicative behavior.* New York: Human Sciences Press.

Diamond, S. (1957). *Personality and temperament.* New York: Harper.

Duncan, S., & Fiske, D. W. (1977). *Face-to-face interaction: Research methods and theory.* New York: John Wiley.

Ferguson, N. (1977). Simultaneous speech, interruptions and dominance. *British Journal of Social and Clinical Psychology, 16,* 295-302.

Field, T. (1985). Attachment as psychobiological attunement: Being on the same wavelength. In M. Reite & T. Field (Eds.), *The psychobiology of attachment and separation.* New York: Academic Press.

Fiske, D. W. (1979). Two worlds of psychological phenomena. *American Psychologist, 34,* 733-739.

Goodwin, B. (1970). Biological stability. In C. H. Waddington (Ed.), *Toward a theoretical biology* (Vol. 3). Chicago: Aldine.

Gottman, J. M. (1979). *Marital interaction: Experimental investigations.* New York: Academic Press.

Gottman, J. M. (1981). *Time series analysis: A comprehensive introduction for social scientists.* New York: Cambridge University Press.

Gottman, J. M., & Bakeman, R. (1978). The sequential analysis of observational data. In M. Lamb, S. Suomi, & G. Stephenson (Eds.), *Methodological problems in the study of social interaction.* Madison: University of Wisconsin Press.

Gottman, J. M., & Ringland, J. T. (1981). The analysis of dominance and bidirectionality in social development. *Child Development, 52,* 393-412.

Hayes, D. P., & Cobb, L. (1979). Ultradian biorhythms in social interaction. In A. W. Siegman & S. Feldstein (Eds.), *Of speech and time: Temporal speech rhythms in interpersonal contexts.* Hillsdale, NJ: Erlbaum.

Hayes, D. P., & Meltzer, L. (1972). Interpersonal judgments based on talkativeness. I: Fact or artifact? *Sociometry, 35,* 538-561.

Hayes, D. P., Meltzer, L., & Wolf, G. (1970). Substantive conclusions are dependent upon techniques of measurement. *Behavioral Science, 15,* 265-268.

Hofer, M. A. (1984). Relationships as regulators: A psychobiological perspective on bereavement. *Psychosomatic Medicine, 46,* 183-197.

Hoskins, C. N. (1979). Level of activation, body temperature, and interpersonal conflict. *Nursing Research, 28,* 154-160.

Iberall, A. S., & McCulloch, W. S. (1969). The organizing principle of complex living systems. *Journal of Basic Engineering, 91,* 290-294.

Jaffe, J., Breskin, S., & Gerstman, L. (1972). Random generation of apparent speech rhythms. *Language and Speech, 15,* 68-71.

Jaffe, J., Dahlberg, C. C., Luria, J., & Chorosh, J. (1973). Effects of LSD-25 and dextroamphetamine on speech rhythms in psychotherapy dialogues. *Biological Psychiatry, 6,* 93-96.

Jaffe, J., & Feldstein, S. (1970). *Rhythms of dialogue.* New York: Academic Press.

Kagan, J. (1967). Biological aspects of inhibition systems. *American Journal of Diseases of Children, 114,* 507-512.

Kaplan, H. B., Burch, N. R., & Bloom, S. W. (1964). Physiological covariation and sociometric relationships in small peer groups. In P. H. Liederman & D. Shapiro (Eds.), *Psychobiological approaches to social behavior.* Stanford, CA: Stanford University Press.

Kimberly, R. P. (1970). Rhythmic patterns in human interaction. *Nature, 228,* 88-90.

Lenneberg, E. (1967). *Biological foundations of language.* New York: John Wiley.

Lester, B. M., Hoffman, J., & Brazelton, T. B. (1985). The rhythmic structure of mother-infant interaction in term and preterm infants. *Child Development, 56*, 15-27.

Levenson, R. W., & Gottman, J. M. (1983). Marital interaction: Physiological linkage and affective exchange. *Journal of Personality and Social Psychology, 45*, 587-597.

Lund, R. (1974). Personality factors and desynchronization of circadian rhythms. *Psychosomatic Medicine, 36*, 224-228.

Lynch J. J. (1985). *The language of the heart: The body's response to human dialogue.* New York: Basic Books.

Lynch, J. J., Thomas, S. A., Mills, M. E., Malinow, K., & Katcher, A. H. (1974). The effects of human contact on cardiac arrhythmia in coronary care patients. *Journal of Nervous and Mental Disease, 158*, 88-99.

Maxim, P. E., Bowden, D. M., & Sackett, G. P. (1976). Ultradian rhythms of solitary and social behavior in rhesus monkeys. *Physiology and Behavior, 17*, 337-344.

McClintock, M. (1971). Menstrual synchrony and suppression. *Nature, 229*, 244-245.

McGowan, J., & Gormly, J. (1976). Validation of personality traits: A multicriteria approach. *Journal of Personality and Social Psychology, 34*, 791-795.

McGrath, J. E., & Kravitz, D. A. (1982). Group research. *Annual Review of Psychology, 33*, 195-230.

Moore-Ede, M. C., Sulzman, F. M., & Fuller, C. A. (1982). *The clocks that time us.* Cambridge, MA: Harvard University Press.

Parsons, T. (1951). *The social system.* New York: Free Press.

Patterson, M. L. (1976). An arousal model of interpersonal intimacy. *Psychological Review, 83*, 235-245.

Pittendrigh, C. (1975). Circadian oscillations in cells and circadian organization of multicellular systems. In C. S. Pittendrigh (Ed.), *Circadian oscillations and organization in nervous systems.* Cambridge, MA: MIT Press.

Porges, S. W., Bohrer, R. E., Cheung, M. N., Drasgow, F., McCabe, P. M., & Keren, G. (1980). New time-series statistics for detecting rhythmic co-occurrence in the frequency domain: The weighted coherence and its applications to psychophysiological research. *Psychological Bulletin, 88*, 580-587.

Richman, C. L., Patty, R. A., & Fisher, T. D. (1976). Mind-body revisited: Every 28 days. *Psychological Reports, 39*, 1311-1314.

Scherer, K., & Giles, H. (Eds.). (1979). *Social markers in speech.* Cambridge: Cambridge University Press.

Strauss, A. (Ed.). (1965). Introduction. In G. H. Mead, *On social psychology.* Chicago: University of Chicago Press.

Takala, M. (1975). Consistencies of psychomotor styles in interpersonal tempo. *Scandinavian Journal of Psychology, 16*, 193-202.

Thomas, A., Chess, S., & Birch, H. G. (1970). The origin of personality. *Scientific American, 223*, 102-109.

Thrall, T., & Engleman, L. (1981). Univariate and bivariate spectral analysis. In Dixon et al. (Eds.), *BMDP: Biomedical Computer Programs.* Berkeley, CA: University of California Press.

Wade, M. G., Ellis, M. J., & Bohrer, R. E. (1973). Biorhythms in the activity of children during free play. *Journal of the Experimental Analysis of Behavior, 20*, 155-162.

Waid, W. M. (Ed.). (1984). *Sociophysiology.* New York: Springer-Verlag.

Warner, R. M. (1979). Periodic rhythms in conversational speech. *Language and Speech, 22*, 381-396.

Warner, R. M. (1982). The psychologist as social systems consultant. In T. Millon, C. Green, & R. Meagher (Eds.), *Handbook of clinical health psychology*. New York: Plenum.

Warner, R. M., Kenny, D. A., & Stoto, M. (1979). A new round robin analysis of variance for social interaction data. *Journal of Personality and Social Psychology, 37*, 1742-1757.

Warner, R. M., Malloy, D., Schneider, K., Knoth, R., & Wilder, B. (1986). *Rhythmic organization of social interaction and observer ratings of positive affect and involvement*. Manuscript submitted for publication.

Warner, R. M., Waggener, T. B., & Kronauer, R. E. (1983). Synchronized cycles in ventilation and vocal activity during spontaneous conversational speech. *Journal of Applied Physiology: Respiratory, Environmental and Exercise Physiology, 54*, 1324-1334.

Watts, B. L. (1982). Individual differences in circadian activity rhythms and their effects on roommate relationships *Journal of Personality, 50*, 374-384.

Wehr, T. A., & Goodwin, F. K. (Eds.). (1983). *Circadian rhythms in psychiatry*. Pacific Grove, CA: Boxwood Press.

Yates, F. E. (1974). Modeling periodicities in reproductive, adrenocortical and metabolic systems. In M. Ferin, F. Halberg, R. N. Richart, & R. L. Van de Wiele (Eds.), *Biorhythms and human reproduction*. New York: John Wiley.

5

Entrainment in Individual and Group Behavior

JANICE R. KELLY

Temporal factors permeate much of our lives. Our culture tends to live by the clock, and schedules and deadlines are common parts of our experience. Yet relatively little is known about the effects of such time pressure on our behavior.

Recently, McGrath and colleagues have embarked on a program of research to investigate these effects. The program deals, generally, with how time influences our thought and behavior. One aspect of the program, however, deals specifically with the effects of temporal constraints on the task performance and interaction of groups and individuals. This chapter will report a number of these studies. I would first like to introduce the concept of entrainment, and later a "social entrainment" model of behavior that we have found to be useful in exploring questions of time and behavior.

Entrainment

The term *entrainment* is used in the biological sciences to refer to the process by which one internal (or endogenous) rhythmic process is captured and modified by another (endogenous or exogenous) rhythmic process. When a rhythm becomes strongly entrained, it is modified in periodicity and/or phase to or toward the entraining cycle. Once established, the new, modified rhythm persists, even when the external cycle is removed, until the modified cycle becomes decoupled from the entraining cycle or until it becomes entrained to a new cycle.

McGrath and colleagues (Kelly & McGrath, 1985; McGrath & Kelly, 1986; McGrath, Kelly, & Machatka, 1984; McGrath & Rotchford, 1983) have used this term, by analogy, to describe many processes of human social behavior. On an individual level, for example, there are physiological processes that adjust (become entrained) to various circadian rhythms in one time zone. These can become disrupted when jet travel takes a person rapidly to a new time zone. The physiological processes eventually reentrain to the rhythms dominant in the new time zone. On a dyadic level, Jaffe and Feldstein (1970) have found that individuals in conversation modify their "natural" activity levels toward that of their partners. On an even more macro level, there is an entrainment in life activity patterns that becomes disrupted when a worker is shifted to an off-time shift.

In this chapter, I will focus on the entraining effects of temporal constraints—in the form of task time limits—on the behavior patterns of individuals and groups. A number of studies have been conducted that demonstrate how time constraints can alter some rhythms of behavior, such as the rate of performance of some task activity. These studies will be reviewed and will be interpreted within a "social entrainment" model of social behavior.

The Social Entrainment Model

The social entrainment model (see Kelly & McGrath, 1985; McGrath & Kelly, 1986; McGrath, Kelly, & Machatka, 1984) rests on four major propositions:

(1) that much of human behavior, at individual, group, and organization levels, is temporal (cyclical, periodic, or rhythmic) in character;
(2) that these are endogenous or naturally occurring rhythms;
(3) that these rhythms become mutually entrained to one another; and
(4) that they become collectively entrained to some powerful external oscillators or pacers.

These propositions have been combined into a model of social entrainment (see Figure 5.1).

The first component of the model is a set of multiple endogenous temporal (rhythmic) processes. These processes can be found on many levels of behavior—individual, interpersonal, and organizational—and can range in their periodicities from fractions of a second to lifespans.

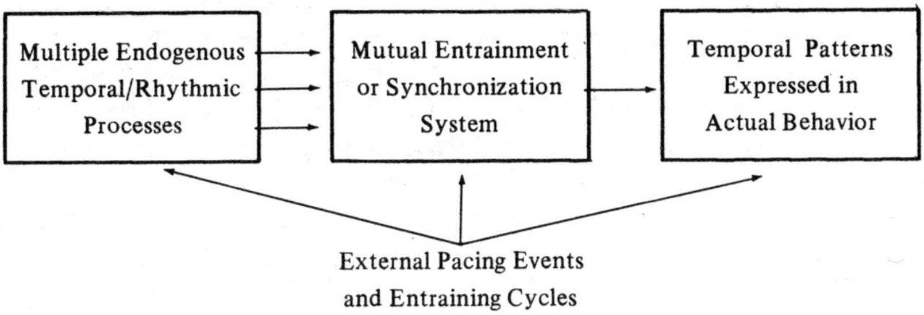

Figure 5.1. The Social Entrainment Model

The second component of the model is some system that acts to couple and synchronize the endogenous rhythmic processes. For instance, the system responsible for the coupling between the core body temperature cycle and the rest/activity cycle is apparently located in the superchiasmic nuclei of the lateral hypothalamus (see Moore-Ede et al., 1982). On the social level, the location of the entraining process is not as clear. It is clear, however, that entrainment does occur, and this component simply describes the entraining process.

The third component of the model refers to patterns of behavior resulting from such entrainment processes. These could include, for example, the pattern of sound and silence during a conversation between two people, a pattern of individual task performance, or daily recurrent patterns of activity and rest.

The fourth component of the model, which is of most concern here, refers to the set of all external (or exogenous) pacing cycles or events that can have an impact on the individual's endogenous patterns of behavior. For instance, a change in work schedule can have an impact on a worker's life activity pattern both in and out of the workplace, or an abrupt change in time zones can have an impact on an individual's sleep pattern. These events can operate so as to change the onset or offset of some activity, or to alter the phase and/or periodicity of some temporal cycle.

Studies of External Pacing Events

We have conducted a series of studies to examine the concept of entrainment in the task performance patterns of groups and individuals.

We have focused on task time limits as potentially strong, external pacing events that can have an impact on performance. A number of the studies have used rate as the performance measure. Rate is a measure of the completion of some unit of performance per some unit of time, and thus can be used as an index of performance over time. We assume that most individuals have a natural (most comfortable) rate at which they perform any given task. A time limit can alter this rate by inducing the individual to work at a faster or slower pace than their natural rate. Thus a time limit can alter (entrain) a person's rate of performance by shifting it to a new level. The effects of entrainment can then be examined by looking at rate measures over time. If the external pacer is powerful enough, the new rate of performance induced by the time limit should persist over time.

We have investigated these entrainment effects in a number of studies all based on the same basic paradigm. Individuals or groups are given tasks to work on during each of several trials. The time limits given for the successive trials differ in length so that each group or individual works during trials with time limits that are too short, too long, or about optimal for the given task. For many of the studies we have used sets of five-letter anagrams. Through pretesting, we have found that 10 minutes is about optimal for completing 40 five-letter anagrams. Thus a 5-minute time limit is not enough time for that task, and a 15-minute time limit is more than enough time for that task. For some subjects, the time limits over the three trials are arranged in order of increasing length (5, followed by 10, followed by 15 minutes). For others, the time limits over the three trials are arranged in order of decreasing length (15, followed by 10, followed by 5 minutes). For still others, the time limits do not differ over the three trials (10, followed by 10, followed by 10 minutes).

Using this paradigm, we have identified a number of effects that we consider important. First, different time limits imposed on the initial trial alter the rate at which subjects perform the given task on that trial. Subjects who are initially given short time limits work at a higher rate than those initially given longer time limits. Second, these differences in initial performance rates are maintained over the later trials. That is, if subjects are given short time limits on the first trial, and thus begin working at a higher rate of performance, this higher rate is maintained on later trials, as compared to subjects who are given longer time limits on the first trial, even though those later trials no longer have such short time limits.

Entrainment in Individual Performance

An example may clarify these effects. Table 5.1 presents the results of a typical experiment. In this experiment, individuals worked on three sets of 40 anagrams, one during each of three trials. Three orders of time limits for the three trials were used: (condition 1) 5 minutes, followed by 10 minutes, followed by 20 minutes; (condition 2) 10 minutes, followed by 10 minutes, followed by 10 minutes; or (condition 3) 20 minutes, followed by 10 minutes, followed by 5 minutes. Subjects in this study were only informed about the time limit on the first trial, but they were aware that the time limits on the later trials might differ.

The first column demonstrates the effect of initial time limit on rate of performance. The subjects in condition 1, who began with a 5-minute time limit, worked at a significantly higher rate of performance (M= 4.68) than either the subjects who began with a 10-minute trial (M= 3.34) or those who began with a 20-minute trial (M = 1.79). Note that the *total number* of anagrams completed is greater as the time limit is longer, but the *rate of work* in anagrams per minute is faster for the shorter time limit.

The second effect is demonstrated by a comparison of rates in column 2, which were all 10 minutes. Column 2 shows the highest rate in condition 1 (M = 3.64), followed by condition 2 (M = 3.27), and the lowest rate in condition 3 (M = 2.56). Thus even though all subjects are working under the same time limit for the second trial, the differences in rate produced by the different time limits on the initial trial are maintained on trial 2. Note that these differences cannot be explained by fatigue or practice effects. The rates produced in the three trials in condition 2 are virtually identical, showing no evidence of fatigue or practice effects. In addition, although they worked for different periods of time, all subjects had sets of 40 anagrams, and thus had equivalent experience in terms of task load.

Two other comparisons show this persistence or entrainment effect. A comparison of the first trial in condition 1 and the last trial in condition 3, each 5 minutes in length, again shows a higher rate of performance in condition 1 (M = 4.68 for condition 1 and M = 3.89 for condition 3). A comparison of the last trial in condition 1 and the first trial in condition 3, each 20 minutes in length, also shows a higher rate of performance in condition 1 (M = 2.22 for condition 1 and M = 1.79 for condition 3). Thus the slower rate established by the initial, longer time

TABLE 5.1
The Entrainment Study

	Trial 1	*Trial 2*	*Trial 3*
Condition 1:			
5-10-20 rate	4.68	3.64	2.22
Condition 2:			
10-10-10 rate	3.34	3.27	3.31
Condition 3:			
20-10-5 rate	1.79	2.56	3.89

NOTE: The dependent variable of rate is measured in number of anagrams per person per minute.

limit for the first trial in condition 3 is maintained over all three trials, and the higher rate of performance established by the initial, shorter time limit for the first trial in condition 1 is also maintained over all three trials.

The pattern of these results are interpretable within the social entrainment model. First, let us assume that the "natural," endogenous rate of performance for this task is that exhibited in condition 2, the control condition. A 10-minute time limit is about optimal for performance of this task. In each condition, the time limits on the initial trials operate as external pacers that alter these endogenous rhythms. A shorter time limit increases the natural rate to a faster pace. A longer time limit decreases the natural rate to a slower pace. Once established at a new level, the new rate tends to persist over later trials, despite changes in the actual time limits imposed.

The study to be reported next replicates these entrainment findings in a slightly different context.

Dyadic Entrainment

Another study demonstrated an even stronger entrainment effect. This study was similar to the one described above with several key differences. First, we used dyads instead of individuals. (Individuals and four-person groups were also used; these results can be found in McGrath, Kelly, & Machatka, 1984.) Second, we altered the task load conditions. Dyads were given three sets of either 20, 40, or 80 anagrams to solve during three trials. Third, the participants were told the conditions of each trial (how much time they would have and how many anagrams they would be given to solve) prior to each trial. In the previous study, the participants were only told the conditions of the initial trial. The time limits for the three trials were: (1) 5 minutes, followed by 10 minutes, followed by 20 minutes; (2) 10 minutes, followed by 10 minutes, followed by 10 minutes; or (3) 20 minutes, followed by 10 minutes, followed by 5 minutes. Task load remained constant at one of the three levels over the three trials. Thus, for example, one condition comprised dyads solving 20 anagrams in 5 minutes, then 20 anagrams in 10 minutes, and then 20 anagrams in 20 minutes. Another condition comprised dyads solving 80 anagrams in 20 minutes, then 80 anagrams in 10 minutes, and then 80 anagrams in 5 minutes. These results are reported in Table 5.2.

In this study, all participants knew the amount of time that they would be given for each trial. Therefore, there should be a strong pull *against* the persistence of the work pace established on the initial trial. That is, the time limits in the second and third trials should actually act as "reentraining" signals, pulling the subjects toward slower or faster work rates. Even so, there is clear evidence that the higher rates set on the initial trials for those conditions starting with the shorter time limit are maintained over the next two trials. And this is true over all three load conditions. Similarly, the slower rate set on the initial trials for those conditions starting with the longer time limit are maintained over the next two trials. For all of the middle, 10-minute trials, those preceded by 5-minute trials have higher rates of performance than those preceded by 10-minute or 20-minute trials. Again, this effect cannot be explained by fatigue effects, because the control conditions (the 10-10-10 order) show little evidence of either fatigue or learning, and because the number of anagrams given to solve on the preceding trial were constant within each load condition.

Figure 5.2 reports additional information collected in this study. Observers recorded the cumulative number of anagrams solved by each dyad after every minute of work. This cumulative total is plotted against time. Therefore, the slopes of the lines represent the dyads' rates of performance for the different conditions. In order to simplify the graph, only the 40-item task load conditions are reported, and the control group (the 10-10-10-minute time order condition) has been left out. If graphed, the slopes for the control conditions would have fallen between the other two sets of conditions.

These data show that the entrainment findings for rate are not a function of unequal distributions of anagram solving over time. The

TABLE 5.2
Dyadic Entrainment Study

Order of Time Limits	*Trial 1*	*Trial 2*	*Trial 3*
Task Load 20:			
5-10-20	1.85	1.28	1.10
10-10-10	0.91	1.12	1.02
20-10-5	1.19	1.07	1.54
Task Load 40:			
5-10-20	2.64	1.85	0.96
10-10-10	1.58	1.54	1.51
20-10-5	1.08	1.55	1.88
Task Load 80:			
5-10-20	3.08	2.85	1.78
10-10-10	2.19	2.37	2.22
20-10-5	1.59	2.32	2.50

NOTE: The dependent variable is rate calculated in number of anagrams solved per person per minute.

slopes for all three trials for the ascending time limit order condition (5-10-20 minutes) are steeper than the slopes for all three trials for the descending time limit order condition (20-10-5 minutes). The control condition—the 10-10-10-minute time limit order falls in between these two sets of slopes. The steeper slope indicates a faster rate of anagram solving. Therefore, the rate of anagram solving is higher for each minute of work in the ascending condition compared to comparable conditions in the descending condition.

An entrainment interpretation for the above study would suggest that the endogenous rates of performance for the dyad, involving a coordination between individual rates of performance for the pair, are altered by the external pacing demands of the situation (the time limits). This entrainment effect is comparable for conditions in the descending condition, evidenced by the fact that the faster or slower rates produced by the different time limits, as compared to the control, persist over the later trials.

Taken together, these findings seem to suggest that groups and individuals entrain to a work pace that fits the temporal constraints of the work situation. Furthermore, once this pace is established, it is maintained over a period of time.

The results of the dyadic entrainment study also suggest that task load may alter initial rates of performance. The study to be presented next explores differences in task load as a potential pacing condition. It

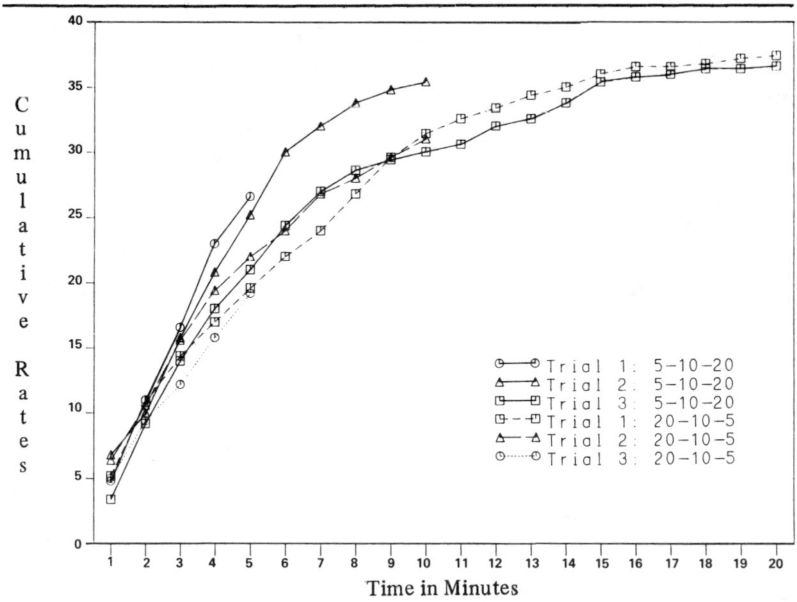

Figure 5.2. Cumulative Rates of Anagram Solutions (dyads, load 40, 5 letters)

addresses the question of whether all forms of task demand act as entraining cycles, or whether temporal demands are in some way especially likely to entrain.

Three Meanings of Task Difficulty

To say that some factor affects the *rate* at which people perform a task is to say that the factor somehow affects the task's *difficulty*. But the idea of *task difficulty* turns out to be a more complex concept than one might assume from its wide and frequent use. Researchers have used many methods for making one task more difficult than another. For instance, you can increase the difficulty of a task by increasing demands of the situation within which the task is done, such as increasing task load or decreasing time limits. Alternately, you can increase task difficulty by increasing demands that are internal to the task, such as changing item characteristics. The findings reviewed above suggest that making tasks vary in difficulty by changing time limits has particular implications for later rates of performance. Other definitions of difficulty may have different implications for performance, both in terms of a person's perception of the difficulty of the task and in terms of implications for rates and quality of performance of the task over time.

In order to investigate some of these effects, I conducted a study that used three different definitions of difficulty: task load differences, time limit differences, and item characteristic differences. Three conditions were created for each definition of difficulty. For the three task load conditions, subjects worked on tasks over the three trials that either increased in size (sets of 20, then 40, then 60 anagrams), decreased in size (sets of 60, then 40, then 20 anagrams), or remained the same in size (sets of 40, then 40, then 40 anagrams). For the three time limit conditions, subjects worked under time limits over the three trials that either increased (5 minutes, then 10 minutes, then 15 minutes), decreased (15 minutes, then 10 minutes, then 5 minutes), or remained the same (10 minutes, then 10 minutes, then 10 minutes). For the three item characteristic conditions, the number of letters in the anagrams over the three trials either increased (4 letters, then 5 letters, then 6 letters), decreased (6 letters, then 5 letters, then 4 letters), or remained the same (5 letters, then 5 letters, then 5 letters). Only one thing varied at a time over the three trials. For instance, when load varied for the three trials, time was held constant at 10 minutes and anagram size was held constant at 5 letters. Similarly, when item size varied over the three trials, time was held constant at 10 minutes and load was held constant at 40 anagrams.

This design allowed us to explore some different aspects of the entrainment question. For instance, it allowed us to look at whether temporal constraints were unique in generating entrainment effects, or whether other forms of task difficulty (such as task load or item size) could potentially serve as pacing events to produce these effects. The results of this study are presented in Table 5.3.

A number of effects are evident. First, note that while the most difficult initial conditions induced the fastest rates of anagram solving for parts A and B, the most difficult initial trial in part C induced the slowest rate of anagram solving. It appears that increasing external demands of the task (by time limits or task loads) increases work rate, presumably by increasing effort, whereas increasing internal task demands (by item size) decreases work rate, presumably by making each item qualitatively more difficult.

Second, there is, in general, a replication in part A of the entrainment effects for time limits found in previous studies. The faster rate induced

TABLE 5.3
Three Meanings of Difficulty

	Trial 1	*Trial 2*	*Trial 3*
Part A–Differing time limits with task load held constant at 40 and item size held constant at five letters			
Order of time limits:			
5-10-15	4.60	3.29	2.55
10-10-10	2.71	2.82	2.51
15-10-5	2.55	3.00	3.62
Part B–Differing task loads with time limit held constant at 10 minutes and item size held constant at five letters			
Order of task loads:			
60-40-20	3.58	2.82	1.63
40-40-40	2.71	2.82	2.51
20-40-60	1.80	2.37	3.78
Part C–Differing item sizes with time limit held constant at 10 minutes and task load held constant at 40 anagrams			
Order of item sizes:			
6-5-4	1.54	2.44	3.38
5-5-5	2.71	2.82	2.51
4-5-6	3.32	2.83	1.46

NOTE: The dependent variable is rate calculated as number of anagrams per person per minute.

by the initial 5-minute trial is maintained over the later trials, whereas the slower rate induced by the initial 15-minute trial is also maintained over the later trials. This entrainment effect, however, is not found for parts B and C. Although the initial task load of 60 anagrams induced a faster rate of performance, as compared to initial loads of 40 and 20 anagrams, this superior performance is not maintained on later trials. The rate for the 20-anagram third trial is slower than the rate for the 20-anagram first trial, while the rate for the 60-anagram third trial is faster than the rate for the 60-anagram first trial. (The lack of evidence for entraining effects using task load has been replicated by Murphy & McGrath, 1984.)

For the item size conditions, the least difficult initial condition induced the fastest rate of anagram solving. This performance is not maintained over the later trials, however. The rate for the initial 4-letter anagram trial is slower than the rate for the last 4-letter anagram trial.

Similarly, the rate for the last 6-letter anagram trial is slower than the rate for the initial 6-letter anagram trial.

In sum, two condition were created that manipulated task difficulty by altering aspects of the situation in which the task was performed. The first of these, shorter time limits, initially led to increases in work rate. Furthermore,this faster work rate was maintained on later trials. The second of these, higher task loads also initially led to increases in work rate. This faster rate, however, was not maintained on later trials. The third manipulation of difficulty altered internal task characteristics, the number of letters in the anagrams presented. The most difficult condition here, the six-letter anagrams, initially led to slower work rates. These work rates were not maintained on later trials. It does appear, then, that temporal constraints are distinctive in their ability to induce entrainment effects.

It was suggested at the beginning of this section that task difficulty is not as simple a concept as it might appear to be. This study has shown a complex relation between task difficulty and rate of performance. I would like to turn now to some of the psychological implications of task demands—perceptions of task difficulty, satisfaction with performance, and performance goals. Of main interest is whether there is a connection between the effects that task demands have on work rate and the effects that task demands have on perceptions.

An Analysis of Task Difficulty

There appears to be two types of difficulty involved in these anagram tasks and, more generally, in intellective and perhaps other types of tasks. These are "quantitative difficulty" and "qualitative difficulty." A task is quantitatively difficult when it presents too much to do in the time allowed. A task is qualitatively difficult when the elements of the task are difficult relative to the competence of the person performing the task. I hypothesized that a task will be judged as quantitatively more difficult as the proportion of unsolved elements of the set increases. I hypothesized that a task will be judged as qualitatively more difficult as the time needed to solve each item increases, or as the time spent before solving an item increases. Kahn and colleagues (Kahn, Wolfe, Quinn, Snoek, & Rosenthal, 1964), in their book on stress in organizations, make a similar distinction between qualitative and quantitative overload.

In the "three meanings of difficulty" study, we seem to be dealing with both "quantitative difficulty" and "qualitative difficulty." We manipulated quantitative difficulty most clearly when we altered task load. A task is seen as more quantitatively difficult, in the sense of requiring more effort (or faster rate), when you have more than you can do in the time allowed. The proportion of the set remaining unsolved can serve as an index of this difficulty.

Our clearest manipulation of qualitative difficulty is altering the number of letters in the anagrams. If you use as an index of qualitative difficulty the number of possible anagrams—that is, the number of permutations of letters possible in the anagrams—then a four-letter anagram is much easier (24 permutation) than a five-letter anagram (120 permutation), which in turn is much easier than a six-letter anagram (720 permutation). As the number of possible permutations increases, the time needed (on the average) to solve each item increases, and therefore the task is judged as more difficult.

What the difficulty study seems to show is that our conditions that change time limits contain elements of both quantitative difficulty and qualitative difficulty. We have found, in previous pretesting, that ten minutes is about optimal for completing a set of forty, five-letter anagrams. When an individual is given five minutes to solve a set of forty anagrams, that individual encounters "quantitative difficulty." That is, the individual has too much to do in the time allowed. The most common strategy for solving sets of anagrams is to first go through the set rapidly, solving only the ones that are immediately recognizable. These can be solved in a smaller amount of time per anagram than the rest of the set. With a short time limit, the "easy" ones are still being done. Therefore, there is little opportunity to encounter qualitative difficulty because the more difficult items are not attempted. When the five minutes are up, there are usually a number of anagrams left unsolved (a certain proportion of the set of forty). Therefore, the judgment of difficulty is based on quantitative difficulty—the number or proportion of the task set left unsolved. The individual has not spent much time puzzling over the unsolved items of the set, and therefore there is little qualitative difficulty.

When the individual is then given ten minutes to solve a set of forty, they can usually complete most of them, often as many as 38 of the 40. A small proportion of the set is left. Therefore quantitative difficulty is relatively low. But qualitative difficulty is also low, since the individual has spent relatively little time puzzling over the remaining unsolved anagrams.

When the individual is then given fifteen (or twenty) minutes to solve a set of forty anagrams, they can usually complete most of the set. Since the proportion remaining is small, there is little quantitative difficulty. However, the participants often get stuck on the remaining items. They are likely to spend relatively more time on each of the remaining items in order to try to solve them, and still may fail to do so. Therefore, they judge the task to be difficult, and this judgment is based on the qualitative difficulty of the remaining unsolved items.

In the "three meanings of difficulty" study, I administered questionnaires to the subjects after each trial to assess their perceptions of the difficulty of the task and their satisfaction with their own performance. These results are reported in Table 5.4.

Difficulty Judgments

Part A of Table 5.4 offers some support for the above reasoning. For the increasing time series (5-10-15 minutes), both the five minute initial trial and the fifteen minute final trial are judged as more difficult than the middle ten minute trial. We would argue that the participants encounter quantitative difficulty on the initial five minute trial, since the proportion of items in the set left unsolved is high. However, there is little qualitative difficulty, since the time spent in solving each item is low and work rate is relatively constant across the entire five minute trial (see Figure 5.2 for evidence of this). The difficulty judgment for the final fifteen minute trial is most likely based on qualitative difficulty. The proportion of items solved is high (96%). But the time spent attempting to solve the last few items is high. The curve in Figure 5.2 appears to asymptote between ten and fifteen minutes. Thus, relatively few items are being solved in the last five minutes of the trial.

For the decreasing time series (15-10-5 minutes), the final five minute trial is judged most difficult, and this judgment is most likely based on quantitative difficulty, since the proportion of unsolved items is quite high (55%). In this series, the initial fifteen minute trial is judged least difficult. The proportion of items left unsolved is very low, and therefore there is little quantitative difficulty. However, since the rate of anagram solving in the early parts of the trial is also low for this trial, the individual does not have much time to spend puzzling over the few unsolved items, and therefore there is also little qualitative difficulty.

As proposed, part B shows evidence for quantitative difficulty and part C shows evidence for qualitative difficulty. Except for the initial 60

TABLE 5.4
Number of Items Solved and Judgments of Difficulty and Satisfaction with the Task for the Three Meanings of Difficulty Study

	Question	*Trial 1*	*Trial 2*	*Trial 3*
Part A–Order of time limits:				
5-10-15	number solved	23.00	32.90	38.25
	proportion solved	.58	.82	.96
	difficulty	5.00	4.75	6.12
	satisfaction	5.88	8.12	7.50
10-10-10	number solved	27.10	28.20	25.10
	proportion solved	.68	.70	.63
	difficulty	5.22	4.89	5.67
	satisfaction	5.33	5.89	4.44
15-10-5	number solved	38.25	30.00	18.10
	proportion solved	.96	.75	.45
	difficulty	4.00	4.22	7.44
	satisfaction	7.89	7.22	4.00
Part B–Order of task loads:				
60-40-20	number solved	35.80	28.20	16.30
	proportion solved	.60	.70	.82
	difficulty	5.44	5.67	5.44
	satisfaction	5.22	5.33	5.56
40-40-40	number solved	27.10	28.20	25.10
	proportion solved	.68	.70	.63
	difficulty	5.22	4.89	5.67
	satisfaction	5.33	5.89	4.44
20-40-60	number solved	18.00	23.70	37.80
	proportion solved	.90	.59	.63
	difficulty	5.22	6.22	6.56
	satisfaction	6.78	5.89	5.67
Part C–Order of item sizes:				
6-5-4	number solved	15.40	24.40	33.80
	proportion solved	.38	.61	.84
	difficulty	6.00	4.86	3.14
	satisfaction	4.29	5.86	7.00
5-5-5	number solved	27.10	28.20	25.10
	proportion solved	.68	.70	.63
	difficulty	5.22	4.89	5.67
	satisfaction	5.33	5.89	4.44
4-5-6	number solved	33.20	28.30	14.60
	proportion solved	.83	.71	.36
	difficulty	3.78	5.78	8.33
	satisfaction	6.56	5.00	3.78

NOTE: Difficulty and satisfaction are measured on a nine-point scale, with (1) being "not at all" and (9) being "extremely."

item trial, judgments of difficulty in part B increase as the proportion of items left unsolved decreases. Judgments of difficulty in part C increase as the number of letters in the anagrams increase.

Notice also that judgments of satisfaction are closely tied to judgments of difficulty in an inverse relation. Over all conditions, as judgments of difficulty increase, judgments of satisfaction decrease. As judgments of difficulty decrease, judgments of satisfaction increase. While this finding is not surprising, the regularity of these judgments gives some confidence regarding the stability of the difficulty judgments.

Further Explorations of Difficulty

Table 5.5 shows the results for judgments of difficulty for the first study reported, the entrainment study. Looking at trial 1 results only, you can see that the initial ten minute trial is judged as less difficult than either the initial five minute trial or the initial twenty minute trial. We would argue that the difficulty judgment for the initial five minute trial is based on quantitative difficulty, while the difficulty judgment for the initial twenty minute trial is based on qualitative difficulty. In addition, for the increasing time limit series (5-10-20 minutes), the middle ten minute trial is judged as least difficult. Again, we would argue that the difficulty judgment for the initial five minute trial for this series is based on quantitative difficulty and the difficulty judgment for the final twenty minute trial is based on qualitative difficulty.

Table 5.5 shows again that judgments of satisfaction are clearly tied to judgments of difficulty in an inverse relation. As a task becomes more difficult, through either qualitative or quantitative difficulty, judgments of satisfaction decrease. As a task becomes less difficult, judgments of satisfaction increase.

In sum, variations in judgments of difficulty for a series of trials that manipulate task load are based on quantitative difficulty. Variations in judgments of difficulty for a series of trials that manipulate item characteristics are based on qualitative difficulty. Variations in judgments of difficulty for a series of trials that manipulate time limits are based on quantitative difficulty when the time limit is too short and qualitative difficulty when the time limit is too long. Judgments of satisfaction are inversely tied to judgments of difficulty, regardless of whether the difficulty judgments are based on qualitative or quantitative difficulty.

TABLE 5.5
Judgments of Task Difficulty and Satisfaction with Performance on the Entrainment Study

		Trial 1	*Trial 2*	*Trial 3*
Condition 1				
5-10-20	difficulty	5.67	4.67	6.42
	satisfaction	5.17	7.42	7.58
Condition 2				
10-10-10	difficulty	4.50	4.75	5.12
	satisfaction	7.12	6.00	5.12
Condition 3				
20-10-5	difficulty	5.00	5.93	5.93
	satisfaction	6.79	4.50	3.71

NOTE: Both dependent variables are measured on nine-point scales with (1) meaning "not at all" and (9) meaning "extremely."

Goals

In the "three meanings of difficulty" study, participants were also asked, prior to each trial, to estimate the number of anagrams that they could solve on that trial. Goal is reported in Table 5.6 as both the number of anagrams that the subjects estimated that they could solve on that trial and that number's translation into proportion of the set presented. Goals for trial 1 on part A were very similar across all time limit conditions. That is, subjects' initial estimates of how many they could solve were not dependent on the time limits that they were given. There is, however, a great divergence over trials for the increasing and decreasing time limit conditions. When time limits increased, goals also increased. When time limits decreased, goals also decreased. In fact, goals on the final 15-minute trial for condition 1 were about 20% higher than the goals on the initial 15-minute trial for condition 3, whereas goals on the final 5-minute trial for condition 3 were about 20% lower than the goals on the initial 5-minute trial for condition 1. Apparently time limits affect goals as well as rates.

A similar pattern is found for part B on the proportion indexes. The goal for the final 20-item set for condition 1 is about 17% higher than the goal for the initial 20-item set for condition 3, whereas the goal for the final 60-item set for condition 3 is about 15% higher than the goal for the initial 60-item set for condition 1. In terms of number of anagrams, however, this pattern is reversed. On the initial trials, task load affected

TABLE 5.6
Goals for the Three Meanings of Difficulty Study

	Question	*Trial 1*	*Trial 2*	*Trial 3*
Part A–Order of time limits:				
5-10-15	goal	25.00	30.12	34.50
	proportion	.62	.75	.86
10-10-10	goal	25.11	26.33	27.67
	proportion	.63	.66	.69
15-10-5	goal	26.88	21.25	16.44
	proportion	.67	.53	.41
Part B–Order of task loads:				
60-40-20	goal	36.00	27.22	15.44
	proportion	.60	.68	.77
40-40-40	goal	25.11	26.33	27.67
	proportion	.63	.66	.69
20-40-60	goal	12.11	18.56	26.89
	proportion	.61	.46	.45
Part C–Order of item sizes:				
6-5-4	goal	18.00	20.00	28.86
	proportion	.45	.50	.72
5-5-5	goal	25.11	26.33	27.67
	proportion	.63	.66	.69
4-5-6	goal	26.11	23.00	17.44
	proportion	.65	.58	.44

NOTE: Goal is reported in total number of anagrams that the participants estimated that they could complete under the conditions specified on each trial. Proportion is the number of anagrams estimated divided by the total number of items in the set presented.

goal estimates in terms of number of anagrams; higher task loads increased estimates. Task load also affected goal estimates in terms of number of anagrams across trials; those series that started with higher task loads maintained higher goal estimates across later trials. Thus either increasing the time limit for the same number of items or increasing the number of items for the same time limit increases subjects' expectations for their performance in terms of the *number* of anagrams they think they can solve. That is, changes in either task load or time limit seems to *entrain* the level of goals set for the next trial. Decreasing task load for the same time limit, however, increases the *proportion* of the anagram set that subjects expected to solve.

For item difficulty in part C of Table 5.6, there is very little difference in subjects' expectations for performance goals between initial and final trial goals for equivalent anagram size conditions. Goals increased over trials as anagram size decreased and vice versa. There is no relative advantage in goal estimates for the final trial when item size decreases (when difficulty decreases), however, such as was found when time limit increased or task load decreased. In other words, goal levels *do not* entrain for changes in item difficulty.

Entrainment of Interaction Patterns

We have shown some evidence for the entrainment of task performance by the use of time limits. One logical next step is to investigate what subjects are doing to increase their work rate when time is short and to decrease their work rate when time is abundant. We conducted a study (Kelly, 1984; Kelly & McGrath, 1985) that looked at interaction patterns in groups in order to investigate this question. We hypothesized that, when time was short, work groups would cut down on all nontask interactions (i.e., would cut down on interpersonal interaction), and, when time was abundant, would engage in more interpersonal interaction. We also hypothesized that the interaction patterns established on initial trials would be maintained (that is, they would be entrained) on later trials. Finally, we were interested in whether the quality of performance would vary inversely with rate, and whether quality would show entrainment effects such as were found for rate measures.

Four-person groups were given two tasks to work on, one in each of two time periods. Although three different pairs of tasks were used, all of the tasks required written solutions that could be scored on quality and quantity dimensions, such as creativity, originality, and length. These tasks and product quality dimensions were taken from Hackman (1966). Any one group worked on two tasks of the same task type for the two trials. Half of the groups worked on the first task for 10 minutes and on the second task for 20 minutes, while the other half worked on the first task for 20 minutes and the second task for 10 minutes. As the group worked, an observer recorded what kind of behavior was occurring at the tenth second of each ten-second interval throughout the two task performance periods. Each observation was coded into one of eight categories adapted from Bales (1950): answers, questions, agreements, disagreements, positive interpersonal comments, negative interpersonal comments, neutral comments, and silence.

The question of entrainment of interpersonal interaction was examined by looking at the distribution of observations over the eight interaction categories as a function of task, time, and time order. The full results and analyses may be found in Kelly and McGrath (1985). The results for the first trial showed significant differences in the distribution of interaction acts as a function of time limit. As predicted, there were relatively fewer agreements, disagreements, and positive and negative interpersonal comments in the 10-minute condition as compared to the 20-minute condition. This pattern was reversed, however, on the second trial. On the second trial, there were relatively fewer agreements, disagreements, and positive and negative interpersonal comments in the 20-minute condition. That is, the second trial 20-minute condition was more similar to the 10-minute trial preceding it than it was to the initial 20-minute trial. These results suggest that the pattern of interaction in a group can be altered by imposing different time limits on the group's work, and that this pattern of interaction is maintained in later sessions. In other words, the pattern of interaction was entrained to an externally imposed temporal constraint, and that entrained pattern persisted beyond the single task performance.

The time limits and interaction patterns also had effects on the quality of the group product. Products produced in the initial 20-minute time periods were significantly higher in quality as measured by scores on the dimensions of quality of presentation, originality, creativity, and issue involvement than were products produced in the initial 10-minute time periods. The 20-minute products were also longer than the 10-minute products. (Three other dimensions—outlook, action orientation, and adequacy of the solution—showed no difference.) Furthermore, the differences in quality between the 10- and 20-minute time periods for the second trial were sharply attenuated, in the direction expected by an entrainment interpretation, although they did not completely reverse as did the interaction patterns.

A rough rate measure was calculated for the task products by computing an index of the number of words written by the group per minute. This index showed a higher rate of performance on the initial 10-minute trial, and this higher rate was maintained on the second 20-minute trial. This suggests that, when time is short, the group may be sacrificing quality of the product for an increased rate of performance.

These results suggest that short time limits induce and entrain interaction patterns that lead to high rates of performance and lower quality of performance, whereas long time limits induce and entrain interaction patterns that lead to low rates of performance and higher quality of performance.

Closing Comments

In this chapter, I have tried to demonstrate the usefulness of the concept of entrainment for explaining variations in rate and quality of task performance over time. The social entrainment model is distinctive in that it makes predictions about patterns of behavior over time. It is flexible in its potential applications. We have found it useful in integrating research in diverse areas ranging from psychophysical judgments of time intervals to aspects of behavior in organizational settings (see McGrath & Kelly, 1986).

This chapter has focused on one aspect of the model—the influence of external pacing events on task performance. We used time limits as external pacers, and conducted studies examining the effects of time limits on the pattern of task behavior of groups and individuals over time. The results of the studies show that time limits exert an interesting influence over behavior. Time limits initially entrain work rates, with short time limits producing faster rates and longer time limits producing slower rates. These new rates of performance persist over later trials. Further, we have found that these effects generalize over group size and task types. We have also found evidence of entrainment in interaction patterns of groups. And the effects of time limits seem to be distinctive—other external and internal task demand manipulations have not elicited such entrainment effects.

Time limits also seem to affect perceptions of the task. When time limits are too short for the amount of work, the task is judged to be difficult, and we believe that this judgment is based on the amount of work that is left undone (quantitative difficulty). When the time limits are too long for the amount of work, the task is also judged to be difficult, and we believe that this judgment is based on the relatively greater amount of time that is needed to solve the last few items of the set (qualitative difficulty). When the time limit more or less matches the task, the task is judged to be less difficult. Obviously more research is needed in order to be confident about this effect and our interpretation of it.

This chapter offers some new ways of looking at task performance. An increasing number of researchers are interested in looking at behavior over time. This chapter has introduced a model that makes predictions of behavior over time, and has presented evidence of effects that fit the model. It is my hope that the chapter will stimulate more research along these lines.

REFERENCES

Bales, R. F. (1950). *Interaction process analysis*. Cambridge, MA: Addison-Wesley Press.

Hackman, R. J. (1966). *Effects of task characteristics on group products* (Technical Report No. 5; Contract AFOSR AF-49 [638]-1291). Urbana: University of Illinois, Department of Psychology.

Jaffe, J., & Feldstein, S. (1970). *Rhythms of dialogue*. New York: Academic Press.

Kahn, R. L., Wolfe, D. M., Quinn, R. P., Snoek, J. D., & Rosenthal, R. A. (1964). *Organizational stress: Studies in role conflict and ambiguity*. New York: John Wiley.

Kelly, J. R. (1984). *Time limit and task type effects on individual and group performance and interaction*. Unpublished master's thesis, University of Illinois, Urbana.

Kelly, J. R., & McGrath, J. E. (1985). Effects of time limits and task types on task performance and interaction of four-person groups. *Journal of Personality and Social Psychology, 49,* 395-407.

McGrath, J. E., & Kelly, J. R. (1986). *Time and human interaction: The social psychology of time*. New York: Guilford.

McGrath, J. E., Kelly, J. R., & Machatka, D. E. (1984). The social psychology of time: Entrainment of behavior in social and organizational settings. *Applied Social Psychology Annual, 5,* 21-44.

McGrath, J. E., & Rotchford, N. (1983). Time and behavior in organizations. *Research in Organizational Behavior, 5,* 57-101.

Moore-Ede, M. C., Sulzman, F. M., & Fuller, C. A. (1982). *The clocks that time us*. Cambridge, MA: Harvard University Press.

Murphy, S., & McGrath, J. E. (1984). *The effects of group size and task load demands on task performance*. Unpublished study, University of Washington, Seattle, WA.

PART III

Time Allocation

6

Time Pressure, Task Performance, and Enjoyment

JONATHAN L. FREEDMAN
DONALD R. EDWARDS

Time pressure has often been considered a major element producing stress. Although everyone seems to have a somewhat different definition of the term *stress*, at least in this context, it generally seems to mean a negative reaction to the environment caused by too much pressure on the individual. Many of the complaints about the stress of modern life revolve around the lack of time, the pressure to move quickly, the too-fast pace of life, and so on. In work settings, stress is typically considered to be inherent in jobs that involve time pressure (Frankenhaeuser & Gardell, 1976). In the psychological literature, time pressure is also usually considered a source of stress. Weitz (1970) mentions speeded information processing first in a short list of situations that are thought to be stressful. Hackman (1970) notes that time sequencing is one of the most common manipulations by which task-related stress is induced. McGrath (1970) mentions it prominently in a general discussion of stress. And, in a somewhat different context, the work on the type A

AUTHORS' NOTE: The research reported in this chapter was part of a dissertation submitted by D. Edwards as partial fulfillment of the master's degree at the University of Toronto. This study was supported in part by a grant from the Social Science and Humanities Research Council of Canada to the senior author, and was conducted while the junior author held a graduate fellowship from the same agency. We are grateful for this support. We are also extremely grateful to Deborah Rutman and Heather Wilson for their advice, encouragement, and help in conducting the study.

behavior pattern (Friedman & Rosenman, 1974; Glass, 1977) often focuses on time pressure and time urgency as important elements producing stress and eventually increasing the likelihood of coronary heart disease.

In much of this literature, there is an implicit or explicit assumption that the greater the time pressure, the more stress it creates. Some of the research appears to support this view. For example, Palermo (1957) and others have used variations in the amount of response time allowed as a means of inducing what they refer to as stress. Sales (1970) found that subjects who were given more work than they could handle experienced more stress and were less satisfied than subjects who were given less work that they could complete. Caplan and Jones (1975) compared people's responses during a period of high work activity and a time of relatively low activity, and found more stress during the former. These studies have typically involved only two levels of time pressure, however, with one being extremely high. Therefore, they do not provide strong support for the assumption that time pressure is generally stressful.

We have taken quite a different view of the relationship between time pressure and stress. Rather than viewing time pressure as inherently negative, it seems more plausible to consider it a factor in the environment that can have either positive or negative effects depending on the situation. Under some situations it will, indeed, exert too much pressure on people and, therefore, cause them to experience stress. But under other circumstances, it can have an energizing or challenging effect and can increase satisfaction. The effect it has should depend on a wide variety of factors, including the amount of time pressure, the particular activity being engaged in, and the personalities of those involved.

This view of time pressure is based on two different, though related, perspectives. First, it is derived from an analysis in terms of the Yerkes-Dodson law. According to the Yerkes-Dodson law (1908), for any task, optimal performance occurs at neither the maximum nor the minimum level of arousal but at some intermediate level. Empirical research has provided support for this analysis with a variety of tasks (Berry, 1962; Sjoberg, 1977; Stennett, 1957). If we assume that time pressure produces arousal, and that greater time pressure produces greater arousal, the Yerkes-Dodson law leads to the prediction that the relationship between time pressure and performance should be an inverted U-shaped function, with best performance occurring at an intermediate level of time pressure.

McGrath (1976) has presented an analysis of the relation between stress and performance that, while not inconsistent with the Yerkes-Dodson law, provides a plausible explanation of it. He suggested that performance actually increases monotonically with increasing arousal and that the inverted-U relation between arousal and performance occurs only when increased demand also makes the task more difficult. He noted, however, that under many circumstances, increased arousal is produced by increased demands of the situation, and that this often means that the task becomes more difficult as demand increases. When this is so, performance should depend on the precise relation between the amount of arousal and the difficulty of the task. At lower levels of arousal, the task may still be quite easy and the increased arousal will improve performance, but, at some point, the increased demands will make the task so difficult that performance will get less good. This will produce the typical inverted-U relation between arousal and performance. McGrath would say, however, that the degradation of performance at high levels of demand occurs despite the high level of arousal, not because of it.

Although this seems clear in terms of actual performance, our focus is more on the psychological reactions than on the amount of work that is performed. This brings us to the second basis for our view of time pressure, which concerns the enjoyment and satisfaction people derive from work. We begin with the assumption that people enjoy and get satisfaction from their work and other activities to the extent that they are interesting, pleasurable, important, or challenging. Clearly, some activities are inherently satisfying for the people involved in them. Artistic and intellectual creation are probably rewarding more or less regardless of the conditions under which they occur. For these activities, the amount of time allowed will have little effect on general satisfaction, as long as sufficient time is provided.

Unfortunately, many of the tasks people perform in the world, especially work-related tasks, are not inherently interesting or pleasurable, or at least not to any great extent. Although they may be important from the point of view of society or business or some other perspective, they are important to the worker primarily as a means of earning an income or advancing in a career. Satisfaction must be based primarily on a sense of accomplishment, competency, or achievement, which ordinarily can be experienced only when the task is to some extent challenging. With many of these tasks, if the person has the necessary skill, the task can be performed perfectly as long as there is enough time and the person has sufficient motivation. We would argue that with these activities there is little sense of accomplishment, competency, or achievement derived simply from completing the task, because completion was never in doubt and there is another equivalent task just ahead. Picking all of the ripe beans off a plant does not mean much when there are thousands of other similar plants left, and the same can be said of a great many tasks, both mechanical and intellectual.

Therefore, for all of these tasks, the time element is critical to one's satisfaction. This is because what is simple with no time pressure can become exceedingly difficult under high time pressure. In other words, a trivial, meaningless task can become challenging when speed of performance is an issue, so that a person can derive considerable satisfaction from the task by completing it under time pressure.

For example, consider the difference between chess and a typical electronic game. Chess is played by experts with some time limitation, but it is enjoyed by a great many people without one. Chess cannot be played perfectly even with all the time in the world, and thus is satisfying even when there is no time pressure. The kind of computer game found in game arcades offers a direct contrast. Most of these games require the player to manipulate buttons or levers in order to shoot down enemy ships, avoid traps, or run an obstacle course. In PAC-Man, for example, the player moves an object that eats dots. The objective is to eat as many dots as possible, while keeping out of the way of danger. The player must decide what direction on a maze to take in order to accomplish this. Without a time element, PAC-man is trivial and boring. This is because, given enough time, virtually anyone can manage to devour all of the dots and avoid getting eaten. With no time limit on individual moves, everyone would get a perfect score. And no one would want to play. A limitation on the time allowed to make decisions is absolutely essential to the game. In a sense, it is not really a game without some pressure of time.

Because of the differences in the structure, purpose, and complexity of the games, we would expect the effect of time limitations to be quite different for chess and for a computer game. For most people, chess will be most enjoyable with relatively little time pressure, perhaps with no pressure at all. Probably for experts, and perhaps for many good players, chess is somewhat more interesting and exciting with some limit on time. But if there is too little time allowed, it becomes less satisfying. Thus, even for chess, we would expect a curvilinear relationship between time and satisfaction, but the point of optimal enjoyment would be at fairly low time pressure. In contrast, an electronic game offers little or no satisfaction with low time pressure; while only at extreme time pressure does it become unsatisfying. Therefore, in both cases, there should be a curvilinear relationship between time and satisfaction, but the optimal point should be at quite high time pressure.

The important point of this analysis is that despite the differences between the two types of activities, and the corresponding differences in the effect of time pressure, the underlying relation between time and satisfaction is essentially the same. For both games, indeed, for any activity, we would predict that the optimal point of satisfaction will be at some intermediate level of time pressure, with the actual point depending on the nature of the task in relation to the experience, personalities, and abilities of the people involved.

Work on the person-environment (P-E) fit by French, Caplan, and others (e.g., French, Caplan, & Harrison, 1982) extends this prediction to include the psychological reactions of the individuals as well as their performance on the task. The assumption guiding this research is that people have abilities, expectations, goals, and other characteristics that affect their reactions to a wide variety of environmental factors, and that when the particular characteristics of the environment match these characteristics of the individual (i.e., when there is a P-E fit), the response of the individual will be most positive. Applying this general formulation to the effect of time pressure leads to the prediction that, in any given situation, there will be an optimal level of time pressure for each individual, with reactions being less positive under conditions of increased or decreased time pressure.

A major study (Caplan, Cobb, French, Harrison, & Pinneau, 1980; French, Caplan, & Harrison, 1982) dealing with many environmental factors found substantial support for this analysis. People in a variety of occupations who said that their work load was equivalent to their expected or preferred level were least stressed and most satisfied (although the effect was not terribly strong). When there was not a good P-E fit, when the environment was either at a higher level (overload) or a lower level (underload) than preferred or expected, reactions were generally more negative.

This is an impressive study in a natural setting. It has certain limitations however. In the first place, there was no independent measure of time pressure. Subjects rated the work load and presumably this was related to time pressure, but the connection may not have been very close. Many factors other than time pressure can contribute to the perception of work load. The subjects may have felt that they had a great deal of work because the work was complex or difficult or too diverse rather than because they were under time pressure. It would be desirable to have an independent measure or manipulation of time pressure in order to assess its effect on performance and satisfaction. A more basic problem is that the study is, by its nature, not experimental. Neither time pressure nor work load was deliberately varied. Instead, subjects rated the naturally occurring situation and their own reactions to it. This leaves open the question of causation. It is possible, for example, that feeling satisfied caused people to rate the work load as fitting their expectations rather than the other way around. It would therefore be helpful to have an experimental test of the hypothesis.

Unfortunately, there is little experimental research that is directly relevant. Pepinsky, Pepinsky, and Pavlik (1960) gave teams of workers either complex or simple tasks to perform under low, moderate, or high time pressure. For both kinds of tasks, performance was best with moderate time pressure, but none of the effects was significant. All subjects were actually given the same amount of time, however, with the manipulation of time pressure being how often they were reminded of the time remaining. Thus perceived rather than actual time pressure was varied, which might explain the weakness of the effects.

In one of a series of studies, Streufert, Streufert, and Gorson (1981) investigated the relation among time urgency, information load, and the quality of decision making. Subjects were given low, moderate, or high amounts of information and were asked a series of questions about which they had to make decisions. The subjects were told that they had to respond quickly (almost immediately) on varying numbers of these decisions. The inverted-U function appeared under low urgency, with the greatest number of high quality decisions being made at intermediate levels of information load; but under high urgency, the greater the load, the fewer high quality decisions were made. This study did not vary time pressure explicitly (only the number of fast decisions to be made, with a considerable amount of time between them), but it does suggest an interaction of urgency and other factors that is similar to that predicted here for time pressure.

Thus none of the available work provides an experimental demonstration of the predicted relationship between time pressure and psychological reactions. The results of French et al. suggest that there may be such a relation, and some of the other research is also promising. But there is no experimental study in the literature that employs three or more levels of time pressure, measures psychological reactions, and shows the predicted inverted-U relation. That is what we attempted to accomplish in the study we are about to describe.

A second focus of this research was the role played by characteristics of the individual in determining reactions to time pressure. The type A behavior pattern would seem to be a prime candidate for affecting reactions to time pressure, because the type A pattern has been described as one that includes, among other qualities, a general and persistent sense of time urgency (Glass, 1977). This built-in feeling of urgency should affect responses to time pressure situations. In a sense, it might be argued that type A individuals always function under a certain degree of self-imposed time pressure. It seems plausible that this internal time pressure summates with externally imposed pressure, causing type A people to react to a low time pressure situation as if it were moderate time pressure, and to a moderate time pressure situation as if it were high time pressure.

If this analysis is correct, we would expect several differences between type A and type B persons in their reactions to time pressure situations. Under low time pressure, because of their internal sense of urgency, type As should experience some time pressure and should therefore work harder and presumably accomplish more than type Bs. In fact, Burnam, Pennebaker, and Glass (1975) found that, with no time limit, type As worked more rapidly than Bs, perhaps because of their internal feeling of time urgency. As time pressure increases, however, type A persons should reach the optimal level of time pressure sooner than type Bs. Thus the overall effect would be that type As would perform better at low and moderate levels of time pressure, but their performance should peak at a lower level of time pressure than for type Bs.

It is difficult to make predictions about the relation between type A and B, and subjective experience. Although there is some evidence (e.g., Brunson & Matthews, 1981) that type As respond less well to failure and are more self-blaming, there is also reason to believe that type As are less willing to admit experiencing negative reactions (e.g., Carver, Coleman, & Glass, 1976). Moreover, if type A individuals generally perform better than type Bs, clearly this will have some effect on their experience of stress. Thus we leave open the question of how this personality variable might affect stress and other subjective reactions to time pressure.

Another personality variable that might affect reactions to time pressure is neuroticism. Although the connection is less clear than with the A/B pattern, it seems plausible that highly neurotic individuals will have more difficulty coping with time pressure. If we see neuroticism as a general difficulty in coping or as a high level of tension, the burden of time limitations would impose an added problem for those high in neuroticism. Accordingly, we would expect that the optimal point of satisfaction and performance would be at lower levels of time pressure for high neurotic individuals than for those lower on this trait.

In our study, subjects performed a task under varying degrees of time pressure. The primary measures of interest were performance on the task and self-reports of reactions to the experience, including enjoyment, satisfaction, tension, and boredom. The major predictions were that the relationship between performance and time pressure would describe an inverted-U function, with optimal performance occurring at intermediate levels of time pressure and that a similar relation would hold for subjective reactions. In addition, it was expected that type As would perform better at low levels of time pressure than type Bs, but that the performance of the former would peak before that of the latter. Finally, we expected high neurotic subjects to achieve peak performance and satisfaction at lower levels of time pressure than low neurotic subjects.

Method

Overview

Subjects performed a simple task under five conditions of time pressure, ranging from very low to very high. The type A/B behavior pattern was assessed with a version of the Jenkins Activity Scale; trait neuroticism was measured by Form B of the Eysenck Personality Inventory (Eysenck & Eysenck, 1968). The main dependent variables were performance on the task and self-reports of enjoyment, tension, boredom, and other psychological reactions to the experience.

Subjects

The study was conducted at the Ontario Science Centre in Toronto. The subjects were recruited by means of a sign that was posted asking people who were visiting the centre to participate in a study on task performance. Of the 191 subjects who began the study, 22 failed to complete it and they are not included in the data analysis. The final sample consisted of 73 males and 96 females ranging in age from 14 to 76 with a mean age of 34.

Time Pressure Manipulation and Task

The task consisted of a series of four-letter anagrams that the subjects had to form into an acceptable English word. The words on which the anagrams were based ranged from very common to quite rare, but none was obscure. Most of the anagrams were quite easy.

Time pressure was varied by giving subjects different numbers of anagrams within the same time period of 22 minutes. Pretesting suggested that a subject who was not working terribly hard, felt under little pressure, but was trying to work reasonably quickly could solve the average anagram in about 10 seconds. Because we were predicting a curvilinear relationship, it seemed important to have many levels of time pressure so that we would not have to rely on choosing precisely the right values in order to test our prediction adequately. Accordingly, five values of time pressure were employed that bracketed the 10-second estimate. The five conditions allowed 25, 14, 10, 6, and 2.5 seconds per anagram. With a .5 second intertrial interval, this required 48, 88, 128, 220, and 460 anagrams in the five time pressure conditions. The actual number of anagrams presented varied slightly from these figures, because minor delays due to changing slide trays and interruptions occurred in some sessions and every effort was made to keep the total time exactly the same for all subjects.

Procedure

Groups of subjects completed a standard consent form, provided some demographic information, and were then briefed on the anagram task. They were shown two anagrams with their solutions and then four without solutions to introduce them to the task. The instructions noted that all of the anagrams had solutions, but that the subjects might not find them all. They were asked to work as quickly and accurately as possible. The anagrams were projected onto a screen at the front of the room. They appeared in large uppercase black letters against a white background. Subjects wrote their answers in answer booklets, each page of which contained 36 numbered blanks. The instructions told the subjects to draw a line next to an item if they could not solve it. The anagrams were presented for the time intervals described above. A warning beep sounded 1.5 seconds before the end of the interval. The first 10 anagrams were treated as practice trials and excluded from all analyses. Every 40 items there was a brief pause and the number of the next anagram was announced in order to make it easier for subjects to make certain they were answering in the right place on their sheets.

After the anagram task, subjects were given a questionnaire designed to assess their psychological reactions. It contained items relating to physical and psychological strain as well as more positive feelings. The precise wording was "This task is making me feel" followed by a series of descriptors, for each of which the subjects were to indicate "very little" to "very much" on a seven-point unmarked scale. A final question asked subjects to give their overall reaction to the task from very negative to very positive. After this, subjects completed a modified form of the Jenkins Activity Survey (JAS; Glass, 1977; Jenkins, Zyzanski, & Rosenman, 1979), which measures type A/B behavior pattern, and Form B of the Eysenck Personality Inventory (Eysenck & Eysenck, 1968), which measures neuroticism. The study was then explained to the subjects and they were thanked for their help.

Results

Task Performance

Table 6.1 presents the proportion of items and the absolute number of anagrams solved in each time condition. As might be expected, these measures show quite different relations with time pressure. The proportion of anagrams solved decreased as time pressure increased, though the decrease was sharpest from 6 to 2.5 seconds per item: F linear $(1, 166) = 111.03$, $p < .001$. This is a trivial result because, except under very unusual circumstances, the more time there is for a task, the more likely it is that the task will be successfully completed.

Of more interest is that, as predicted, the relation between time pressure and the number solved described an inverted-U function, with performance optimal at an intermediate level of time pressure. As shown in Figure 6.1, the number of anagrams solved increased as time pressure increased from 25 seconds per item to 6 seconds per item, and then declined: F quadratic $(1, 166) = 10.69$, $p < .001$; F linear $(1, 166) =$

TABLE 6.1
Task Performance in Each Condition

	Time Pressure (in seconds)				
	2.5	*6.0*	*10.0*	*14.0*	*25.0*
Number correct	86.81	123.91	91.89	67.82	41.26
Percent correct	18.89	56.48	71.81	76.97	85.71
N in condition	36	33	36	33	31

28.69, $p < .001$. This too is hardly surprising, because the higher the time pressure, the more items the subjects are given to solve. Nevertheless, it does demonstrate that under some circumstances time pressure can produce higher productivity as measured by the amount of work completed in a given period, and that time pressure that is too great will eventually reduce productivity.

Psychological Reactions

The major focus of the study was on the relation between time pressure and the psychological reaction to the experience. Again, the hypothesis was that the relationship would be curvilinear, specifically an inverted-U function, with the most positive reactions occurring at intermediate levels of time pressure. The 10 relevant self-ratings by the subjects were grouped into four indices on the basis of a principal components factor analysis with varimax rotation (though various other factor analyses produced quite similar results). These four indices can be described as measures of general positivity (enjoyment, confidence, sense of accomplishment, energetic); tension (tension and anxiety); physical discomfort (tired, headachy, physical discomfort); and boredom. In addition, three measures were expressly concerned with enjoyment. They were so similar to each other that only one of them was included in the factor analysis, but they were also all combined into one enjoyment index consisting of the sum of the responses to the three measures. The means for the five indices are presented in Table 6.2. With minor variations, the individual items composing these indices show patterns similar to the pattern of the overall indices.

The clearest measures of overall reaction to the task would seem to be the combined enjoyment measure and the index of general positivity. These two measures are very similar and produced almost identical results, so we will present only the former. Figure 6.2 shows the relation

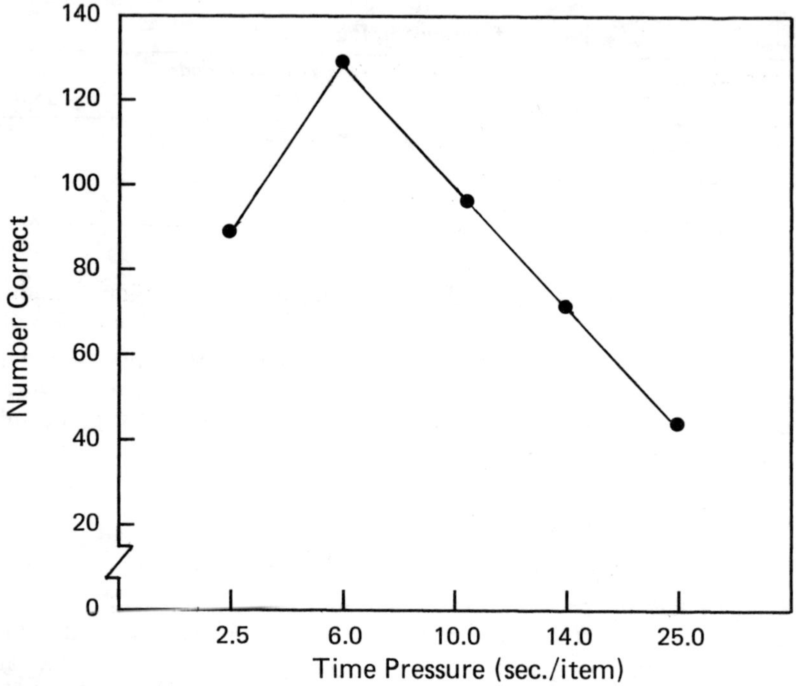

Figure 6.1. Number of Items Solved in Each Time Pressure Condition

between time pressure and enjoyment. Enjoyment was greatest in the 10-second condition, with both faster and slower pacing producing less enjoyment. The quadratic trend is the only effect that approaches significance, and it is highly significant: $F(1, 165) = 11.36$, $p < .001$. Enjoyment was significantly greater in the 10-second condition than in either the 2.5-second condition ($t\,[157] = 3.63$, $p < .01$) or the 25-second condition ($t\,[157] = 2.54$, $p < .05$).

Although the index just described is probably the best measure of the overall response to the experience, other data provide additional details about subjects' psychological responses. There was little tension or physical discomfort reported in any condition. Greater time pressure was generally associated with increases on both indices, however. For tension, only the linear trend was significant: $F(1, 164) = 29.62$, $p < .001$. For physical discomfort, both linear and quadratic trends were significant (F linear $[1, 166] = 11.64$, $p < .001$ and F quadratic $[1, 166] = 5.14$, $p < .05$) because the 2.5-second condition was significantly higher than any of the others, which did not differ appreciably.

TABLE 6.2
Mean Scores on Indices of Reactions to the Task

	Time Pressure Condition (in seconds)				
Index	*2.5*	*6.0*	*10.0*	*14.0*	*25.0*
Enjoyment	2.61	3.26	3.89	3.22	3.11
Positivity	2.18	2.64	3.25	2.89	2.72
Tension	3.22	2.38	2.04	1.58	1.19
Physical discomfort	2.25	1.27	1.09	1.03	1.09
Boredom	1.19	1.00	0.77	2.70	2.76
Perceived control	0.81	2.30	3.11	3.28	3.55

NOTE: Range of all indices is 0-6. Higher numbers mean that the subject reported experiencing more of the reaction indicated by the label. Number of subjects on which the means are based vary from 29 to 36 because not all subjects answered all questions.

There is an interesting contrast between measures of boredom and perceived control. As might be expected, boredom was inversely related to time pressure. Both linear and quadratic trends were significant: F linear $(1, 164) = 25.04$, $p < .001$ and F quadratic $(1, 164) = 9.26$, $p < .01$. Examination of the means indicates that the three fastest conditions did not differ appreciably and were significantly lower in boredom than the two slowest conditions ($t[157] = 6.31$, $p < .01$), which also did not differ from each other. Perceived control showed the opposite pattern, with less control at faster speeds: $F(1, 166) = 36.48$, $p < .01$. On this measure, however, the only significant effect was that the fastest condition led to lower control than any of the others, which did not differ among themselves.

In summary, our hypothesis regarding the psychological effects of time pressure seems well supported, although different types of reactions produced quite different effects. Faster conditions tended to produce more tension, and the fastest produced more physical discomfort and less perceived control than the others, whereas slower conditions produced more boredom. Of perhaps greatest importance, overall, subjects had the most positive experience and reported the most enjoyment and satisfaction in the 10-second condition, with lower ratings in both faster and slower conditions.

Type A/B Behavior Pattern

Subjects were divided into type A and type B on the basis of a median split on scores on the modified JAS. Although this produced a somewhat uneven distribution of the two types within each time

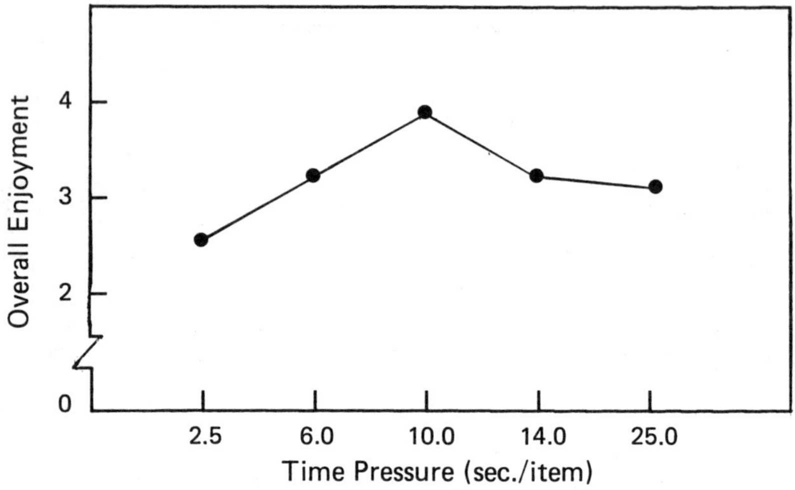

Figure 6.2. Enjoyment of the Task in Each Time Pressure Condition

pressure condition, the numbers were close enough to allow analyses of variance with personality type as a variable. When such analyses were performed on all of the measures described above, there was only one significant effect: Type A subjects solved more anagrams ($F[1, 159] = 8.80$, $p < .01$) and a greater percentage of anagrams ($F[1, 159] = 18.92$, $p < .001$). There were no significant interactions with level of time pressure, however, nor were there any significant effects on any measure of psychological reaction.

Other Individual Differences

That the only difference between type A and type B subjects was on performance suggested that the effect might be due to differences in motivation rather than to any other characteristic that is supposed to distinguish between the groups. To test this, a need for achievement score was calculated for each subject on the basis of the seven items on the JAS that clearly relate to achievement. Subjects were then split into high and low achievement groups using a median split, and analyses of variance were performed as before. As expected, the high motivation group solved more items and a higher percentage of items than the low motivation group, with the difference between the groups being very similar to that found for the type A/B groups. In addition, the high motivation group was significantly more positive ($F[1, 153] = 11.69$, $p < .001$) and enjoyed the experience more ($F[1, 157] = 6.83$, $p < .01$). No other effects were significant.

Subjects were also split into two groups on the basis of their scores on the JAS with the motivation items excluded. This residual JAS division showed a substantially smaller relation with the measures than did the achievement measure. On the residual JAS, those with high scores solved more items and a higher percentage of items on the anagram task, although these effects were weaker than for the achievement measure. Unlike the achievement measure, there was no relation between the residual JAS and any measure of psychological reaction.

Neuroticism was unrelated to task performance, but higher neuroticism was correlated with physical discomfort ($r = .27$, $p < .01$), negativity ($r = .20$, $p < .05$), and boredom ($r = .17$, $p < .05$). In addition, when subjects were divided into high and low neurotic, there was an interaction between neuroticism and tension: $F(4, 156) = 2.50$, $p < .05$. The high and low groups reported equal amounts of tension at low time pressure (25 and 14 seconds per item) and very high time pressure (2.5 seconds per item), but the high neurotic subjects felt more tension at intermediate levels of time pressure (10 and 6 seconds per item).

Discussion

Time Pressure and Productivity

Although time pressure is often considered a disruptive force, especially in work situations, we have found that its effect depends on the degree of time pressure as well as the particular reaction being considered. In terms of performance, time pressure increased productivity substantially. Those who were given an item every 6 seconds solved more than three times as many as those given an item every 25 seconds, and even those in the fastest condition (2.5 seconds) solved almost twice as many anagrams as those in the slowest condition. As predicted, however, the best performance was not in the fastest condition. Rather, those in the 6-second condition solved the most anagrams, with those in the 10-second condition solving the next most. In other words, increasing time pressure improved performance up to a point and then interfered with it. Presumably increases beyond our fastest condition would degrade performance still further, so that the inverted-U relation between time pressure and performance would be even clearer.

This finding is quite consistent with the analysis of stress and performance presented by McGrath (1976). In his terms, greater demand produces greater arousal, which in turn improves performance as long as the task does not also become more difficult. In the present study, demand was varied by reducing the amount of time available to perform the task (i.e., by increasing time pressure), which clearly made the task more difficult as demand increased. Thus it would seem that the analysis would predict that performance would improve up to a point because of the increased arousal, but would then decline because of increased difficulty of the task.

In one sense, this effect of time pressure is trivial, yet in another sense it is important. It is trivial because productivity must depend to some extent on the amount of work attempted and the level of motivation of the worker. If an assembly line allows a worker 20 minutes to do a task that can readily be performed in 10 minutes by the average worker, there is little or no time pressure, and productivity is necessarily very low. Speeding up the assembly line so that only 10 minutes are allowed for the task will exert time pressure, because workers who are slower than average will have some difficulty completing the task and even those at the average will have to work steadily to keep up. But productivity will almost certainly increase. Further decreases in the amount of time allowed for the task will lead to increasing time pressure, which at some point must begin to cause a decline in productivity, because the workers cannot perform the task in the time allowed. In other words, whatever the task, as long as it is possible for those working on it to perform it at all, there must be some amount of time in which the average person can perform it easily. Giving more time than this will reduce productivity; giving less time will increase productivity, but eventually will again decrease it. Therefore, the inverted-U function describing the relation between time pressure and task performance is inevitable and trivial.

Nevertheless, this finding is important because the potentially positive effects of time pressure are not generally recognized. Anyone who has ever had to meet a deadline or worked on a piece-rate basis will understand that time pressure can have an energizing, motivating effect on people that causes them to work harder and be more productive. The present study shows this. Thus the important aspect of the result is the demonstration that time pressure is not always a source of disruption—that under the right circumstances it can have the positive effect of increasing productivity.

There are, however, two crucial limitations on the positive effect of time pressure on task performance. First, as we have seen, beyond a certain point, increasing time pressure will produce a decline in productivity. The optimal point will presumably depend on many factors. It is likely that the type of task, the motivation and skill of the workers, their attitudes and personalities, and other factors will determine their reactions to time pressure. But in any situation and with any people, there will be some optimal level of time pressure, and further increases will reduce the amount of work completed.

Individual Differences in Reaction to Time Pressure

What of individual differences in response to time pressure? It seems likely that there are consistent individual differences in these reactions. We investigated two personality characteristics and found little of great interest. Type A and type B individuals did not differ in their reactions to varying degrees of time pressure, and the only effect of neuroticism was that high neurotic subjects felt more tension than low neurotic subjects at intermediate levels of time pressure. The usual descriptions of the type A personality include a sense of time urgency, so that it seemed a good candidate to explain some of the individual variation. That we did not find this could be due to any of a number of factors. Perhaps the written form of the Jenkins is not as good as the interview procedures. We should note, however, that our own study of this (Edwards, 1983) as well as that by others (Dembroski, 1978) showed a high degree of agreement in classifications by the two methods. Also, many investigators have found consistent effects using the Jenkins. So it seems unlikely that our failure to find an effect was due solely or mainly to the particular measuring instrument we employed.

The current study provides little on which to base an explanation of the failure to find more substantial effects of our two personality variables. It may be that the task and experimental conditions did not engage these particular dimensions of individual differences. For example, type As may have a greater sense of time urgency and may react differently to time pressure, but only when they are more involved in the outcome than they were here. Similarly, neuroticism may have greater effects on reactions to time pressure when the people involved are more concerned about performing well or when the time period is longer. There are many other possible explanations about which one could speculate.

On the other hand, it may be that these two personality characteristics do not, in fact, have much impact on reactions to time pressure. Even if type As feel a greater sense of time urgency than type Bs, this urgency may not change as a function of time pressure. It may be merely superimposed on any condition of time pressure without interacting with it. This is consistent with our finding that As performed better at all levels of time pressure. In the same way, neuroticism may not interact with time pressure, because such pressure is not an especially relevant factor in the arousal of neurotic feelings. A considerable amount of additional research will be necessary in order to determine which, if any, of these possible explanations is correct.

Time Pressure and Stress

Although we have discussed this study entirely in terms of time pressure, it is important to consider it from a somewhat different point of view. The actual manipulation consisted of allowing subjects varying amounts of time to solve a cognitive task, in this case, anagram puzzles. We conceptualized this manipulation as a means of varying time pressure, but, of course, all that varied was the amount of time allowed. It is possible that subjects did not experience any degree of time pressure when more time was allowed than they would have used if they had paced themselves. A pretest indicated that, on average, people took about 10 seconds per item, so most subjects should have found that amount of time sufficient. The psychological experience of pressure due to limited time may have occurred only when subjects were pushed to work faster than they ordinarily would. Thus they may have felt time pressure only when the amount of time provided per item was 10 seconds or less.

Conceptualized in this way, the curvilinear relationship we predicted and found would not indicate the effects of time pressure alone. Rather, as also suggested by McGrath's (1976) analysis, the relationship between amount of time and enjoyment could be seen as being due to the operation of two quite different processes. Those who are given more time than they require feel bored and therefore do not enjoy the task; whereas those who are given less time than they need experience time pressure, and the greater the pressure, the more tension is felt and the less they enjoy the task. Once there is enough time, boredom increases when still more time is given. Once there is too little time, pressure and tension increase when less time is given. At the optimal point, the amount of time is just about right—people are neither terribly bored nor very stressed. In other words, perhaps we are dealing with two quite different processes—boredom when there is "too much" time, pressure when there is "too little," and optimal satisfaction when there is just enough.

One of the difficulties in discussing time pressure and its relation to stress is that neither is well defined. This is not the place to get involved in a long discussion of what is meant by *stress*. The term has been used in many different ways in different situations. Probably no single definition will suit all circumstances. For our purposes, let us assume that stress involves too much of some kind of stimulation, not too little. Thus too much excitement, stimulation, work, or almost anything else is consistent with our conceptualization of stress or a stressor; whereas too little of these is not. Too little stimulation can, of course, produce other effects, but we shall not call them stress. Therefore, in the present context, too much time pressure would be expected to cause stress, but too little time pressure would not. Whereas overstimulation causes stress, understimulation causes boredom or some other negative reaction.

In investigating positive and negative reactions to the amount of time allowed for performing a task, it may be necessary to consider two different response modes that are activated by too much and too little time. It seems to us that the most parsimonious way of describing the relation between the psychological reaction and the amount of time is an inverted-U function, even though the negative reaction at one end of the time continuum may be different from the negative reaction at the other end. This does not preclude the possibility that some degree of time pressure is necessary for maximum satisfaction. The key point is that maximum satisfaction does not always require an absence of tension or stress. It is entirely possible that the optimal point occurs when the sum (or perhaps the product) of boredom and tension is smallest; or when the total of the positive effects of challenge, excitement, and satisfaction are greatest compared to the negative effects of stress and boredom. Thus even if two processes are involved in producing the relation between time and enjoyment, maximum enjoyment may occur only with some amount of time pressure.

Conclusions

Time pressure is generally considered a source of stress in the world. Although there is little doubt that limiting the amount of time to complete an activity can have negative effects and can cause pressure that is experienced as stress, limitations on time need not always be harmful. For some activities, time pressure is absolutely integral to the task, so much so that without some time pressure, the activity becomes meaningless. It is the time pressure that produces the challenge that turns a trivial task into one that may be enjoyable. For simple tasks, the absence of time restrictions may lead to boredom and other associated negative reactions. Time restrictions, whether reasonable or not, add an element of challenge and structure to the task without which motivation and enjoyment may be low. This must be contrasted with the other extreme, with some complex intellectual or artistic activities for which even a small amount of time pressure will interfere with good performance and with enjoyment. We would assert that for all, or virtually all, activities, maximum performance and optimal psychological reactions occur at some intermediate level of time allowed. The ideal amount of time pressure is enough so that the task is challenging and interesting and so that performance is efficient. Any less time pressure reduces the challenge, makes the task less enjoyable, and reduces efficiency; any more time pressure interferes with high quality performance and introduces tension that reduces satisfaction.

The optimal point of time pressure will depend on the type of task (complexity, degree of creativity necessary, inherent interest, necessity for perfect performance, and so on), characteristics of the individual (though what they are has not yet been determined), and presumably other factors such as the consequences of failure and duration of the activity. But the basic relation should hold—time limitations are not inherently bad, rather there is some degree of limitation that will be ideal.

REFERENCES

Berry, R. N. (1962). Skin conductance levels and verbal recall. *Journal of Experimental Psychology, 63,* 275-286.

Brunson, B. I., & Matthews, K. A. (1981). The type A coronary-prone behavior pattern and reactions to uncontrollable stress: An analysis of performance strategies, affect, and attributions during failure. *Journal of Personality and Social Psychology, 40,* 906-918.

Burnam, M. A., Pennebaker, J. W., & Glass, D. C. (1975). Time consciousness, achievement striving and type A coronary-prone behavior pattern. *Journal of Abnormal Psychology, 84,* 76-79.

Caplan, R. D., Cobb, S., French, J.R.P., Jr., Harrison, R. V., & Pinneau, S. R., Jr. (1980). *Job demands and worker health: Main effects and occupational differences.* Ann Arbor, MI: Institute for Social Research.

Caplan, R. D., & Jones, K. W. (1975). Effects of work load, role ambiguity, and type A personality on anxiety, depression, and heart rate. *Journal of Applied Psychology, 60,* 713-719.

Carver, C. S., Coleman, A. E., & Glass, D. C. (1976). The coronary-prone behavior pattern and the suppression of fatigue on a treadmill test. *Journal of Personality and Social Psychology, 33,* 460-466.

Dembroski, T. M. (1978). Reliability and validity of methods used to assess coronary-prone behavior. In T. M. Dembroski, S. M. Weiss, J. L. Shields, S. G. Haynes, & M. Feinleib (Eds.), *Coronary-prone behavior* (chap. 7, pp. 95-106). New York: Springer-Verlag.

Edwards, D. (1983). *The activation of performance and affect by time pressure.* Master's thesis, University of Toronto.

Eysenck, H. J., & Eysenck, S.B.G. (1968). *Manual for the Eysenck personality inventory.* San Diego: Educational and Industrial Testing Service.

Frankenhauser, M., & Gardell, B. (1976). Underload and overload in working life: Outline of a multidisciplinary approach. *Journal of Human Stress, 2,* 35-46.

French, J.R.P., Jr., Caplan, R. D., & Harrison, W. (1982). *The mechanisms of job stress and strain.* New York: John Wiley.

Friedman, M., & Rosenman, R. H. (1974). *Type A behavior and your heart.* New York: Knopf.

Glass, D. C. (1977). *Behavior patterns, stress and coronary disease.* New York: Halsted Division, John Wiley.

Hackman, J. R. (1970). Tasks and task performance in research on stress. In J. E. McGrath (Ed.), *Social and psychological factors in stress.* New York: Holt, Rinehart & Winston.

Jenkins, C. D., Zyzanski, S. J., & Rosenman, R. H. (1979). *The Jenkins' activity survey.* New York: Psychological Corporation.

McGrath, J. E. (1970). Major substantive issues: Time, setting, and the coping process. In J. E. McGrath (Ed.), *Social and psychological factors in stress.* New York: Holt, Rinehart & Winston.

McGrath, J. E. (1976). Stress and behavior in organization. In M. D. Dunnette (Ed.), *Handbook of industrial and organizational psychology* (pp. 1351-1395). New York: John Wiley.

Palermo, D. S. (1957). Proactive interference and facilitation as a function of amount of training and stress. *Journal of Experimental Psychology, 53,* 293-296.

Pepinsky, P., Pepinsky, H., & Pavlik, W. (1960). The effects of task complexity and time pressure upon team productivity. *Journal of Applied Psychology, 44,* 34-38.

Sales, S. M. (1970). Some effects of role overload and role underload. *Organizational Behavior and Human Performance, 5,* 592-608.

Sjoberg, H. (1977). Interaction of task difficulty, activation and work load. *Journal of Human Stress, 3,* 33-38.

Stennett, R. G. (1957). The relationship of performance level to level of arousal. *Journal of Experimental Psychology, 54,* 54-62.

Streufert, S., Streufert, S. C., & Gorson, D. M. (1981). Time urgency and coronary-prone behavior: The effectiveness of a behavior pattern. *Basic and Applied Social Psychology, 2,* 161-174.

Weitz, J. (1970). Psychological research needs on the problem of human stress. In J. E. McGrath (Ed.), *Social and psychological factors in stress.* New York: Holt, Rinehart & Winston.

Yerkes, R. M., & Dodson, J. D. (1908). The relation of strength of stimulus to rapidity of habit formation. *Journal of Comparative and Neurological Psychology, 18,* 459-482.

7

Time-Diary Evidence About the Social Psychology of Everyday Life

JOHN P. ROBINSON

For the social psychologist, the study of time presents many attractive features. First, it presents us with an opportunity to observe normal everyday behavior—with a measure (i.e., time) that has true ratio-scale properties. Second, it can be taken as a behavioral indicator of values and preferences, because individuals are continually presented in their daily lives with activity choices about how to use their time. Third, it allows us to examine individuals in the totality of roles in which they engage in daily life: marital partner, economic provider, parent, family manager, consumer, group/organizational member, citizen, cultural participant, friend, and information user. Study of time use in everyday life also allows social psychologists to study the role of attitudes and perceptions of activities in the stream of "real time"—as individuals are in the actual process of experiencing and engaging in these activities.

One of the important techniques in the study of time use is the "time diary." Time diaries can be seen as a prime example of the "micro-behavioral" approach to survey research. This micro-behavioral approach recognizes the limited ability of respondents to report very complex behavior in a survey context. Thus survey questions are limited to the more elementary experiences about which respondents can accurately report. For example, a micro-behavioral approach would ask about the details of a recent unhappy episode at work or in marriage, rather than just a global question on job or marital dissatisfaction; it would ask for accounts of activities that happened "yesterday" and not "in general" or "typically"; or it would ask direct questions on the specific information the respondent possesses about a topic and the respondent's specific mass media usage and not simply about "main sources" of information about that topic. The micro-behavioral approach thus provides researchers with a more basic and flexible, but also a far more complex, data base from which to draw conclusions about human behavior.

The Time Diary

The chapter first reviews the methodological features of the time-diary approach, including evidence of its basic reliability and validity. It then examines results from four national studies of time use and attempts to extract from them some social psychological generalizations about the nature of daily life in the United States. Finally it suggests some needed direction for new research. The time diary is a technique for collecting self-reports of an individual's daily behavior in an open-ended fashion on an activity-by-activity basis. Individual respondents keep such activity accounts for a short, manageable period such as a day or a week—usually across the 24 hours of a single day. In that way, the technique capitalizes on the most attractive measurement properties of the time variable:

(1) All daily activity is potentially recorded (including that which occurs in early morning hours when most "normal" people may be asleep).
(2) All 1440 minutes of the day are equally distributed across respondents (thus allowing certain "trade-offs" of activities to be examined).
(3) Respondents are allowed to use a time frame and accounting variable that is maximally understandable to them and accessible to memory.

The Time-Diary Method

The open-ended nature of activity reporting means these activity reports are automatically geared to detecting new and unanticipated activities, as well as capturing the flavor of how daily life is experienced. A typical diary page (see Figure 7.1) would leave room for respondents to report each activity they engaged in, and in addition to report where

WHAT YOU DID FROM MIDNIGHT UNTIL 9 IN THE MORNING

Time	What did you do?	Time Began	Time Ended	Where?	List Other People With You	Was This An Activity That You Had to Do	Was This An Activity That You Planned Ahead	Enjoyment Scale 0 = Dislike 10 = Like	Doing Anything Else?	Check If Using: Phone	TV	Radio
Midn ↓		12:00										
1 AM ↓												
2 AM												
3 AM												
4 AM												
5 AM ↓												
6 AM ↓												
6 AM ↓												
8 AM ↓												

Figure 7.1. Sample Time-Diary Page

they were, who they were with, and what other activities they were doing at the same time.

These open-ended diaries can be coded and arranged in a variety of ways. Table 7.1 outlines the activity coding scheme developed for the 1965 Multinational Time Budget Research Project (Szalai, Converse, Feldheim, Scheuch, & Stone, 1972). This scheme, which was developed by social researchers in Eastern Europe, first distinguishes non-free time activities (codes 00-49) from free time activities (codes 50-99). It then further subdivides non-free activities into paid work (codes 00-09), family care (codes 10-39), and personal care (codes 40-49). Free time activities are subdivided into five general categories: adult education, organizational activity, social life, recreation, and communication activities. More fine-grained distinctions within these 10 categories are reflected in the second digit of the Table 7.1 code, and this code has more recently been expanded to nearly 250 categories to reflect further distinctions within activities. Nonetheless, this is not the only category scheme that has been developed, and the value of the open-end diary approach (as well as the Table 7.1 scheme) is that activities can be recoded or recombined depending on the analyst's particular assumptions or purposes.

These diary data can provide generalizable aggregate estimates for the full range of alternative daily activities: from "contracted" time (e.g., work and commute to work), to "committed" time (e.g., family care), to personal care (e.g., sleeping, eating, hygiene), and to all the types of activities that occur in free time: adult education, cultural participation, recreation, use of the mass media, and the daily activities that ought to be of major interest to social psychologists—participation in formal and informal social life.

Some Features of Time-Diary Data

The multiple uses and perspectives afforded by time-diary data have led to a recent proliferation of research and literature in this field. Comparable national time-diary data have been collected in over 25 countries over the last two decades, including virtually all Eastern and Western European countries.

Several methodological studies have provided evidence of the basic reliability and validity of the time-diary approach, both in the United States and in other countries (Juster, 1985; Robinson, 1977, 1986;

TABLE 7.1
Basic Code Categories
(additional details in third digit of code—not shown)

Complete Two-Digit Activity Code

Code		Code	
	Working time and time connected to it (00-09)		Private needs: meals, sleep, and so on (private and nondescribed activities) (40-49)
00	Regular work	40	Personal hygiene
01	Work at home	41	Personal medical
02	Overtime	42	Care to adults
03	Travel for job	43	Meals, snacks
04	Waiting, delays	44	Restaurant meals
05	Second job	45	Night sleep
06	Meals at work	46	Daytime sleep
07	At work, other	47	Resting
08	Work breaks	48	Private, other
09	Travel to job	49	Travel, personal
	Domestic work (10-19)		Adult education and professional training (50-59)
10	Prepare food	50	Attend school
11	Meal cleanup	51	Other classes
12	Clean house	52	Special lecture
13	Outdoor chores	53	Political courses
14	Laundry, ironing	54	Homework
15	Clothes upkeep	55	Read to learn
16	Other upkeep	56	Other study
17	Gardening, animal care	57-58	Blank
18	Heat, water	59	Travel, study
19	Other duties		Civic and collective participation activities (60-69)
	Care to children (20-29)	60	Union, politics
20	Baby care	61	Work as officer
21	Child care	62	Other participation
22	Help on homework	63	Civic activities
23	Talk to children	64	Religious organization
24	Indoor playing	65	Religious practice
25	Outdoor playing	66	Factory council
26	Child health	67	Miscellaneous, organization
27	Other, babysit	68	Other organization
28	Blank		Spectacles, entertainment, social life (70-79)
29	Travel with child	70	Sports events
	Purchasing of goods and services (30-39)	71	Mass culture
30	Marketing	72	Movies
31	Shopping	73	Theatre
32	Personal care	74	Museums
33	Medical care	75	Visiting with friends
34	Administrative service		
35	Repair service		
36	Waiting in line		

Continued

TABLE 7.1 Continued

37	Other service	76	Party, meals
38	Blank	77	Cafe, pubs
39	Travel, service	78	Other social
		79	Travel, social
	Sports and active leisure (80-89)		Passive leisure (90-99)
80	Active sports	90	Radio
81	Fishing, hiking	91	TV
82	Taking a walk	92	Play records
83	Hobbies	93	Read book
84	Ladies' hobbies	94	Read magazine
85	Artwork	95	Read paper
86	Making music	96	Conversation
87	Parlor games	97	Letters, private
88	Other pastime	98	Relax, think
89	Travel, pastime	99	Travel, leisure

Szalai et al., 1972). These validity studies have involved "outside" observational techniques, such as participant observation (Chapin, 1974); reports of other household members (Juster, 1985); television cameras in the home (Bechtel, Achepohl, & Akers, 1972); and beepers that alert respondents to report their activities at specific points in time by means of random alarms during the day (Robinson, 1986). Correlations of time expenditures between these observational measures and time-diary estimates have usually been over .80, and often over .90.

Time-diary data have been especially useful in identifying aggregate societal trends in time expenditures, particularly because if time spent on one free time activity increases, time on some other activity must decrease. Time-diary data can be construed as evidence of the value people put on the activities in which they engage and in very real behavioral terms. Table 7.2 shows some cross-time American data on time use from two national time-diary studies, done in 1965 and 1975. These data indicate certain important structural changes in the nature of daily life in America over that decade: declines in both paid work time (mainly for men) and in family care activities (mainly for women). This left more time available, not only for free time activities (particularly television and rest) but for personal care activities as well (e.g., sleep and grooming). This pattern of shifts in activity suggested more movement toward a "postindustrious" society than a "postindustrial" one.

TABLE 7.2
1965-1975 Differences in Time Use by Sex, Employment Status, and Marital Status

	Employed Men		Employed Women		Housewives		
	Married	*Single*	*Married*	*Single*	*Married*	*Single*	*Total Sample*
1965 Urban Data	(N = 448)	(N = 73)	(N = 190)	(N = 152)	(N = 341)	(N = 14)	(N = 1218)
Sleep	53.1	50.6	53.8	52.6	53.9	58.8	53.3
Work for pay	51.3	51.4	38.4	39.8	.5	1.6	33.0
Family care	9.0	7.7	28.8	20.6	50.0	45.7	25.4
Personal care	20.9	22.2	20.3	21.7	22.6	23.0	21.5
Free time	33.7	36.1	26.7	33.3	41.0	38.9	34.8
organizations	2.6	3.6	1.4	3.7	3.4	3.4	2.8
media	17.1	13.9	10.7	11.1	15.3	19.1	14.7
social life	7.2	10.4	7.9	9.6	12.6	10.2	9.4
recreation	1.4	1.3	.6	.5	.6	1.1	.9
other leisure	5.4	6.9	6.1	8.4	9.1	5.1	7.0
Total (free)	168.0 (33.7)	168.0 (36.1)	168.0 (26.7)	168.0 (33.3)	168.0 (41.0)	168.0 (38.9)	168.0 (34.8)
1975 Urban Data	(N = 245)	(N = 87)	(N = 117)	(N = 108)	(N = 141)	(N = 28)	(N = 726)
Sleep	53.4	54.1	55.1	54.3	56.8	58.6	54.7
Work for pay	47.4	40.0	30.1	38.8	1.1	0.0	32.5
Family care	9.7	9.0	24.9	16.6	44.3	42.8	20.5
Personal care	21.4	20.0	26.2	21.9	21.4	19.2	21.8
Free time	36.1	44.9	31.7	36.4	44.4	47.4	38.5
organizations	3.7	4.8	2.2	4.4	4.8	3.0	3.8
media	18.9	18.5	15.6	14.5	20.4	27.2	18.2
social life	6.4	8.9	6.6	8.9	10.1	9.1	7.8
recreation	1.3	4.1	.8	.5	.7	.4	1.3
other leisure	5.8	8.6	6.5	8.1	8.4	7.7	7.4
Total (free)	168.0 (36.1)	168.0 (44.9)	168.0 (31.7)	168.0 (36.4)	168.0 (44.4)	168.0 (47.4)	168.0 (38.5)

SOURCE: Robinson (1976).

Some Major American Time-Diary Studies

To date, a total of four major national time-diary studies have been conducted in the United States. The studies and the data-collection organizations involved are as follows:

(1) Mutual Broadcasting Corporation (1954) study, in which more than 8000 American adults aged 15-59 kept time diaries for a two-day period in the spring of that year (more exact details are given in DeGrazia, 1962).
(2) Survey Research Center, University of Michigan (1965) study, in which 1244 adult respondents aged 18-64 kept a single-day diary of activities in the fall of that year (and the spring of 1966); respondents in rural and nonemployed households were excluded (details described in Robinson, 1977, and Szalai et al., 1972).
(3) Survey Research Center, University of Michigan (1975) study, in which 1519 adult respondents (and 788 of the spouses of those respondents who were married) aged 18 and over kept diaries for a single day in the fall of that year (Robinson, 1976). These respondents became part of a panel that was subsequently reinterviewed three times by telephone in the winter, spring, and summer months of 1976, with about 1500 of the original respondents remaining through four waves of the study. Some 677 of the original respondents were subsequently reinterviewed in 1981 and again across all four seasons of the year (Juster & Stafford, 1985).
(4) Survey Research Center, University of Maryland (1985) study, in which single-day diary data will be available from more than 3500 adults aged 18+ across the entire calendar year 1985. In most households, diary data were collected for all members of the household aged 11 and older. This will be the first national diary study to include extensive diary data of psychological states during activity (more extensive data of this type were collected in the community study of Csikszentmihalyi & Kubay, 1981).

In general, these time-diary studies have not encountered severe response rate problems, particularly if the respondents are not asked to report on more than a single day's activities at one time. Response rates of over 70% have been achieved in each of the last three studies described above.

Some Conclusions About the Social Psychological Nature of Daily Life

Analysis of several social psychological variables included in the 1965 and 1975 national time-diary studies has led to certain tentative conclusions about the general social psychological nature of daily life. These include questions about the relations between attitudes and behavior and about discrepancies between perceived and actual use of time.

In particular, time-diary data collected to date have shown that there seems to be a clear relation between general attitudes toward activities and time spent on those activities as reported independently in time diaries. Respondents in both the 1965 and the 1975 studies were asked about the amount of satisfaction and enjoyment they generally obtained from engaging in various daily activities (e.g., reading, watching TV, housework). How people felt about activities were among the strongest correlates of time spent in these activities (at the individual level). In other words, people who said they derived more enjoyment from reading also recorded more reading time in their diaries (than people who derived less enjoyment from reading). Moreover, this relation held across time: enjoyment ratings obtained at one point in time were predictive of time reported in time diaries filled out three to six months later (Robinson, 1983).

At the same time, this relation held up much less well at the aggregate level across time. Between 1965 and 1975, for example, time spent watching TV increased significantly, while time spent visiting and in social interaction declined. Yet, TV was among the activities rated below average for enjoyment overall, while social interaction was among the highest rated activities in terms of enjoyment. Obviously, other factors came into play (such as the effort or barriers involved in the two activities); but it is important to be aware of this example of an "ecological fallacy" in the relation of attitudes and behavior at the short-term individual level and at the long-term aggregate level.

These activity-attitude data have also shown that there are important similarities in the attitudes toward free time and non-free time activities. A common impression from the literature on work attitudes is that many (if not most) workers put up with the job dissatisfaction and low enjoyment inherent in their jobs in order to earn the money and opportunity to maximize enjoyment of life in their free time. Yet activity enjoyment ratings show work to be above average in terms of pleasurable activities, being above such free time activities as organizational participation and watching television. And, when asked directly whether they enjoyed themselves more in their work or in their free time activities, most American respondents could not choose between the two, with more than 60% of employed people saying they enjoyed both about equally (Robinson, 1984).

This may say less about the high quality of work life in America than about the poor quality of free time, but it does serve as a reminder of certain incomplete and misleading assumptions that social psychologists and other social observers may have about the interrelation between work and the rest of life.

Some Inferences from Time-Diary Data

Turning to the time-diary data themselves, there is little evidence of America turning into the "self-actualizing" society that many psychologists saw in the "postindustrial" America of the 1960s and 1970s. While that may have indeed occurred, time-dairy entries reported between 1965 and 1981 indicate that instead of increased time in such self-actualizing activities as arts participation, recreational activity, and reading, the major gain in free time was found for television viewing—a relatively low involvement, low enjoyment activity. (In examining the elasticity of time categories in the 1965 study, for example, Robinson and Converse, 1972, found television to be the activity respondents overwhelmingly considered most expendable in the context of all of their daily activities.)

Nonetheless, time-diary data do remind us of important contextual factors in certain self-actualizing activities. For example, far more helping behavior is accomplished through informal arrangements (e.g., caring for the sick, helping someone move) than through formal philanthropic organizations. Moreover, people spend more direct time in arts activities (such as painting or playing music) than in going to art museums or concerts, or in playing sports rather than attending sports events (Robinson, 1977).

It has often been presumed that there would be marked social class differences in time use. Social class differences in having free time available have been found to be minimal, however. None of the four time-diary studies to date has found significant differences in total reported free time activities by educational attainment, by level of income, or by occupational prestige. All these class groups have about 40 hours per week of free time on the average, and much greater differences are found *within* these social classes depending on whether that class member is married or single, is male or female, or has a longer or shorter work week.

At the same time, more highly educated and middle-class people are more likely to describe their lives as being "rushed," and not having enough time to complete routine activities. That may mean that they have more ambitious schedules of both free time and non-free time activities, or that they are able to accomplish more in the time available to them. But objectively, they have no less free time, according to their own diary accounts of daily activity. Moreover, more highly educated people have reported greater gains than less educated people in the least harried activity (television viewing) since 1965. This suggests an interesting, and basic, social psychological paradox for future research: Middle-class people feel more harried but they can afford more time on the least harried of activities.

There are significant sex-role differences in certain time expenditures, particularly doing housework. Historically, women in our society have done more housework than men. Time-diary data make it clear that however much these sex-role differences may have come under attack, we are a long way from gender equality. To the extent that the ratio of housework has shifted, it is due far more to women doing less housework than to men doing more. Men may be doing two or three more hours of housework per week than they did 20 years ago, but women are doing five to ten hours a week less; and that change is not solely due to women marrying later or having smaller families.

There remain certain deep-rooted sex-role orientations toward housework. Single women without children spend three times as much time doing housework than do single men. And although the situation is changing, only a minority of women who are married say they wish the husbands would do more housework (or more child care). Part of the reason appears to be that these women feel their husbands work hard enough at their paid jobs. But another main reason suggested from research is that husbands are unable to perform these tasks to the standards that women expect. Reductions of these standards may be necessary before one sees more significant shifts toward gender equality in time doing housework. In any event, these inequalities do not seem to be major determinants of marital dissatisfaction or life dissatisfaction.

And even with the large increase in women's participation in the labor force, women in society still average about the same amount of free time as do men (Robinson, 1977).

Outputs from and Organization of Daily Time

There does not appear to be a strong, or even moderate, relation between time spent and productivity from this time expenditure. There is much evidence to support C. Northcote Parkinson's famous "law" that work length is primarily determined by the "time available for its completion." For example, there seems little relation between the time women (and men) spent in doing housework and the cleanliness of the household—either in terms of the respondent's own criteria or interviewer ratings. There is also no difference in rated cleanliness between women who work and those who do not, even though employed women devote only 60% as much time to housework as do full-time homemakers and many have larger families and living facilities to manage. (At the same time, having "labor-saving" technology or household cleaning sessions in the household also has no effect on these household output indicators.)

Nor does there seem to be much relation between the time parents "invest" in their children and their children's academic performance; for example, as a group, Jewish parents (who generally have higher achieving children) spent below-average amounts of time in child care activities in the 1965 study (Robinson, 1977). Unpublished studies of college students have similarly found minimal relations between the time students spent studying and their course performance. Finally, there are several studies that indicate that availability of free time is not an important determinant of whether people will engage in such "quality" free time activities as arts participation, sports and recreation, and reading.

Such findings bring to mind recent book titles (such as *The One Minute Manager*) that suggest that it is the quality and organization of time that is important to performance and not merely the quantity of time that is spent. Careful study of work life may reveal a surprisingly small correlation between hours spent at the workplace and occupational performance or rewards (such as nonhourly income). An intriguing explanation of the failure of technology to increase free time was suggested in the "harried leisure" hypotheses of Swedish economist

Staffan Linder (1970): The more technology we obtain to relieve the burdens of daily life, the more time we give up to maintain and repair it.

What kind of organization lies behind these time expenditure patterns? Few distinct clusterings, or life-styles, of activities appear from factor analyses of the data. Despite the many efforts that have been undertaken to study the "psychographics" of the American public, time-diary data reveal few distinctive or fundamental clusterings across activities. The most basic seems to be an at-home (versus away-from-home) distinction, with younger, better educated, and unmarried people being more likely to participate in activities outside the home. Better educated people are also more active in more "cultural" activities such as reading, arts participation, interacting with friends (but not relatives), and adult education courses—and are less likely to spend free time in front of the television set. But these correlations are modest at best and usually explain less than 10% of the variance in time spent in these activities.

Nor, moreover, are these activity clusterings related in any truly significant way to life satisfaction, happiness, or other subjective quality-of-life variables in the way in which certain objective life circumstances are (e.g., marital status). Rating of one's leisure time as satisfactory is related less to time spent watching television or attending arts events or social interaction than simply to being able to identify at least one leisure activity that one does enjoy (Robinson, 1977).

Some Directions for Future Research

The above conclusions are almost entirely based on self-reports in time diaries using the single method of the social survey—with all of its limitations regarding depth of understanding of underlying social process and causal inference. They stand in need of replication, therefore, using other research methodologies, such as naturalistic observation or in-depth interpretative interviews.

Such observational studies could also tell us much more that we need to know about the social psychological context of everyday life. How much constraint is associated with particular activities that we now code as "free" time? Some preliminary data from one small sample to address these questions show that, as expected, there is more personal choice involved in free time activities than in non-free time activities (particularly for use of the mass media). There are several interesting exceptions to this distinction, however, with more than a third of respondents describing shopping, helping others, and cooking as activities they "wanted to do" rather than something they had to do. Conversely, up to a quarter of participating respondents described a hobby, conversation, or organizational activity as something they had to do rather than wanted to do.

What is not known, however, are the circumstances that lead to these unexpected ratings of activities by respondents. Under which circumstances is work considered primarily something that people want to do, or social life something they have to do? Are these circumstances something that would be obvious to an outside observer or coder, or do they mainly exist in some idiosyncratic interpretation of individual respondents? For example, how many workers report to work mainly because of the psychological satisfaction they derive from the social contacts with coworkers? How many social or organizational activities are engaged in mainly because of others' expectations and not one's own choice? These are important questions because of the easy, perhaps facile, interpretations that are afforded by the activity coding scheme in Figure 7.1. That may lead us to misleading conclusions about changes in the nature of everyday life, including possibly the increased leisure scenario suggested by the data in Table 7.2.

Nor do these objective time expenditure data reflect the flavor of many of the subtle contextual changes that may have occurred since the 1960s—the increasing informality or variety of dress, the increased use of profane or standardized language across classes or geographic locations, the increased emphasis on quality or status factors in life goals, or the increased use of "do-it-yourself" approaches (such as home technology, self-service gasoline pumps, or self-reliant solutions to individual problems).

Observational studies could also suggest some worthwhile experimental research into the nature and organization of time experience. Given a set of hypothetical tasks of varying enjoyment and complexity levels, how would different individuals go about organizing these tasks for completion? What social class differences would one find in such an exercise, and would such a "middle-class" experiment evoke different problems among working-class respondents than among middle-class respondents? Such an experiment could be made more realistic if it could be made to involve "actual life" situations, such as in a summer camp or a behavioral workshop.

More detailed observational studies can also serve two other useful purposes: further validation of the diary time expenditures and integration of these single-day time expenditures and experiments into the life-styles or "life spaces" of individuals. As it stands now, time-diary figures provide aggregate data with fairly primitive social psychological or individual-level interpretation. Nonetheless, to move much beyond this situation will require a greater commitment of social psychologists to the study of the mundane circumstances of everyday life. The other chapters in this volume should do much to start us in this direction.

REFERENCES

Bechtel, R., Achepohl, C., & Akers, R. (1972). Correlates between observed behavior and questionnaire responses on television viewing. In E. A. Rubinstein, G. A. Comstock, & J. P. Murray (Eds.), *Television and social behavior: Vol. 4. Television in day-to-day life: Patterns and use*. Washington, DC: Government Printing Office.

Chapin, S. (1974). *Human activity patterns: Things people do in time and space*. New York: John Wiley.

Csikszentmihalyi, M., & Kubay J. (1981). Television and the rest of life: A systematic comparison of subjective experience. *Public Opinion Quarterly, 45*, 317-328.

DeGrazia, S. (1962). *Of time, work and leisure*. New York: Twentieth Century Fund.

Juster, F. T. (1985). The validity and quality of time use estimates obtained from recall diaries. In F. T. Juster & F. P. Stafford (Eds.), *Time, goods, and well-being*. Ann Arbor: University of Michigan, Institute for Social Research.

Juster, T., & Stafford, F. (1985). *Time, goods, and well-being*. Ann Arbor: University of Michigan, Institute for Social Research.

Linder, S. (1970). *The harried leisure class*. New York: Columbia University Press.

Robinson, J. (1976). *Changes in Americans' use of time: 1965-1975*. Cleveland, OH: Cleveland State University Communication Research Center.

Robinson, J. (1977). *How Americans use time: A social-psychological analysis of everyday behavior*. New York: Praeger. (Further analyses were published in *How Americans used time in 1965-66*, 1977, Ann Arbor: University Microfilms, Monograph Series)

Robinson, J. (1983). Environmental differences in how Americans use time: The case for subjective and objective indicators. *Journal of Community Psychology*, 11, 171-180.

Robinson, J. (1984). *Free time in Western countries*. College Park, MD: University of Maryland, Survey Research Center.

Robinson, J. (1986). Testing the validity and reliability of diaries versus alternative time use measures. In T. Juster & F. Stafford (Eds.), *Time, goods, and well-being*. Ann Arbor: University of Michigan, Institute for Social Research.

Robinson, J., & Converse, P. (1972). Social change as reflected in the use of time. In A. Campbell & P. Converse (Eds.), *The human meaning of social change*. New York: Russell Sage.

Szalai, A., Converse, P., Feldheim, P., Scheuch, E., & Stone, P. (1972). *The use of time*. The Hague, Netherlands: Mouton.

PART IV

Developmental Cycles

8

Group Dynamics Over Time

Development and Socialization in Small Groups

RICHARD L. MORELAND
JOHN M. LEVINE

During the 1970s, a number of social psychologists lamented the lack of new and interesting research on small groups (e.g., McGrath, 1978; Steiner, 1974; Zander, 1979). Many researchers, however, are now beginning to study such groups once again. Greater research attention is being given to traditional topics, such as decision making in groups and leadership, as well as newer topics, such as attribution in groups and minority influence.

One particularly interesting topic that has not yet received the attention that it deserves concerns temporal changes in small groups. Although several observers (e.g., McGrath & Kravitz, 1982; Ziller, 1977) have criticized the static nature of most research on small groups, little effort has yet been made to study the dynamic properties of such groups. This lack of attention to temporal changes in small groups is surprising, given efforts to understand such changes in dyads (e.g., Altman, Vinsel, & Brown, 1981; Duck & Gilmour, 1981; Levinger,

---

AUTHORS' NOTE: Preparation of this chapter was supported by grant BNS-8316107 from the National Science Foundation. Because we contributed equally to the chapter, our order of authorship was determined arbitrarily.

1980) and organizations (e.g., Feldman, 1976; Van Maanen & Schein, 1979; Wanous, 1980).

In order to understand temporal changes in small groups, two distinct phenomena must be considered. The first phenomenon is *group development*, which concerns changes over time in the group as a whole. The second phenomenon is *group socialization,* which concerns changes over time in the relationship between the group and each of its members. Although group development and group socialization both involve temporal changes in small groups, their similarities (and differences) have seldom been recognized, much less analyzed.

We have two major goals in this chapter. First, we want to review briefly the theoretical and empirical work that has been done on group development and group socialization. Second, we want to discuss some of the ways in which group development might affect group socialization and group socialization might affect group development. Our discussion focuses primarily on small, autonomous, voluntary groups whose members interact on a regular basis, have affective ties with one another, share a common frame of reference, and are behaviorally interdependent. Development and socialization in other kinds of groups have been studied less often and thus may operate somewhat differently.

Group Development

Modern research on group development began in the early 1950s and was stimulated primarily by the work of Bales (1950, 1953) and Bion (1948a, 1948b, 1961). Although they were interested in very different kinds of groups, both Bales and Bion described what they regarded as the basic problems facing small groups and speculated about the temporal order in which those problems are solved by group members. Their ideas focused attention on group development, and soon a great deal of work on that topic began to appear (e.g., Bales & Strodtbeck, 1951; Bennis & Shepard, 1956; Borgatta & Bales, 1953; Heinicke & Bales, 1953; Martin & Hill, 1957; Philp & Dunphy, 1959; Schutz, 1958; Stock & Thelen, 1958). Interest in group development remained strong during the 1960s and 1970s (e.g., Dunphy, 1968; Lundgren & Knight, 1978; Mabry, 1975; Mann, 1967; Mills, 1964; Shambaugh, 1978; Slater, 1966; Winter, 1976), producing methodological refinements and new theories. Less work on group development has appeared in recent years, yet the topic clearly remains intriguing to those who study small groups (e.g., Baker, 1983; Bell, 1982; Davies & Kuypers, 1985; Eklof, 1984; Gersick, 1983; Lewis & Beck, 1983; Obert, 1983).

Over the years, several attempts have been made to review the literature on group development (e.g., Braaten, 1974; Cissna, 1984; Hare, 1973; Lacoursiere, 1980; Tuckman, 1965; Tuckman & Jensen, 1977). Although none of these reviews is comprehensive, together they provide a clear picture of how research on group development has been conducted. That picture reveals a focus on one particular category of small groups, which are typically studied using a single research methodology. Most of the research on group development involves therapy, training, or self-analytic groups. These groups generally consist of intelligent and highly motivated members who agree to work together for a while, under the guidance of a specially trained leader, to improve their understanding of themselves and other people. Field studies are the most common means of studying these groups. Such studies involve observations of how group members behave toward one another from the beginning of the group until its ending. These observational data are then analyzed in ways that reveal temporal patterns in intragroup relations. Finally, the group's development is either compared with the predictions of existing theories or (more often) used as the basis for some new theory.

A prototypical study of group development was carried out by McMurrain and Gazda (1974). Gazda organized and led a small group of eight psychiatric residents, who met weekly for two semesters to obtain some counseling experience. At each meeting, group members discussed their personal problems and tried to help one another solve those problems. Audiotapes were made of every meeting, so that detailed information about the interactions among group members would be available for analysis. These tapes were later coded by trained judges, who evaluated the quantity and quality of helping behavior exhibited by group members during each of their meetings. The judges' evaluations revealed four distinct stages in the group's development. During an initial "exploratory" stage, group members behaved rather tentatively toward one another, apparently in an effort to become better acquainted before discussing their private lives. A "transition" stage followed, beginning with arguments about how meetings should be conducted and ending with general agreement that everyone should be as empathic and open as possible. The group next entered an "action" stage, when members settled down to the real work of trying to solve their problems. Finally, there was a brief "termination" stage; as the last meeting of the group approached, members tried to cope with their conflicting feelings of joy (at creating such a rewarding group) and sadness (at disbanding that group). These four stages were identical to those that Gazda (1972) had proposed in an earlier theoretical analysis of group development.

Clearly, research of this sort has both strengths and weaknesses. The major strength of most research on group development is the rich descriptive information that it provides. When extensive data on the behavior of group members are collected throughout a group's history, it becomes possible to detect even complex patterns of development. As a result, researchers can evaluate the predictive accuracy of theories about group development and then either modify those theories or propose new ones. The major weakness of most research on group development is the rather narrow way in which it is carried out. Therapy, training, and self-analytic groups are both interesting and important, but their development may well differ from that of other groups. When a broader range of groups is observed, it becomes possible to discover at least some of these developmental differences. Researchers can then propose more general theories of group development that explain *why* some groups develop differently than others. Field studies are a valuable source of information about small groups, but other research methodologies may reveal more about the causes of group development. When laboratory or field experiments on group development are performed, it becomes possible to investigate some of the variables that might influence that development, such as the size of the group, the composition of its membership, the frequency with which group members meet, the kinds of tasks that the group performs, the success or failure of the group at achieving its goals, and the group's physical and social environment. Researchers can then propose new theories that go beyond description to the explanation of group development.

There are a great many theories of group development; nearly everyone who does research on this topic (and some who do not) eventually theorizes about it. Unfortunately, most of these theories are based on weak or unspecified empirical evidence (e.g., Battegay, 1977; Berkowitz, 1974; Bonney, 1974; Burghardt, 1977; Caple, 1978; Chadbourne, 1980; Mills, 1978; Pedigo & Singer, 1982) and are primarily descriptive rather than explanatory in nature. Even at a descriptive level, theorists disagree about several basic issues regarding group development. For example, what does group development really mean: Does the passage of time always improve a group, as the term "development" implies, or merely change a group in various ways? How do developmental trends in different aspects of a group, such as its composition, structure, dynamics, and performance, relate to one another? What form does group development take: Does it always involve a one-way passage of the group through some neatly ordered series of stages, or are more complex forms of development possible (see Shambaugh, 1978)? Why do some groups develop more slowly than others or even cease to develop at all? Amid all this theoretical confusion, it is difficult to choose a single theory of group development that is clearly better than all the others. Perhaps the best choice is a theory proposed by Tuckman (1965). In addition to being based on an impressive amount of empirical evidence, this theory has been tested several times since it was first proposed (e.g., Berger, 1976; Tuckman & Jensen, 1977) and is rather widely accepted (see Forsyth, 1983; McGrath, 1984; Napier & Gershenfeld, 1985; Ridgeway, 1983; Shaw, 1981).

Tuckman (1965) derived his theory from a careful review of 50 studies of small group development. These studies involved therapy, training, laboratory, and natural groups. Tuckman looked for evidence of developmental trends in both the social/emotional and the task activities of group members.[1] Social/emotional activities showed a clear pattern of development across different kinds of groups. During an initial "dependence" stage, group members sought out someone willing to serve as their leader. A "conflict" stage followed, in which group members argued with one another and criticized their leader's guidance. The group next entered a "cohesion" stage, when everyone began to feel more positive about membership in the group. Finally, during a "role-taking" stage, group members adopted social roles that made the group more rewarding for them all. Task activities also showed a clear pattern of development across groups of different kinds. During an initial "orientation" stage, group members discussed the nature of their task and how it might be performed. An "emotionality" stage followed, in which group members resisted the need to work closely with one another. The group next entered an "exchange" stage, when everyone shared ideas about how to improve the group's level of performance. Finally, during a "problem-solving" stage, group members solved their performance problems and worked together productively.

Tuckman (1965) was distressed by the generally poor xternal validity of research on group development, he was also impressed by the fact that developmental trends in both social/emotional and task activities seemed to generalize across different kinds of groups. He also noted that these two general developmental trends were rather similar to one another, both in the number of phases involved and in the kinds of interactions that occurred during those phases. These insights led Tuckman to propose a new theory of group development that he hoped could be applied to the activities of any small group.

The original version of this theory contained four distinct stages. According to Tuckman (1965), the first stage of group development is *forming*, which involves dependence and orientation. During this stage, everyone is anxious and uncertain about belonging to the group, and there is a tendency to be rather cautious as a result. The second stage of group development is *storming*, which involves conflict and emotionality. During this stage, everyone becomes more assertive and tries to change the group to satisfy personal needs. As a result, resentments and hostilities erupt among group members with different needs. The third stage of group development is *norming*, which involves cohesion and exchange. During this stage, everyone tries to resolve earlier conflicts, often by negotiating clearer guidelines for group behavior. The fourth stage of group membership is *performing*, which involves role-taking and problem solving. During this stage, everyone works together cooperatively to achieve mutual goals.

A subsequent review of more recent research on the development of small groups (Tuckman & Jensen, 1977) led Tuckman to revise his theory by adding another stage of group development, *adjourning*. During this stage, everyone gradually disengages from both social/emotional and task activities within the group. This disengagement reflects group members' efforts to cope with the approaching end of the group.

Tuckman (1965; Tuckman & Jensen, 1977) offers a clear and simple description of group development. The apparent generalizability of the theory is appealing, and the fact that recent research seems to confirm its predictions is reassuring. The theory might be made more precise by specifying how long each stage of group development lasts or why different kinds of groups develop in slightly different ways, but that may be asking too much of a theory that is meant to apply so broadly. Perhaps the greatest disadvantage of Tuckman's theory is its inability to explain why groups develop at all and why they must develop in the way that his theory describes. Tuckman did not have much to say about these issues, other than to make some oblique references to possible parallels between the development of groups and individuals. The claim that group development "recapitulates" individual development is intriguing (see Grunebaum & Solomon, 1982; Long, 1984; Pedigo & Singer, 1982; Rice & Rutan, 1984; Saravay, 1978; Slater, 1966; Tucker, 1973), but so are claims that group development reflects changes in leader-member relations (see Mann, 1967; Winter, 1976), the occurrence of certain critical events (see Cohen & Smith, 1976; Mills, 1978; Pridham, 1975), and the group's efforts to adapt to internal and external pressures (see Hare, 1973; Mabry, 1975). Until such explanations are refined and tested, theories of group development will remain incomplete.

Group Socialization

Research on group socialization also has a long and rich history. One of the earliest and best-known studies of group socialization was conducted by Newcomb (1943), who found that freshmen entering Bennington College with conservative political attitudes generally became more liberal by the time they were seniors. Newcomb attributed this shift in attitudes to social pressures arising from the liberal norms of the college community. In the four decades since Newcomb's classic study was published, a great deal of research on group socialization has been performed (e.g., Aronson & Mills, 1959; Feldman, 1977; Feshbach & Sones, 1971; Insko, Gilmore, Moehle, Lipsitz, Drenan, & Thibaut, 1982; Jacobs & Campbell, 1961; Moreland, 1985; Putallaz & Gottman, 1981; Scott, 1965; Trice, 1957). A comprehensive review of this literature by Moreland and Levine (1982) provides a clear picture of how research on group socialization has been conducted.

Unlike research on the development of small groups, research on group socialization is eclectic in both the types of groups that are studied and the methodologies that are employed. Socialization has been studied in a wide variety of groups, including military units (e.g., Zurcher, 1965), churches (e.g., Roozen, 1980), self-help groups (e.g., Lofland & Lejeune, 1960), college fraternities (e.g., Wallace, 1964), laboratory groups (e.g., Ziller & Behringer, 1960), school classrooms (e.g., Feldbaum, Christenson, & O'Neal, 1980), therapy groups (e.g., Gauron & Rawlings, 1975), and work groups (e.g., Vaught & Smith,

1980). The research methodologies used to study group socialization have also been varied. These methodologies include laboratory experiments (e.g., Fromkin, Klimoski, & Flanagan, 1972; Gerard & Mathewson, 1966), field experiments (e.g., Hazer & Alvares, 1981; Lofland & Lejeune, 1960), surveys (e.g., Bouma, 1980; Rusbult, 1980), field studies (e.g., Bartell, 1971; Feldbaum, Christenson, & O'Neil, 1980), and archival studies (e.g., Kanter, 1968; Snyder, 1958).

Because of the magnitude and diversity of research on group socialization, it is difficult to select prototypical studies. Nevertheless, two quite different examples of research on group socialization might serve to illustrate some of the ways in which the topic has been investigated. The first example is a longitudinal field study by Ziller and Behringer (1961) on the assimilation of newcomers into elementary school classrooms (grades one to six). On the first day that a new child entered a classroom and on six additional days, spaced one to four weeks apart, both old-timers (who had been in the classroom for several months) and newcomers were asked to name their five favorite classmates. The newcomers were also asked to compare their current classrooms to their previous ones, and teachers were asked to rate the newcomers' adjustment to their current classrooms. Newcomers were reasonably popular when they first entered their classrooms, but their popularity declined sharply for several weeks thereafter and only rose again toward the end of the study. The popularity of old-timers showed nearly the opposite pattern of changes. Early in the study, newcomers tended to choose less popular classmates than did old-timers, and the consistency of their choices was lower than that of old-timers as well. These differences disappeared by the end of the study. Finally, new girls were assimilated into their classrooms more readily than new boys, and younger newcomers were assimilated more readily than older ones. Apparently, assimilation into elementary school classrooms can require several weeks and can be influenced by such demographic variables as the sex and age of the new child.

Another example of how group socialization has been studied is a laboratory experiment by Levine, Saxe, and Harris (1976) on reactions to opinion deviance in groups of male college students. The four subjects in each group were seated in separate booths containing signal lights and answer switches and asked to vote several times on the proper treatment for a juvenile delinquent (whose case was known to them). Each subject believed that the lights in the booth accurately reflected the votes of fellow group members, but the experimenter actually simulated those responses. Two members of each group appeared to vote consistently with the subject's own position on the issue. The other (target) member exhibited one of four voting patterns: consistent agreement with the modal opinion of the group, consistent disagreement with that opinion, movement from disagreement to agreement, or movement from agreement to disagreement.[2] Between votes, each subject exchanged notes with the target. The target's "notes" to the subject were prepared by the experimenter and defended the target's most recent "vote." Following the voting, the subject evaluated the target and made attributions for the target's behavior.

The results showed that the target's pattern of responses affected the subjects' reactions to the target in several ways. Target attractiveness in the four conditions was rank-ordered in the following way: consistent agreement > disagreement-agreement > agreement-disagreement > consistent disagreement. Attributions for the target's behavior also differed across conditions. For example, in the disagreement-agreement condition, the target was viewed as seeking group approval and as being influenced both by the votes of the other group members and by the subject's own notes. In the agreement-disagreement condition, the target was viewed as trying to demonstrate assertiveness. The subjects communicated most with the consistent disagreer, a moderate amount with the disagreer-agreer and the agreer-disagreer, and least with the consistent agreer. Finally, subjects shifted their own votes toward the target's final "vote" (and away from the modal group opinion) only in the agreement-disagreement condition. Apparently, even though deviates are rejected by their fellow group members, they still can influence opinions under some conditions.

Research on group socialization clearly has both strengths and weaknesses. Interestingly enough, these are almost a mirror image of those associated with research on group development. The major strength of group socialization research is that many different socialization activities have been studied using a wide variety of groups and methodologies. This diversity is valuable, not only because it allows researchers to evaluate the generalizability of their findings, but also because it can lead to the development of theories that both describe *and* explain group socialization. Research on group socialization also has two major weaknesses, however. First, most researchers have adopted a rather narrow temporal perspective on group socialization, focusing on only one phase of the socialization process. So although there has been a great deal of work on such topics as entry into groups, the experiences of new group members, conformity and deviance within groups, and exit from groups, few researchers have studied how the entire socialization process develops over time. Second, most researchers have exhibited a rather narrow social perspective on group socialization; their work nearly always reflects the viewpoint of the group rather than that of the individual. For example, studies of newcomers have typically focused on how they are assimilated into the groups that they join, rather than on how these groups accommodate to the entry of those new members.

A great deal of theoretical work on group socialization has also been done. This work deals with such issues as the recruitment and socialization of new members (e.g., Feldman, 1981; Louis, 1980; Van Maanen & Schein, 1979; Wanous, 1980; Wheeler, 1966; Zander, 1976; Ziller, 1965), feelings of commitment to a group (e.g., Becker, 1960; Farrell & Rusbult, 1981; Gordon, Philpot, Burt, Thompson, & Spiller, 1980; Kanter, 1968; Salancik, 1977), conformity and reactions to deviance among group members (e.g., Allen, 1965, 1975; Levine, 1980; Levine & Russo, 1987; Moscovici, 1985), and departures from a group (e.g., Mobley, Griffeth, Hand, & Meglino, 1979; Staw, 1980; Steers & Mowday, 1981; Zander, 1976; Ziller, 1965). Much of this theoretical work is quite elegant and informative. Nevertheless, like the research on which it is based, this work generally suffers from narrow temporal and social perspectives. That is, theories involving group socialization generally deal with only a single aspect of the entire socialization process and emphasize the viewpoint of the group rather than that of the individual.

To address some of these problems, we have recently developed a theory of group socialization that views both the individual and the group as active social influence agents and assumes that their relationship changes in systematic ways over time (Levine & Moreland, 1985; Moreland & Levine, 1982, 1984). The theory is based on three psychological processes, each of which can be viewed from the perspectives of both the group and the individual. *Evaluation* reflects efforts by groups and individuals to assess and alter one another's rewardingness. The rewardingness of the relationship for both parties is based on the degree to which each fulfills the other's normative expectations. Although evaluations usually focus on the present relationship between the group and the individual, they may also be extended to the past and the future. In addition, groups and individuals may evaluate the past, present, and future rewardingness of their available alternative relationships. *Commitment* depends on the outcome of the evaluation process. As the perceived rewardingness of their past, present, and future relationships increases, the group and the individual become more committed to one another. In contrast, as the perceived rewardingness of their past, present, and future alternative relationships increases, the group and the individual become less committed to one another. Finally, a *role transition* occurs when commitment rises or falls to a previously established decision criterion, which reflects some specific level of commitment. If the group's and the individual's commitment to one another rise or fall to their decision criteria, then the individual will undergo a role transition and his or her relationship with the group will change.

Within our theory, group membership can be described as a series of phases separated by role transitions. Within each of these phases, evaluations produce changes in commitment, which in turn lead to a role transition when a decision criterion is reached. Once a role transition has occurred, a new phase is entered and evaluations begin again, often on different dimensions than before. The theory thus involves a temporal process that is basically recursive in nature. Figure 8.1 illustrates how the socialization process might unfold. The dotted line in the figure represents the personal "history" of a hypothetical person who has passed through all five phases of group membership. Of course, socialization does not proceed in exactly the same way for every group member. The dotted line in Figure 8.1 is thus only one of many possible lines that could be drawn. A more complete discussion of alternative passages through a group can be found in Levine and Moreland (1985) and Moreland and Levine (1982, 1984).

As the figure indicates, group membership begins with an *investigation* phase, when the individual is a *prospective member* of the group. During investigation, the group looks for people who seem likely to contribute to the attainment of group goals (*recruitment*), and the individual looks for groups that seem likely to contribute to the satisfaction of personal needs (*reconnaissance*). If the group's and the individual's commitment levels rise to their respective entry criteria (*EC*), then the role transition of entry occurs.

After entry, the individual becomes a *new member* of the group, and the *socialization* phase begins. During this phase, the group attempts to change the individual so as to maximize his or her contributions to the attainment of group goals; to the extent that the group succeeds, the individual undergoes *assimilation*. Similarly, the individual attempts to

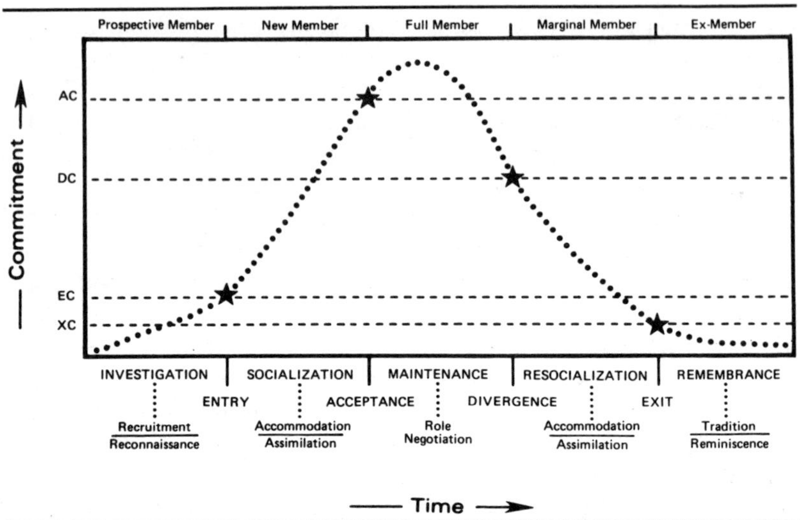

Figure 8.1 A Theoretical Model of Group Socialization (Moreland and Levine, 1982)

change the group so as to maximize its contributions to the satisfaction of personal needs; to the extent that the individual succeeds, the group undergoes *accommodation.* The socialization phase ends when the group's and the individual's commitment levels rise to their respective acceptance criteria (*AC*) and the individual undergoes the role transition of *acceptance.*

During the *maintenance* phase, the individual is a *full member* of the group, and both parties engage in *role negotiation.* The group attempts to define a specialized role for the individual that maximizes his or her contributions to the attainment of group goals, and the individual attempts to define a special role that maximizes the satisfaction of personal needs. If role negotiation fails, then the group and the individual regard their relationship as less rewarding and feel reduced commitment to one another. If their commitment levels fall to their respective divergence criteria (*DC*), then the role transition of *divergence* occurs.

After divergence, the individual becomes a *marginal member* of the group, and the *resocialization* phase begins. During this phase, both the group and the individual try to restore the previous rewardingness of their relationship together. To the extent that both parties are successful, *assimilation* and *accommodation* again occur. If the group's and the individual's commitment levels rise again to their respective divergence criteria, then a special role transition (*convergence*) occurs, and the individual returns to full membership. If, however, the group's and the individual's commitment levels fall to their respective exit criteria (*XC*), then the individual undergoes the role transition of *exit,* as depicted in Figure 8.1.

Group membership ends with a *remembrance* phase, when the individual is an *ex-member* of the group. During this phase, the group develops a consensus about the individual's previous contributions to the attainment of group goals. That consensus becomes part of the group's *tradition.* Similarly, the individual engages in *reminiscence* about how much the group satisfied his or her personal needs. Groups and individuals may also engage in ongoing evaluations of one another during remembrance, insofar as they continue to provide mutual rewards and costs. Feelings of commitment between the group and the individual eventually stabilize at some level.

Our theory has several major advantages. First, it explicitly considers all major group socialization activities and allows for reciprocal influence between the group and its members throughout their relationship. Second, through the basic psychological processes of evaluation, commitment, and role transition, the theory provides an explanatory as well as a descriptive account of group socialization. Third, although the theory was developed to deal with small, autonomous, voluntary groups, many aspects of it are relevant to other kinds of groups as well. Finally, the theory draws attention to some issues, such as role transitions (Moreland & Levine, 1984), that have been neglected by researchers who study small groups, and offers a fresh approach to other issues, such as minority influence (Levine & Moreland, 1985), that have already been studied extensively by those same researchers. Our theory also has at least one major disadvantage. Because it was developed only recently and has such a broad scope, neither the theory as a whole nor many of its propositions have yet been tested empirically.

Group Development and Group Socialization

Although group development and group socialization both involve temporal processes, they have been studied quite independently of one another. Researchers in one area have rarely mentioned the work of those in the other area, and few efforts have been made to integrate research in the two areas (but see Wanous, Reichers, & Malik, 1984). By overlooking the possible relationships between group development and group socialization, researchers have almost certainly limited their understanding of both phenomena. It is thus worthwhile to consider how group development and group socialization might affect one another, even though such an endeavor must be rather speculative.

Some Effects of Group Development on Group Socialization

Researchers who study group socialization have ignored many aspects of group development. Most important, they have failed to recognize that the group can pass through several distinct stages of development (forming, storming, norming, performing, adjourning) and that the process of group socialization can vary as a function of those stages. Most theories of group socialization implicitly assume that the group is in the performing stage of development. This assumption probably stems from an interest in how groups evaluate and control their members. In order for a group to perform these activities, it must have clear norms and a desire to enforce these norms. Before it reaches the performing stage, the group has not yet evolved a clear set of norms, and after it leaves the performing stage, the group may not be strongly motivated to enforce its norms. Thus it is only during its performing stage that the group is fully prepared to evaluate and control its members.

Failure to consider group development poses problems for those who seek to understand group socialization. These problems arise because (a) some kinds of group socialization activities rarely (if ever) occur in certain stages of group development and (b) group socialization activities that do occur in more than one stage of group development may operate differently in those stages.

Some group socialization activities occur infrequently, if at all, in certain stages of group development. All group members seem to be in a single phase of group socialization during the forming, storming, and adjourning stages of group development. During forming, when members are deciding whether they wish to join the group, investigation activities predominate. Because group norms have not yet evolved, socialization, maintenance, and resocialization activities cannot occur. Moreover, if someone leaves the group during this stage, neither that person nor the rest of the group is likely to engage in many remembrance activities. During storming, when members are attempting to force their own views on the group, socialization activities predominate. In the absence of group norms, maintenance and resocialization activities are once again impossible. Because group members have completed reconnaissance before storming and rarely engage in recruitment during that stage, investigation activities are also unlikely to occur. Remembrance activities are also uncommon during the storming stage, even if members leave the group. Socialization activities are again dominant in the early portion of the norming stage, before the majority has been able to impose its will on the minority. During adjourning, when members are often preparing for the demise of the group, remembrance activities predominate. Investigation, socialization, maintenance, and resocialization activities do not occur during this stage because members have little motivation to strengthen a group that seems destined to "die." Thus it is only at the end of the norming stage and during the performing stage of group development that the full range of group socialization activities can be observed.

Group socialization activities that occur in more than one stage of group development may also operate quite differently in each stage. Consider, for example, how the group's level of development can affect its socialization of new members and resocialization of marginal members. These two kinds of activities can change considerably as the group develops. Such changes are particularly striking when the group moves from its performing to adjourning stage of development.

To understand how socialization and resocialization activities are carried out during adjourning, it is necessary to distinguish between two different types of adjourning that groups may experience. Group development researchers have generally studied groups (e.g., therapy, training, self-analytic) that have formal termination dates. Members of such groups believe that, no matter what they do, their group will die at some specified time in the near future. It is not surprising, then, that they disengage from both task and social/emotional activities as a way of coping with this anticipated event. Although adjourning of this type certainly occurs, group development researchers have ignored a more common type of adjourning, which occurs when members are *not* reconciled to the inevitability of their group's demise. Members of most groups believe that their group has the potential to survive indefinitely, albeit with some turnover in membership. In these kinds of groups, "optimistic adjourning" occurs when members fear that the group may die in the near future, but believe that they have the power to prevent (or at least forestall) this event. When the group is in its optimistic adjourning stage, members engage in vigorous activities designed to strengthen the group and prevent (or at least delay) its death. Should these activities fail, of course, then the group will probably move on to a "pessimistic adjourning" stage, much like that described by most group development researchers.[3]

When the group is in the pessimistic adjourning stage of its development, socialization and resocialization activities simply do not occur. The knowledge that the group will die has profoundly disturbing effects on its members. These effects include a refusal to admit that the group will end; an inability to perform conventional tasks, coupled with regression to earlier stages of group development; a communicated desire to continue the group; reminiscence about past events in the group; evaluations of the group's worth; and "flight," defined as a rejection of the group and a search for new experiences outside of it (see Garland, Kolodny, & Jones, 1965; Lewis, 1978). Group members may also exhibit depression, anxiety, reduced commitment to the group, hostility, absenteeism, and exit during pessimistic adjourning (see Eklof, 1984; Greenhalgh, 1983; Krantz, 1985). In other words, they behave much like ex-members who are in the remembrance phase of group socialization. Neither socialization nor resocialization activities take place under these conditions, because there is little incentive to influence other group members or to be influenced by them. During pessimistic adjourning, all members are more concerned with improving their lives outside the group than in it. The resulting absence of any socialization and resocialization activities during pessimistic adjourning contrasts sharply with the prevalence of these activities during the performing stage of group development.

When the group is in the optimistic adjourning stage of its development, socialization and resocialization activities nearly always occur. In some ways, these activities are similar to those that take place during the performing stage of group development. During both optimistic adjourning and performing, the group seeks to produce assimilation in new members while those members seek to produce accommodation in the group. If the commitment levels of both the group and its new members rise to their respective acceptance criteria, then the new members become full members of the group. During both optimistic adjourning and performing, the group also seeks to produce assimilation in marginal members while these members seek to produce accommodation in the group. If the commitment levels of both the group and its marginal members rise to their respective divergence criteria, then the marginal members return to full membership. But if the commitment levels of both parties fall to their respective exit criteria, then the marginal members become ex-members of the group.

There are other ways, however, in which socialization and resocialization activities differ in the optimistic adjourning and performing stages of group development. When dealing with new members, the group must decide how much assimilation it will demand and how much accommodation it will allow. Because a "sick" group feels more threatened than a "healthy" one, the potential contributions of new members are regarded as more valuable and the group is more willing to compromise during optimistic adjourning than during performing. As a result, during its optimistic adjourning stage, the group may (a) put less pressure on new members to assimilate; (b) lower its acceptance criterion; and (c) show more willingness to accommodate. By behaving in this way, the group can reduce the length of newcomers' assimilation prior to acceptance. The group may also reduce the breadth and depth of newcomer's assimilation during optimistic adjourning by decreasing the number of dimensions on which they are required to change and by demanding change primarily on behavioral (rather than affective and cognitive) dimensions.

When dealing with the group, new members must decide how much accommodation they will demand and how much assimilation they will allow. Because new members are less eager to join a sick group than a healthy one, they will be less cooperative and more assertive during optimistic adjourning than during performing. As a result, during the optimistic adjourning stage, new members may (a) put more pressure on the group to accommodate; (b) raise their acceptance criteria; and (c) show less willingness to assimilate. By behaving in this way, new members can increase the length of the group's accommodation prior to acceptance. They may also increase the breadth and depth of the group's accommodation during optimistic adjourning by increasing the number of dimensions on which it is required to change and by demanding change on affective and cognitive (as well as behavioral) dimensions.

When dealing with marginal members, the group must again decide how much assimilation it will demand and how much accommodation it will allow. Because marginal members are more likely to be blamed for a group's problems when it is sick rather than healthy, the group will be more eager to get rid of such members during optimistic adjourning than during performing. As a result, during its optimistic adjourning stage, the group may (a) put more pressure on marginal members to assimilate; (b) raise its divergence and/or exit criteria; and (c) show less willingness to accommodate. By behaving in this way, the group can reduce the length of marginal members' assimilation prior to exit. The group may also increase the breadth and depth of marginal members' assimilation during optimistic adjourning by increasing the number of dimensions on which they are required to change and by demanding change on affective and cognitive (as well as behavioral) dimensions.

When dealing with the group, marginal members must again decide how much accommodation they will demand and how much assimilation they will allow. Because marginal members of a sick group are more likely to feel guilty about contributing to the group's problems than marginal members of a healthy group, they will ask for less and offer more during optimistic adjourning than during performing. As a result, during the optimistic adjourning stage, marginal members may (a) put less pressure on the group to accommodate; (b) lower their divergence and/or exit criteria; and (c) show more willingness to assimilate. By behaving in this way, marginal members can reduce the length of the group's accommodation prior to convergence. They may also decrease the breadth and depth of the group's accommodation during optimistic adjourning by decreasing the number of dimensions on which it is required to change and by demanding change primarily on behavioral (rather than affective and cognitive) dimensions.

Finally, there are at least two aspects of socialization and resocialization that are unique to the optimistic adjourning stage of group development. First, the presumed life expectancy of the group during optimistic adjourning may influence full members' motivation to retain and promote new members versus marginal members. If full members believe that the group will probably survive for some time, then they may behave more favorably toward new members because their potential contributions to the group are greater than those of marginal members. If full members believe that the group will probably die soon unless some drastic action is taken, however, then they may behave more favorably toward marginal members because their prior contributions were valuable to the group and they may still possess useful skills. These preferences for socializing/resocializing new and marginal members also can be affected, of course, by the perceived abilities and motivations of the particular new and marginal members under consideration. Second, the desire of new and marginal members to demand accommodation from full members during optimistic adjourning may be influenced by the full members' past behavior. For example, new and marginal members may be particularly interested in producing accommodation if they hold full members personally responsible for the group's current predicament (see Greenhalgh, 1983). The perception that full members are responsible for the group's problems may be more prevalent among new members, who have not yet had the opportunity to hurt the group, than among marginal members, who may have contributed to the group's weakness themselves. Finally, the motivation to demand accommodation from full members may be especially high among new members who feel that they were deceived about the group during their recruitment (see Greenhalgh, 1983).

Some Effects of Group Socialization on Group Development

Researchers who study group development have ignored many aspects of group socialization. Most important, they have failed to recognize that individuals pass through several distinct phases of group membership (investigation, socialization, maintenance, resocialization, remembrance) and that members of the same group can be in different membership phases. This failure to consider group socialization poses problems for those who seek to understand group development. These problems are more serious in regard to some stages of group development than in regard to others.

In the forming, storming, and adjourning stages of group development, the assumption that all members are in the same phase of group socialization seems plausible. During forming, each member cautiously tries to ascertain whether the group will meet his or her needs. The behavior of group members toward one another is tentative, and their commitment to the group is rather low. Thus they behave much like prospective members who are in the investigation phase of group socialization. During storming, each member attempts to persuade the others to adopt group goals that will fulfill his or her needs. The behavior of group members toward one another is assertive, and their commitment to the group is higher than it was before. They now behave much like new members who are in the socialization phase of group socialization. Finally, during (pessimistic) adjourning, each member disengages from group activities and remembers his or her past experiences in the group. Group members interact less closely with one another, and their commitment to the group falls to a relatively low level. They thus behave much like ex-members who are in the remembrance phase of group socialization.

But when the group is in the norming and performing stages of development, the assumption that all of its members are in the same phase of group socialization becomes much less plausible. During norming, group members resolve the conflicts that arose during their storming stage. The outcome of norming is typically the creation of a majority, which "won" most of those conflicts and thus had a strong influence on the group's goals, and a minority, which "lost" most of those conflicts and thus had little influence on those goals. At the end of norming and the beginning of performing, members of the majority are perceived as full members of the group and are in the maintenance phase of group socialization. In contrast, members of the minority are perceived as marginal members of the group and are in the resocialization phase of group socialization. During performing, full members cooperate with one another to attain their mutual goals, recruit prospective members, socialize new members, and resocialize marginal members. If their resocialization efforts fail, then those marginal members leave the group and enter the remembrance phase of group socialization.

There are many ways in which a group's socialization activities can affect its development. Consider, for example, some of the important changes in membership that occur in small groups. As time passes, new members enter the group and their socialization begins. The resocialization of marginal members ends (unsuccessfully) and they exit from the group. These changes are rarely discussed in the literature on group development, perhaps because they occur infrequently in therapy, training, and self-analytic groups. When changes in the membership of such groups are discussed, they generally are regarded as damaging to group development. Yalom (1970), for instance, argues that stability in membership is essential for the proper development of a therapy group. According to him, the socialization of new members and the resocialization of marginal members inevitably require time and energy that would otherwise be devoted to attaining the group's therapeutic goals. Goodman (1981) describes both the "intrusions" of new members into a therapy group and the "separations" of marginal members from such a group as "dangerous" because they produce threatening feelings with which group members cannot easily cope (see also Kaplan & Roman,

1961). Finally, Saravay (1978, 1985) suggests that the assimilation of new members into a therapy group is often difficult because group members have already developed complex ways of relating to their leader and to one another. As a result, they must either reject the new members or try to accommodate to them by regressing to an earlier and simpler stage of group development.

Whether all of these concerns are justified is unclear. The actual effects of membership changes on the development of groups have seldom been studied, and the few studies that have been done are inconclusive. Borgatta and Bales (1953), for example, studied the development of laboratory groups containing military men who met four times over a two-day period to perform role-playing tasks. Subjects were rotated across groups so that no two men worked together more than once. Analyses of the social-emotional and task activities within each group revealed few clear developmental trends. None of the groups progressed beyond its initial stage of development; at each group meeting, the men treated one another like strangers, as indeed they were. Hill and Gruner (1973) studied the development of long-term therapy groups containing delinquent boys who met regularly with a counselor to discuss their adjustment problems. As time passed, some of the boys improved so much that they were allowed to leave their groups; newcomers (with no prior experience in such groups) then took their places. Analyses of the interaction styles exhibited by the boys at each meeting revealed developmental trends that the researchers described as "continuation effects." When old-timers left a group and newcomers took their places, there was no apparent regression of the group to an earlier stage of development. Instead, the group continued in the same developmental stage that it had reached before the change in membership took place. Finally, Bailis, Lambert, and Bernstein (1978) studied the development of long-term self-help groups that met regularly to allow the family members of hospitalized psychiatric patients to talk about their problems. As some patients were admitted to the hospital and others were discharged, newcomers entered these groups and old-timers left them. An analysis of the conversations among group members at each meeting suggested that all of the groups developed, despite their constantly changing memberships. Old-timers often spoke directly to newcomers about the norms and values of their groups; as a result, those newcomers were assimilated so quickly and easily that the development of their groups was not impaired.

The results of these studies suggest that changes in a group's membership do not always harm its development. Instead, those changes appear to affect the group's development in a variety of ways, some positive and some negative. A more careful conceptual analysis of what those effects are and why they occur would be helpful. Such an analysis might begin with our theory of group socialization. According to that theory, similar activities occur during both the socialization and the resocialization phases of group membership. During both phases, the group attempts to produce assimilation in the individual so that he or she will contribute more to the attainment of group goals. New members are trained and marginal members retrained about how to think, feel, and act like full members of the group. At the same time, the individual attempts to produce accommodation in the group, so that it will contribute more to the satisfaction of personal needs. New members inform and marginal members remind the group about what they regard as necessary changes in its structure, dynamics, and performance.

The impact of membership changes on group development probably depends on how assimilation and accommodation activities are carried out. The role of assimilation activities in group development seems relatively simple. Efforts to assimilate new or marginal members nearly always have a negative impact on the development of the group. Such efforts often require the use of valuable group resources, such as time, energy, and money, and create conflicts within the group regarding such issues as what form assimilation should take and who will be responsible for producing it. The loss of these resources and resolution of these conflicts usually harm the group's development. Therefore, the more successful the group becomes at assimilating its new and marginal members, the less its development will suffer. The role of accommodation activities in group development seems more complex. The more successful new or marginal members are at producing accommodation in the group, the more its development will be affected. The nature of those effects will vary with the kinds of accommodations that are made, however. In principle, both new and marginal members can change the group in ways that have positive or negative effects on its development. The positive effects of accommodation on group development might include decreasing the length of time that the group spends in its forming, storming, and norming stages; easing the group's transitions from its forming to storming, storming to norming, and norming to performing stages; increasing the group's chances of reaching its performing stage; and helping the group to cope with its (optimistic or pessimistic) adjourning stage. The negative effects of accommodation on group development might take just the opposite forms.

All of this suggests that the effects of membership changes on group development cannot be completely understood until three basic questions are answered. First, what factors influence the ability of the group to produce assimilation in its new and marginal members? Second, what factors influence the ability of those members to produce accommodation in the group? Third, what are some of the positive and negative effects that such accommodation can have on the group? Once these questions are answered, it should be possible to predict how the development of a particular group will be affected by changes in its membership.

Some answers to these questions have already been generated by research on the socialization phase of group membership. Several factors have been found to affect the ability of a group to produce assimilation in new members. In general, such assimilation is more likely to occur when (a) newcomers have been carefully recruited to ensure that they are already as similar as possible to full group members (Etzioni, 1961; Wanous, 1980); (b) there are relatively few newcomers and they have little or no prior experience with similar groups (Becker, 1964; Van Maanen, 1978; Wheeler, 1966); (c) the group has been "open" rather than "closed" (Ziller, 1965) and thus knows about newcomers and their problems; and (d) newcomers have stronger feelings of commitment toward the group than it has toward them (Levine & Moreland, 1985). These same factors may also affect the ability of new members to produce accommodation in the group, although much less research on this topic has been performed. Accommodation should thus be more likely to occur when a relatively large number of newcomers, who differ greatly from full members and are less committed to the group than it is to them, enter a group that previously was closed. Of course, accommodation does not always require the active efforts of new members; the mere presence of newcomers in the group can sometimes change it in a variety of ways (see Levine & Moreland, 1985). Finally, a few studies have documented how accommodation to new members can affect a group. Newcomers often provide old-timers with a fresh perspective on their group (see Schuetz, 1944; Ziller, 1965). If that perspective makes the group appear more positive, then morale may well increase. Morale may decrease, however, if the group appears more negative from the newcomers' perspective. Whether they mean to or not, newcomers often change the relationships among old-timers as well. Under some conditions, those relationships can be strengthened (see Merei, 1949), but they also can be weakened under other conditions (see Fine, 1976; Snyder, 1958; Ziller & Behringer, 1960). It is not difficult to imagine how these and other such effects might aid or harm the group's development.

Research on the resocialization phase of group membership has also generated some answers to the questions posed earlier. Several factors have been found to affect the ability of a group to produce assimilation in marginal members. In general, such assimilation is more likely to occur when (a) there are relatively few marginal members and they deviate in different ways (see Allen, 1975); (b) the group has had previous experience with marginal members and thus knows how to rehabilitate them (see Levine, 1980); and (c) the marginal members are more committed to the group than it is to them (see Levine & Moreland, 1985). These same factors may also affect the ability of marginal members to produce accommodation in the group. Accommodation should thus be more likely to occur when a relatively large number of marginal members, who are less committed to the group than it is to them, challenge a group that has had little or no prior experience with deviance. Some research also suggests that the behavioral "style" of marginal members can affect their ability to produce accommodation within the group (Moscovici, 1985): When marginal members unite with one another to present their viewpoint in a consistent manner, the group is more likely to accommodate to their position. Finally, some observers (e.g., Coser, 1956; Dentler & Erikson, 1959; Levine & Moreland, 1985) have speculated about the effects that accommodation to marginal members might have on a group. On the positive side, accommodation can clarify the group's norms and perhaps lead to constructive normative change. On the negative side, accommodation can encourage other members of the group to violate its norms and perhaps cause the group to lose the respect of outsiders. Once again, it is not difficult to imagine how these and other such changes might aid or harm the group's development.

Conclusion

Researchers have not yet given sufficient attention to the relationship between group development, which concerns temporal changes in the group as a whole, and group socialization, which concerns temporal changes in the relationship between the group and each of its members. In this chapter, we have briefly summarized previous theoretical and empirical work on group development and group socialization. We have also suggested several ways in which group development might affect group socialization and group socialization might affect group development. Although many of our suggestions are speculative, they indicate some interesting directions for future research on temporal changes in small groups. Because an understanding of these changes is so important, we hope that our suggestions will convince researchers that this topic ought to be explored more fully.

NOTES

1. Tuckman (1965) referred to social/emotional activities as "group structure," but we prefer the former terminology. We have also changed a few of Tuckman's other terms in the interests of brevity and clarity. For example, we refer to Tuckman's "open exchange of relevant information" as *exchange* and to his "functional role-relatedness" as *role-taking*.

2. Two additional voting patterns, involving movement from neutrality to either agreement or disagreement, will not be discussed here.

3. The movement of groups from performing to optimistic adjourning is intriguing, but has received little research attention. Several important questions thus remain to be answered. Why, for example, are groups so slow to acknowledge potentially fatal problems and deal with them effectively (see Mintzberg, Raisinghani, & Theoret, 1976)?

REFERENCES

Allen, V. L. (1965). Situational factors in conformity. In L. Berkowitz (Ed.), *Advances in experimental social psychology* (Vol. 2, pp. 133-175). New York: Academic Press.

Allen, V. L. (1975). Social support for nonconformity. In L. Berkowitz (Ed.), *Advances in experimental social psychology* (Vol. 8, pp.1-43). New York: Academic Press.

Altman, I., Vinsel, A., & Brown, B. B. (1981). Dialectic conceptions in social psychology: An application to social penetration and privacy regulation. In L. Berkowitz (Ed.), *Advances in experimental social psychology* (Vol. 14, pp. 107-160). New York: Academic Press.

Aronson, E., & Mills, J. (1959). The effect of severity of initiation on liking for a group. *Journal of Abnormal and Social Psychology, 59*, 177-181.

Bailis, S. S., Lambert, S. R., & Bernstein, S. B. (1978). The legacy of the group: A study of group therapy with a transient membership. *Social Work in Health Care, 3*, 405-418.

Baker, P. M. (1983). The development of mutuality in natural small groups. *Small Group Behavior, 14*, 301-311.

Bales, R. F. (1950). *Interaction process analysis: A method for the study of small groups.* Cambridge, MA: Addison-Wesley.

Bales, R. F. (1953). The equilibrium problem in small groups. In T. Parsons, R. F. Bales, & E. A. Shils (Eds.), *Working papers in the theory of action* (pp. 111-161). New York: Free Press.

Bales, R. F., & Strodtbeck, F. L. (1951). Phases in group problem-solving. *Journal of Abnormal and Social Psychology, 46*, 485-495.

Bartell, G. (1971). *Group sex*. New York: Wyden.

Battegay, R. (1977). Group models, group dynamics, sociological and psychological aspects of group formation and evaluation. *Acta Psychiatrica Scandinavica, 55*, 330-344.

Becker, H. S. (1960). Notes on the concept of commitment. *American Journal of Sociology, 6*, 32-40.

Becker, H. S. (1964). Personal changes in adult life. *Sociometry, 27*, 40-53.

Bell, M. A. (1982). Phases in group problem-solving. *Small Group Behavior, 13*, 475-495.

Bennis, W. G., & Shepard, H. A. (1956). A theory of group development. *Human Relations, 9*, 415-437.

Berger, D. M. (1976). The multidiscipline patient care conference. *Canadian Psychiatric Association Journal, 21*, 135-139.

Berkowitz, B. (1974). Stages of group development in a mental health team. *Psychiatric Quarterly, 48*, 309-319.

Bion, W. R. (1948a). Experiences in groups (Part I). *Human Relations, 1*, 314-320.

Bion, W. R. (1948b). Experiences in groups (Part II). *Human Relations, 1*, 487-496.

Bion, W. R. (1961). *Experiences in groups and other papers*. New York: Basic Books.

Bonney, W. C. (1974). The maturation of groups. *Small Group Behavior, 5*, 445-461.

Borgatta, E. F., & Bales, R. F. (1953). Task and accumulation of experience as factors in the interacting of small groups. *Sociometry, 26*, 239-252.

Bouma, G. D. (1980). Keeping the faithful: Patterns of membership retention in the Christian Reformed Church. *Sociological Analysis, 41*, 259-264.

Braaten, L. J. (1974). Developmental phases of encounter groups and related intensive groups. *Interpersonal Development, 5*, 112-129.

Burghardt, S. (1977). A community organization typology of group development. *Journal of Sociology and Social Welfare, 4*, 1086-1108.

Caple, R. B. (1978). The sequential stages of group development. *Small Group Behavior, 9*, 470-476.

Chadbourne, J. (1980). Training groups: A basic life cycle model. *Personnel and Guidance Journal, 59*, 55-58.

Cissna, K. N. (1984). Phases in group development: The negative evidence. *Small Group Behavior, 15*, 3-32.

Cohen, A. M., & Smith, R. D. (1976). *The critical incident in growth groups: A manual for group leaders*. La Jolla, CA: University Associates.

Coser, L. A. (1956). *The functions of social conflict*. New York: Free Press.

Davies, D, & Kuypers, B. C. (1985). Group development and interpersonal feedback. *Group and Organization Studies, 10*, 184-208.

Dentler, R. A., & Erikson, K. T. (1959). The functions of deviance in groups. *Social Problems, 7*, 98-107.

Duck, S. W., & Gilmour, R. (Eds.). (1981). *Personal relationships: Developing relationships*. New York: Academic Press.

Dunphy, D. C. (1968). Phases, roles, and myths in self-analytic groups. *Applied Behavioral Science, 4*, 195-224.

Eklof, M. (1984). The termination phase in group therapy: Implications for geriatric groups. *Small Group Behavior, 15,* 565-571.

Etzioni, A. A. (1961). *A comparative analysis of complex organizations.* New York: Free Press.

Farrell, D., & Rusbult, C. E. (1981). Exchange variables as predictors of job satisfaction, job commitment, and turnover: The impact of rewards, costs, alternatives, and investments. *Organizational Behavior and Human Performance, 27,* 78-95.

Feldbaum, C. L., Christenson, T. E., & O'Neal, E. C. (1980). An observational study of the assimilation of the newcomer to the preschool. *Child Development, 51,* 497-507.

Feldman, D. C. (1976). A contingency theory of socialization. *Administrative Science Quarterly, 21,* 433-452.

Feldman, D. C. (1977). The role of initiation activities in socialization. *Human Relations, 30,* 977-940.

Feldman, D. C. (1981). The multiple socialization of organization members. *Academy of Management Review, 6,* 309-318.

Feshbach, N. D., & Sones, G. (1971). Sex differences in adolescent reactions toward newcomers. *Developmental Psychology, 4,* 381-386.

Fine, G. A. (1976, August). *The effect of a salient newcomer on a small group: A force-field analysis.* Paper presented at the meeting of the American Psychological Association, Washington, DC.

Forsyth, D. R. (1983). *An introduction to group dynamics.* Monterey, CA: Brooks/Cole.

Fromkin, H. L., Klimoski, R. J., & Flanagan, M. F. (1972). Race and competence as determinants of acceptance of newcomers in success and failure work groups. *Organizational Behavior and Human Performance, 7,* 25-42.

Garland, J., Kolodny, R., & Jones, H. (1965). A model for stages of development in social work groups. In S. Bernstein (Ed.), *Explorations in group work* (pp. 98-127). Boston: Milford House.

Gauron, E. F., & Rawlings, E. I. (1975). A procedure for orienting new members to group psychotherapy. *Small Group Behavior, 6,* 293-307.

Gazda, G. M. (1972). *Group counseling: A developmental approach.* Boston: Allyn & Bacon.

Gerard, H. B., & Mathewson, G. C. (1966). The effects of severity of initiation on liking for a group: A replication. *Journal of Experimental Social Psychology, 2,* 278-287.

Gersick, C.J.G. (1983). *Life cycles of ad hoc task groups* (Tech. Rep. No. 3). New Haven, CT: Yale University, Research Program on Group Effectiveness.

Goodman, M. (1981). Group phases and induced countertransference. *Psychotherapy: Theory, Research, and Practice, 18,* 478-486.

Gordon, M. E., Philpot, J. W., Burt, R. E., Thompson, C. A., & Spiller, W. E. (1980). Commitment to the union: Development of a measure and an examination of its correlates. *Journal of Applied Psychology Monographs, 65,* 479-499.

Greenhalgh, L. (1983). Organizational decline. In S. B. Backarach (Ed.), *Research in the sociology of organizations* (Vol. 2, pp. 231-276). Greenwich, CT: JAI Press.

Grunebaum, H., & Solomon, L. (1982). Toward a theory of peer relationships (Part II): On the stages of social development and their relationship to group psychotherapy. *International Journal of Group Psychotherapy, 32,* 283-307.

Hare, A. P. (1973). Theories of group development and categories for interaction analysis. *Small Group Behavior, 4,* 259-304.

Hazer, J. T., & Alvares, D. M. (1981). Police work values during organizational entry and assimilation. *Journal of Applied Psychology, 66,* 12-18.

Heinicke, C., & Bales, R. F. (1953). Developmental trends in the structure of small groups. *Sociometry, 16*, 7-38.
Hill, W. F., & Gruner, L. (1973). A study of development in open and closed groups. *Small Group Behavior, 4,* 355-381.
Insko, C. A., Gilmore, R., Moehle, D., Lipsitz, A., Drenan, S., & Thibaut, J. W. (1982). Seniority in the generational transition of laboratory groups: The effects of social familiarity and task experience. *Journal of Experimental Social Psychology, 18,* 557-580.
Jacobs, R. C., & Campbell, D. T. (1961). The perpetuation of an arbitrary tradition through several generations of a laboratory microculture. *Journal of Abnormal Social Psychology, 62,* 649-658.
Kanter, R. M. (1968). Commitment and social organization: A study of commitment mechanisms in utopian communities. *American Sociological Review, 33,* 499-517.
Kaplan, S. R., & Roman, M. (1961). Characteristic responses in adult therapy groups to the introduction of new members: A reflection on group process. *International Journal of Group Psychotherapy, 11,* 372-381.
Krantz, J. (1985). Group process under conditions of organizational decline. *Journal of Applied Behavioral Science, 21*, 1-17.
Lacoursiere, R. (1980). *The life cycle of groups: Group developmental stage theory.* New York: Human Sciences Press.
Levine, J. M. (1980). Reaction to opinion deviance in small groups. In P. Paulus (Ed.), *Psychology of group influence* (pp. 375-429). Hillsdale, NJ: Erlbaum.
Levine, J. M., & Moreland, R. L. (1985). Innovation and socialization in small groups. In S. Moscovici, G. Mugny, & E. Van Avermaet (Eds.), *Perspectives on minority influence* (pp. 143-169). Cambridge: Cambridge University Press.
Levine, J. M., & Russo, E. M. (1987). Majority and minority influence. In C. Hendrick (Ed.), *Review of personality and social psychology* (Vol. 8, pp. 13-54). Newbury Park, CA: Sage.
Levine, J. M., Saxe, L., & Harris, H. J. (1976). Reaction to attitudinal deviance: Impact of deviate's direction and distance of movement. *Sociometry, 39,* 97-107.
Levinger, G. (1980). Toward the analysis of close relationships. *Journal of Experimental Social Psychology, 16,* 510-544.
Lewis, B. F. (1978). An examination of the final phase of a group development theory. *Small Group Behavior, 9,* 507-517.
Lewis, C. M., & Beck, A. P. (1983). Experiencing level in the process of group development. *Group, 7,* 19-26.
Lofland, J. F., & Lejeune, R. A. (1960). Initial interaction of newcomers in Alcoholics Anonymous: A field experiment in class symbols and socialization. *Social Problems, 8,* 102-111.
Long, S. (1984). Early integration in groups: "A group to join and a group to create." *Human Relations, 37*, 311-332.
Louis, M. R. (1980). Surprise and sense-making: What newcomers experience in entering unfamiliar organizational settings. *Administrative Science Quarterly, 25,* 226-251.
Lundgren, D. C., & Knight, D. J. (1978). Sequential stages of development in sensitivity training groups. *Journal of Applied Behavioral Science, 14*, 204-222.
Mabry, E. A. (1975). Exploratory analysis of a developmental model for task-oriented small groups. *Human Communication Research, 2,* 66-74.
Mann, R. D. (1967). *Interpersonal styles and group development.* New York: John Wiley.
Martin, E. A., & Hill, W. F. (1957). Toward a theory of group development: Six phases of therapy group development. *International Journal of Group Psychotherapy, 7*, 20-30.

McGrath, J. E. (1978). Small group research. *American Behavioral Scientist, 21,* 651-674.

McGrath, J. E. (1984). *Groups: Interaction and performance.* Englewood Cliffs, NJ: Prentice-Hall.

McGrath, J. E., & Kravitz, D. A. (1982). Group research. In M. R. Rosenzweig & L. W. Porter (Eds.), *Annual review of psychology* (Vol. 33, pp. 195-230). Palo Alto, CA: Annual Reviews.

McMurrain, T. T., & Gazda, G. M. (1974). Extended group interaction: Interpersonal functioning as a developmental process variable. *Small Group Behavior, 5,* 393-404.

Merei, F. (1949). Group leadership and institutionalization. *Human Relations, 2,* 23-39.

Mills, T. M. (1964). *Group transformation: An analysis of a learning group.* Englewood Cliffs, NJ: Prentice-Hall.

Mills, T. M. (1978). Seven steps in developing group awareness. *Journal of Personality and Social Systems, 1,* 15-29.

Mintzberg, H., Raisinghani, D., & Theoret, A. (1976). The structure of "unstructured" decision processes. *Administrative Science Quarterly, 21,* 246-274.

Mobley, W. H., Griffeth, R. W., Hand, H. H., & Meglino, B. M. (1979). Review and conceptual analysis of the employee turnover process. *Psychological Bulletin, 86,* 493-522.

Moreland, R. L. (1985). Social categorization and the assimilation of "new" group members. *Journal of Personality and Social Psychology, 48,* 1173-1190.

Moreland, R. L., & Levine, J. M. (1982). Socialization in small groups: Temporal changes in individual-group relations. In L. Berkowitz (Ed.), *Advances in experimental social psychology* (Vol. 15, pp. 137-192). New York: Academic Press.

Moreland, R. L., & Levine, J. M. (1984). Role transitions in small groups. In V. Allen & E. Van de Vliert (Eds.), *Role transitions: Explorations and explanations* (pp. 181-195). New York: Plenum.

Moscovici, S. (1985) Social influence and conformity. In G. Lindzey & E. Aronson (Eds.), *The handbook of social psychology* (Vol. 2, pp. 347-412). New York: Random House.

Napier, R. W., & Gershenfeld, M. K. (1985). *Groups: Theory and experience.* Boston: Houghton Mifflin.

Newcomb, T. M. (1943). *Personality and social change.* New York: Dryden.

Obert, S. L. (1983). Developmental patterns of organizational task groups: A preliminary study. *Human Relations, 36,* 37-52.

Pedigo, J. M., & Singer, B. (1982). Group process development: A psychoanalytic view. *Small Group Behavior, 13,* 496-517.

Philp, H., & Dunphy, D. C. (1959). Developmental trends in small groups. *Sociometry, 22,* 162-174.

Pridham, K. F. (1975). Acts of turning as stress-resolving mechanisms in work groups. *Human Relations, 28,* 229-248.

Putallaz, M., & Gottman, J. M. (1981). An interactional model of children's entry into peer groups. *Child Development, 52,* 986-994.

Rice, C. A., & Rutan, J. S. (1984). Some developmental characteristics of adult psychotherapy groups. *Group, 8,* 21-25.

Ridgeway, C. L. (1983). *The dynamics of small groups.* New York: St. Marten's.

Roozen, D. A. (1980). Church dropouts: Changing patterns of disengagement and re-entry. *Review of Religious Research, 21,* 427-450.

Rusbult, C. E. (1980). Commitment and satisfaction in romantic associations: A test of the investment model. *Journal of Experimental Social Psychology, 16,* 172-186.

Salancik, G. R. (1977). Commitment and the control of organizational behavior and belief. In B. M. Staw & G. R. Salancik (Eds.), *New directions in organizational behavior* (pp. 1-54). Chicago: St. Clair.

Saravay, S. M. (1978). A psychoanalytic theory of group development. *International Journal of Group Psychotherapy, 28*, 481-507.

Saravay, S. M. (1985). Parallel development of the group and its relationship to the leader: A theoretical explanation. *International Journal of Group Psychotherapy, 35*, 197-207.

Schuetz, A. (1944). The stranger: An essay in social psychology. *American Journal of Sociology, 49*, 499-507.

Schutz, W. C. (1958). *FIRO: A three-dimensional theory of interpersonal behavior*. New York: Rinehart.

Scott, W. A. (1965). *Values and organizations: A study of fraternities and sororities*. Chicago: Rand McNally.

Shambaugh, P. W. (1978). The development of the small group. *Human Relations, 31*, 283-295.

Shaw, M. E. (1981). *Group dynamics: The psychology of small group behavior*. New York: McGraw-Hill.

Slater, P. E. (1966). *Microcosm: Structural, psychological and religious evolution in groups*. New York: John Wiley.

Snyder, E. C. (1958). The Supreme Court as a small group. *Social Forces, 36*, 232-238.

Staw, B. M. (1980). The consequences of turnover. *Journal of Occupational Behavior, 1*, 253-273.

Steers, R. M., & Mowday, R. T. (1981). Employee turnover and post-decision accommodation processes. In B. M. Staw & L. L. Cummings (Eds.), *Research in organizational behavior* (Vol. 3, pp. 235-281). Greenwich, CT: JAI Press.

Steiner, I. (1974). Whatever happened to the group in social psychology? *Journal of Experimental Social Psychology, 10*, 93-108.

Stock, D., & Thelen, H. A. (1958). *Emotional dynamics of group culture*. Washington, DC: National Education Association's National Training Laboratories.

Trice, H. M. (1957). A study of the process of affiliation with Alcoholics Anonymous. *Quarterly Journal of Studies on Alcohol, 18*, 35-54.

Tucker, D. M. (1973). Some relationships between individual and group development. *Human Development, 16*, 249-272.

Tuckman, B. W. (1965). Developmental sequence in small groups. *Psychological Bulletin, 63*, 384-399.

Tuckman, B. W., & Jensen, M.A.C. (1977). Stages of small-group development revisited. *Group and Organization Studies, 2*, 419-427.

Van Maanen, J. (1978). People-processing: Strategies of organizational socialization. *Organizational Dynamics, 7*, 18-36.

Van Maanen, J., & Schein, E. H. (1979). Toward a theory of organizational socialization. In B. Staw (Ed.), *Research in organizational behavior* (Vol. 1, pp. 209-264). Greenwich, CT: JAI.

Vaught, C., & Smith, D. L. (1980). Incorporation and mechanical solidarity in an underground coal mine. *Sociology of Work and Occupations, 7*, 159-187.

Wallace, W. L. (1964). Institutional and life-cycle socialization of college freshmen. *American Journal of Sociology, 70*, 303-318.

Wanous, J. P. (1980). *Organizational entry: Recruitment, selection, and socialization of newcomers.* Reading, MA: Addison-Wesley.

Wanous, J. P., Reichers, A. E., & Malik, S. D. (1984). Organizational socialization and group development: Toward an integrative perspective. *Academy of Management Review, 9*, 670-683.

Wheeler, S. (1966). The structure of formally organized socialization settings. In O. G. Brim & S. Wheeler (Eds.), *Socialization after childhood: Two essays* (pp. 53-116). New York: John Wiley.

Winter, S. K. (1976). Developmental stages in the roles and concerns of group co-leaders. *Small Group Behavior, 7*, 349-362.

Yalom, I. D. (1970). *The theory and practice of group psychotherapy.* New York: Basic Books.

Zander, A. (1976). The psychology of removing group members and recruiting new ones. *Human Relations, 29*, 969-987.

Zander, A. (1979). The study of group behavior during four decades. *Journal of Applied Behavioral Science, 15*, 272-282.

Ziller, R. C. (1965). Toward a theory of open and closed groups. *Psychological Bulletin, 64*, 164-182.

Ziller, R. C. (1977). Group dialectics: The dynamics of groups over time. *Human Development, 20*, 293-308.

Ziller, R. C., & Behringer, R. D. (1960). Assimilation of the knowledgeable newcomer under conditions of group success and failure. *Journal of Abnormal and Social Psychology, 60*, 288-291.

Ziller, R. C., & Behringer, R. D. (1961). A longitudinal study of the assimilation of the new child in the group. *Human Relations, 14*, 121-133.

Zurcher, L. A. (1965). The sailor aboard ship: A study of role behavior in a total institution. *Social Forces, 43*, 389-400.

9

Life Cycles of Behavior Settings

ALLAN W. WICKER
JEANNE C. KING

People's lives unfold while they are working and relaxing in behavior settings—in regularly occurring systems of happenings such as one finds in offices, markets, theaters, and restaurants. To date, researchers have typically assumed that behavior settings, which appear stable upon a single occasion, change very little from one day to the next. The present chapter counters this assumption by focusing on the creation, maintenance, growth, decline, and demise of behavior settings and on the personal and interpersonal processes that accompany these events. The work also is responsive to the lament that research on small groups is predominantly atheoretical, nonprogrammatic, laboratory based, limited to few variables per study, and oblivious to such significant topics as temporal dimensions, member interactions, and group tasks (see McGrath & Altman, 1966, chap. 7; Miller, 1971; Wicker, 1985).

Small, face-to-face working groups are integral components of behavior settings. Work groups (McGrath, 1984, calls such groups *standing crews*) carry out a setting *program*—a regularly patterned, but limited, sequence of activities, such as tasks required to operate a bookstore, an automobile repair shop, or a dentist's office. A behavior

---

AUTHORS' NOTE: We are grateful to Joseph E. McGrath, Urs Fuhrer, Volker Linneweber, and three anonymous reviewers for comments on an earlier version of this chapter. Our research is supported by a grant from the John Randolph Haynes and Dora Haynes Foundation of Los Angeles.

setting is more than a social entity, however. Its other features include a place/time locus, defined by a unique location and hours of operation, and physical objects used by the work group, such as equipment and supplies. (Behavior settings are further described in Barker, 1968, and in Wicker, 1979/1983.)

This chapter first summarizes portions of a recent extension of the behavior setting concept (Wicker, 1987). We then outline our current program of research on life cycles of behavior settings.

The Present Framework

Wicker's revised conception of behavior settings incorporates three analyses of temporal relationships that McGrath and Altman (1966) mentioned as important but neglected in small group research: the history of a group prior to being studied, changes in a group as it forms and reforms over numerous occasions, and finer-grained temporal patterns of group process that are enacted within a single session. The following discussion considers aspects of a behavior setting's "pre-history" (including the distribution of components that subsequently form the setting), as well as longitudinal periods of growth, stability, and decline, and the social dynamics that occur on a daily basis.

Four temporal stages of behavior settings are recognized in the framework: (a) preconvergence, the period prior to founding a setting; (b) convergence, the period during which a setting is being organized and begins to operate; (c) continued existence, the indefinite lifetime of a setting; and (d) divergence, the period during which the setting disintegrates. We summarize in Table 9.1 some topics and events that are important at each stage. Each of these aspects is further discussed below. Our discussion focuses on two broad facets of settings: resources (such as people, equipment, and space) and internal dynamics (including the interplay of person, group, and setting-level events). In the discussion of preconvergence, we also consider the environmental contexts from which settings emerge and within which they exist. (This third facet, setting *contexts*, is more generally discussed in the original presentation of the framework. See Wicker, 1987.)

Preconvergence

Prevailing conditions in the larger social/physical world determine whether a prospective new setting can be created and, if so, how readily.

TABLE 9.1
Important Topics and Events at the Different Temporal Stages of Behavior Settings

Preconvergence:
- –Conditions in the social/physical world
- –Assembly of necessary resources
- –Knowledge, plans, goals of founders and staff

Convergence:
- –Establishment of setting program
- –Adjustments in initial configurations of resources
- –Negotiations by staff
- –Interactive sense-making by staff: acting, interpreting, remembering
- –Evaluations of fit between personal goals and activities required by the setting

Continued Existence
- –Differentiation of functional activities
- –Routinization of maintenance functions
- –Negotiations and sense-making by staff during periods of growth and reorganization
- –The dialectical relationship between setting stability and flexibility

Divergence
- –Coping with deficiencies in resources and programs
- –Negotiations and sense-making by staff during periods of decline and crisis
- –Disengagement of staff from setting

These conditions include general environmental factors such as societal values, levels of literacy, stages of technological development, economic and monetary systems, and more specific conditions such as local labor markets, natural resources, and zoning ordinances (see Stinchcombe, 1965). The resources that behavior settings require include people (staff members and possibly clients), behavior objects (equipment, supplies, raw materials, merchandise), physical spaces (suitable rooms or other built facilities), information (knowledge and knowledge sources), and reserves (money, credit, stored goods).

In order for a behavior setting to come into being, its particular resource needs must be practically obtainable. These resources must be identified, located, assembled at one place and time, and configured into the set of routines that constitutes the setting program. The availability of needed resources must of course be known or knowable to the setting founders. In general, the likelihood that a conceived setting will be actualized is greater when its requisite resources are readily available and when prospective founders are knowledgeable and imaginative about how resource needs can be met. For example, a used bookstore specializing in literature is more likely to be founded in a college town than in a mining town in part because the college town has a large reading public that can serve both as a clientele and as a local source of merchandise. Persons who know how this source can be tapped may be more likely to found such a store than those who lack that knowledge.

Two personal factors that span the preconvergence and subsequent stages of behavior settings are the cognitions and motives of founders and staff members. Founders often have images or conceptions of what a new setting should be like; these conceptions may incorporate detailed plans for establishing the setting. If staff members participate at the preconvergence stage, they too may have well-defined ideas about the proper atmosphere or mission of the setting, how its program should be organized, how tasks are to be performed, and so on. On the other hand, it is possible, and probably more likely, that founders and others have only vague projections of a future setting.

Conceptions and plans for new behavior settings may be driven by a wide variety of motives. Participants may be motivated to gain independence, achieve a lifetime ambition, improve their professional careers, reach a higher social status, avoid unemployment, find outlets for personal interests and skills, use or gain knowledge, become wealthy, escape a bad work situation, be of service to others, and so on.

This brief sketch of the preconvergence stage has not recognized sufficiently the momentary and longer-term changes occurring in the social/physical world and in people's cognitions and motives. For example, goods may be available one day and not the next, and founders may alter their plans as they think through the implications of what they want to do. Beginning with the discussion of convergence, we give greater attention to the dynamic features of behavior settings.

Convergence

In the following paragraphs, we first present some system-level transactions that take place when a behavior setting is being created. Then we shift to a discussion of the momentary interpersonal transactions that characterize this and the remaining stages of behavior settings.

Setting-level events. As a setting is converging, founding members attend to many resource components within a short period of time. Information and reserves are likely to be important considerations at the very beginning of this stage as founders assess whether they have or can acquire necessary financing, knowledge, and other resources. When it appears that information and reserves are adequate to launch the setting, they may become more concerned with particular components that must be brought together and arranged for the setting to operate.

At this early stage, the setting's operation may be hampered by insufficient and inadequate resources. The staff may be too small or too inexperienced to perform the work that needs to be done, merchandise may not be available in the kinds or quantities desired, information on how best to coordinate the staff may be lacking, credit lines may be too limited. In the early life of a setting, the configuration of its components needs to be closely monitored so that adjustments in schedules, task assignments, equipment, and procedures may be made as needed.

Some actions necessary for initiating and sustaining a setting may be classified as primarily "functional" from a setting point of view: assembling resources, identifying tasks and grouping them into jobs, configuring behavior objects, recruiting clients, and performing the various operational and maintenance chores that constitute the setting program. Such activities do not just "happen." Rather they are worked out in a series of social exchanges among setting participants. We consider these social processes in the following paragraphs.

Social processes. In the present framework, behavior settings are viewed as social constructions—as cumulative products of the moment-to-moment and day-to-day interactions and interpretations of founders, the original staff members, and their successors (see Berger & Luckmann, 1967).

This analysis of how behavior settings are socially constructed is based in part on Weick's organizing model (Weick, 1979): Organization members respond to events and conditions on the basis of how they construe those inputs. Their responses are then interpreted and selectively retained in the form of *cause maps* or primitive theories about the events to which they reacted. These cause maps guide the members' subsequent actions. To illustrate, a prospective founder who has a well-developed conception of how her restaurant's furnishings should be configured may reject an incompatible suggestion and may conclude that the person who made the suggestion does not understand her conception. She then may attempt to communicate her conception to the other person or she may dismiss him as not helpful on the matter.

Many actions taken by setting participants are responses to behaviors by their coworkers. Over time, participants will adjust their individual interpretations, actions, and working knowledge to be more congruent with others in the setting. Some agreement will be reached about which features of the environment are appropriate to act upon and about which actions various people will take to deal with them. The number of cycles of acting, interpreting, and remembering that must occur before a setting program is operating smoothly will depend on personal factors such as the flexibility and knowledge of founders and staff, and on extrapersonal factors such as the complexity of the setting program and the number of staff members who carry it out.

Certain qualifications and elaborations on the social construction of behavior settings derive from Strauss's negotiated order theory (Strauss, 1978): Participants in settings have personal needs they wish to satisfy, and these needs will influence how they respond to and interpret events. In particular, staff members may actively seek to modify and shape the prescriptions and definitions of others in ways that are more in keeping with their individual interests and cognitions. Founders who have elaborate cognitions of the program may be less willing to negotiate how the setting is to be structured. Workers with strong preferences for or aversions to certain tasks will be concerned with how tasks are divided up and assigned. Their concerns often arise from perceived fit between task requirements and self- or professional image. Further, staff members with specialized or extensive knowledge of particular aspects of the program are more likely to be more influential than other members (McGrath, 1984, p. 261).

Even though participants generally accommodate one another so that the setting program is carried out, the resulting social structure will be a somewhat fragile, negotiated order conditioned by participants' needs and interests. Behavior setting events will be continually constructed and reconstructed as participants respond to new situations and to one another, and as their interests change. Smaller-scale adjustments, like minor procedural changes, will take place within the more slowly changing larger environment of the behavior setting (Gerson, 1976).

According to the present framework, then, functional activities that occur in behavior settings result from organizing and negotiating actions of participants. In the convergence stage, negotiations are more likely to revolve around division of labor, operating procedures, overall adequacy of the setting program, and similar issues. Typically a large number of negotiable issues and a wide range of potential resolutions characterize a converging setting.

The latitude for negotiation may be considerably reduced, however, when the ratio of constructed to preexisting realities in a setting is low. Constructed realities are meanings and procedures worked out by setting occupants (e.g., how a group task is to be divided and assigned to individuals). Preexisting realities are generally recognized by participants as "givens" (e.g., a legal requirement that a licensed person must perform a particular task). To illustrate, in a franchise operation or in a setting that is a subunit of a larger organization, relatively few alternatives may be negotiable because so much has already been specified in directives, mandates, policies, and procedure manuals. Here the ratio of constructed to preexisting realities would be low. By contrast, the ratio would be high in the case of an independent business founded by an inexperienced owner: Relatively many alternatives are negotiable if routines have not been established and if the staff and behavior objects have not been selected.

Continued Existence

Growth and differentiation. Once a setting has been converged, it may begin an indefinite lifetime or it may immediately begin to decline and then disappear. Settings that continue to exist typically undergo periods of growth and differentiation. The following sketch of these changes draws upon Lewin's model of human development (Barker, Dembo, & Lewin, 1941) and upon Katz and Kahn's analysis of organizational growth (Katz & Kahn, 1978).

Behavior settings may become more differentiated in a number of ways. The variety of functional activities and social negotiations in a setting may increase, and a broader array of satisfactions may become available to participants. Functional activities also may become more specialized and more hierarchically organized: Tasks may be grouped into subprograms that become the responsibility of particular staff members. Boundaries between the work domains of various staff members thus may become more distinct, and may be accompanied by an ordering of staff positions according to their importance for the setting's operation.

Differentiation of tasks and responsibilities may be accompanied by an elaboration of maintenance circuits so that different types of threats are handled by different staff members. Generally the range of threats a setting occupant must deal with corresponds to his or her hierarchical position. For example, a restaurant manager will be concerned with more kinds of threats than will a cook. Routines that meet the personal needs of participants may develop and thereby provide indirect support for functional activities through increased group cohesion and dependence. A waiter who aspires to own a restaurant may show keen interest in the jobs of the cook and the hostess. This interest may lead to closer friendships and to the waiter's occasionally volunteering to substitute for the others. "Side programs" that serve secondary functions also may appear; for example, the kitchen crew and waiters may engage in informal information exchanges in the restaurant's kitchen during slack periods.

Physical growth may accompany some of the changes mentioned. Settings may become physically larger by expanding into adjacent areas, and they may increase personnel, equipment, clients, and output. Another type of growth is temporal expansion: a setting may extend its hours of operation as the variety and volume of functional activities increase. Successful settings do not grow indefinitely, however; eventually they may become too large and unwieldy to operate satisfactorily. In response they are likely either to duplicate themselves or to subdivide into additional, more specialized units.

Social processes. The organizing and negotiating processes described earlier continue throughout the existence of behavior settings. At certain periods, however, these processes will be intensified. In general, any development that disturbs the normal procedures of the setting for more than a short time will have this effect. Differentiation and growth therefore will involve periods of increased organizing and negotiating. For example, when duties normally performed by one person become so burdensome that a second person is hired to assume part of the work load, the incumbent will probably wish to retain some preferred tasks and give away others. The new staff member is also likely to have preferences for particular tasks, and to have skills that do not exactly match those of the incumbent. Consequently, the organizing and negotiating processes that take place will be shaped by the personal interests and skills of the participants, as well as by what the staff regards as the preexisting realities in the setting program.

Precisely what the staff considers to be preexisting realities or "givens" may depend on the age of the setting, whether the staff members were part of the founding staff, and the length of time staff members have worked in the setting. There is the possibility that over time, procedures and interpretations that once were viewed as "one possible way" evolve to "our way" to "the way" to "the only possible way." In other words, social constructions may come to be viewed as objective realities with negotiation latitudes being constricted accordingly (see Berger & Luckmann, 1967, pp. 53-67).

Stability and flexibility. The negotiation latitude in a behavior setting may reflect another setting-level dynamic that is important during the continued existence stage: the balance between stability and flexibility. Both processes are needed for setting survival. When environmental changes are lasting, a setting must be flexible enough to adjust its functional activities appropriately. But a setting also must maintain its identity and continuity by processing normal inputs in a regular fashion (see Weick, 1979, chap. 8).

The primary task in a converging behavior setting is to establish routines that define and deal with present realities in particular ways, including routines for counteracting internal threats to the smooth operation of the setting program. The hard-won stability of a mature setting is not readily relinquished, even when changes would be adaptive. Yet in some settings staff members deliberately attempt to maintain flexibility and to monitor environmental trends. Their efforts may parallel the changing role of founders, whose influence on day-to-day operations diminishes as responsibilities are delegated and more formal procedures are established. Thereafter, founders (or perhaps other staff members) may pay more attention to procedures that maintain internal flexibility and that sense and plan responses to changes in external conditions. They may develop record-keeping and data-gathering schemes to keep track of events within and outside the setting. They may also begin accumulating reserves for such purposes as growth, hiring consultants, improving facilities, and upgrading staff (Smith, 1982).

Divergence

The downside of the life cycle of behavior settings is decline and eventual demise. Behavior settings decline whenever a setting program suffers from relatively long-term deficiencies or interference, or when changes necessary for survival are not incorporated into the program. A setting has diverged when its program ceases to be carried out within specifiable place and time boundaries, and when its configuration of components has been dissembled.

Setting-level events. Among conditions that guarantee the demise of a behavior setting are the loss and prolonged absence of essential resources. The most publicized deficit is insufficient financial resources, but settings can also begin to decline for reasons that are not obviously financial. For example, all job applicants may lack necessary technical knowledge, or raw materials may be unavailable due to depletion or embargo. Decline may also result from lack of timely information or damage from catastrophic events such as fire and flood.

Settings are impaired and may even fail when their operating and regulating processes falter or break down. Poorly designed work areas, defective equipment, and untrained or burned-out employees may be symptomatic of setting decline. If the maintenance actions that normally counteract such deficiencies become ineffective, the setting program may disintegrate. Founders and staff members typically will respond to decline by attempting to correct the perceived problem. If there is a resource deficiency, they will try to locate and supply what is needed, or failing that, they will devise ways to get by. Nevertheless, chronic deficiencies almost always force lasting changes in the internal operations of the setting. A setting also may suffer when it fails to sense or respond to important changes in its environment.

Social processes. The realization that a setting is declining and that adjustments must be made immediately will be stressful for staff members, especially because they face the loss of satisfactions that were previously taken for granted. The status quo will be disturbed when cutbacks in budgets, hours of operation, and personnel must be imposed. A setting's negotiation latitude widens dramatically during such crises. Organizing and negotiating processes are intensified as staff members struggle to cope with the situation. They typically will attempt new procedures, redefine inputs, and alter their cause maps. For example, the staff of a declining social service agency may place more responsibility on clients, narrow the agency's service mission, and recruit more volunteer workers. The staff's understanding of what the agency is and does, and what they themselves can and should do will be altered. In understaffed settings, workers may increase their efforts and consequently experience increased feelings of challenge, competence, and involvement (Barker, 1968). These positive outcomes may not continue, however, if understaffing is severe or long lasting. Employees instead may come to feel exploited, cynical, and alienated.

If it becomes clear that the setting's decline is irreversible, organizing and negotiating activity should decrease substantially. At this point, staff members will begin to disengage mentally from their tasks because the setting is no longer serving their personal interests.

Our discussion thus far illustrates that behavior settings are suitable contexts for studying fundamental social processes such as how people organize for sustained, productive action; how personal needs and cognitions help to shape social microstructures; and how working groups define, plan, implement, interpret, and revise their activities. Discrete behavior settings also can be aggregated into a population, which is useful for considering setting life cycles. At convergence, settings enter the population, during their continued existence they are part of it, and at divergence they exit from it. In the following section, we outline a program of research that describes a population of settings, analyzes changes within that population, and explores social processes in individual settings.

A Program of Research on the Life Cycles of Behavior Settings

Our program of research is broader in scope than the conceptual framework. It includes descriptive studies concerned with policy issues and research designed to test and to refine the framework. The investigations complement one another in method, design, and information yield. Together they will provide more comprehensive information about the substantive area we are investigating than would one or two isolated studies. For this reason we have chosen to present the range of our efforts rather than only those investigations closely tied to the framework.

We are examining the life cycles of retail and service establishments such as grocery stores, restaurants, shoe shops, hardware stores, and automobile repair shops. There are several reasons why such establishments are suitable for studying life cycles of settings. Most retail and service businesses meet the standard criteria for behavior settings, although some types such as department stores and automobile dealerships typically contain several different settings. Retail and service establishments are numerous—there are over 150,000 of them in the five-county Los Angeles region of Southern California, and some limited data on these enterprises are accessible to the public. Most also are open to entry and are at least casually observable. And most are independently owned and operated, which makes for considerable diversity in the population of establishments.

The program of research is mapped out in Table 9.2. The targets of study represent three levels of aggregation of establishments: entire populations, cohort samples, and selected cases (see the top row of Table 9.2). Each of these targets can be studied on a single occasion (cross-sectionally)—or over time (longitudinally). We have conducted or plan to conduct studies in each of the six cells, as sketched below.

Trade-Offs in Research

At this point, we want to note some practical trade-offs that seem to be inherent in the research domain presented in Table 9.2. In general, as one proceeds from left to right in the table (i.e., from populations to cohort samples to selected cases), more data can be obtained on each case but fewer cases can be included. For example, we can obtain a wider range of relevant information on a few selected retail/service establishments than would be available or feasible to collect on a large number of such businesses.

A different trade-off exists as temporal complexity increases as, for example, when researchers repeat their measures over time rather than applying them on a single occasion. Repeated measures allow for the description of temporal patterns in events but at some cost. Timing of successive measures may be critical and may require considerable prior knowledge of the events being studied. Additional costs are the time and expense required to follow events as they unfold and the effort required to process a larger volume of data. Moreover, it may be difficult to discern patterns and to communicate them. For example, to probe various phases in the development of retail/service establishments may require knowledge of what kinds of events are critical to such businesses and when these events are most likely to occur. Researchers will need to be at hand to take measures on the appropriate occasions. Subtle patterns may be difficult to identify, particularly if the timing of the measures did not precisely match critical events.

Cross-Sectional Studies

Since January 1, 1985, we have obtained from the California State Board of Equalization (the agency responsible for collecting and distributing sales tax), a quarterly computer listing of records on all retail/service establishments within five Southern California counties. The first study we conducted (Wicker & King, 1986) is represented in

TABLE 9.2
Research Program Outline

Research Strategy	Target of Study: Population	Cohort Sample	Selected Cases
Cross-sectional	1 Analysis of archival data on all retail/service establishments in 5 Southern California counties	2 Telephone survey of owners/managers of newly founded and recently purchased establishments	3 Face-to-face interviews with owners of new and terminating establishments, with women partners in newly founded family-owned establishments
Longitudinal	4 Identification and description of establishments that enter and leave the Southern California population after various time intervals	5 Comparison of surviving and non-surviving establishments in the telephone survey of newly founded and recently purchased establishments	6 Comparative case study tracing the founding of two or three establishments from pre-convergence through continued existence

cell 1 of Table 9.2. This cross-sectional study of our population of establishments provided background information that will be used in subsequent investigations. From the limited data available on each business, we generated a descriptive profile of the 150,606 establishments in existence on January 1, 1985. We found, for example, that Los Angeles County has the most establishments (64% of the total), that sole proprietorships are the most common type of ownership (44%), that eating and drinking places are the most numerous type of business (18%).

Only one variable in this archive represents temporal information: the start date of the establishment's sales tax account. This date, which is recorded when an establishment is founded or when its ownership changes, indicates the length of time the business has existed under its current ownership. We use the term *age* for this variable, even though when it is aggregated, it underestimates the length of time that establishments have been in operation (i.e., the ages of purchased businesses are based on the most recent change of ownership rather than when the business was first founded). The age distribution for the population of businesses is positively skewed; the mean and median ages are 6.8 and 4.3 years, respectively. More than three-fourths (77%) of the establishments are under 10 years old.

Two- and three-way analyses provided comparative profiles on the variables in the archive. Most relevant here are age comparisons. We found, for example, that department stores and drug stores are among the oldest types of establishments (based on median age), and that various specialty shops and eating and drinking places are among the youngest. We also found that establishments owned by partners were younger (Mdn = 3.2) than single proprietorships (Mdn = 4.2) or corporations (Mdn = 5.5) (Wicker & King, 1986).

The second cross-sectional study we conducted is represented in cell 2 of Table 9.2. In this investigation, we drew a representative sample from the cohort of retail/service establishments whose accounts were opened in January or February 1985. A few months after the opening of these establishments, we telephoned the owners and/or managers to check the accuracy of some of the archival data and to obtain additional information. We confirmed the information on type of business, location, and start date in the archive records. Additionally we determined whether the establishment was newly founded or had recently been purchased, the number and characteristics of paid and unpaid workers, and the prior relevant work and entrepreneurial experience of the owner and other workers.

A report of this research is in preparation. Although the data we obtained from 413 owners and managers of new establishments in Southern California were primarily nonpsychological, they nevertheless provide valuable clues about the social and functional activities in such businesses. We suspect, for example, that the amount of negotiating and sense-making activity in these new establishments is substantially greater than in more mature establishments. *This conjecture is substantiated by our finding that nearly two-thirds of these establishments are newly organized rather than purchased*, that almost a quarter of the workers are teenagers, nearly half are part-time, and *only a small minority of the owners had previous experience operating* the kind of business they now own. We will use our speculations about the psychological consequences of such findings to formulate questions for face-to-face interviews with new owners.

The interviews to be conducted with new owners are represented in cell 3 of Table 9.2—cross-sectional investigations of selected cases. We will focus on establishments in transition—those that are just closing as well as just opening. We will explore the range of events that these owners of newly founded and recently terminated establishments have observed and with which they have dealt. The interviews will cover many of the aspects of the conceptual framework. For example, founders will be asked to describe their earliest conception of the establishment, how it changed over time, and how they came to identify and choose particular setting resources including their business location, equipment, product lines, staff members, and clients. They will describe the process by which the various resources were accumulated and configured in the new establishment. The organizing and negotiating processes that occurred in creating and maintaining the establishment and in developing work routines will also be explored. A related set of issues will be examined in interviews with owners of closing businesses.

The second cross-sectional investigation of selected cases in our research program is a master's thesis project that examines the interactions of wives and husbands at home and in a recently founded family business. The telephone survey described earlier included a question on whether the establishment was family owned and, if so, whether the respondent would be willing to talk further about that aspect of the business. Kim Burley subsequently contacted establishments that were jointly owned and operated by married couples. She interviewed 24 women co-owners whose businesses included restaurants, a computer store, an auto repair shop, clothing stores, and a gas station. The line of questioning was influenced by Wicker's framework and by a recent study of family-owned businesses (Rosenblatt, de Mik, Anderson, & Johnson, 1985). The wives were asked to report how decisions were made about three activities: planning for the future, making major equipment purchases, and division of labor—both at home and in the new business. Ratings of relative influence of the husband and wife in each of these areas were also obtained. The report of this research is in preparation.

Longitudinal Studies

In the remaining investigations, repeated measures are taken over time on the targets of study. In one of these studies (cell 4 of Table 9.2), we will examine the kinds of changes that occur in our population of Southern California retail/service establishments. By comparing successive files from the State Board of Equalization, we can identify three categories of establishments: *continuing* (those present at both Time 1 and Time 2), *entering* (those absent at Time 1 but present at Time 2), and *exiting* (those present at Time 1 but absent at Time 2). A variety of comparative statistics can be calculated from the quarterly records we are obtaining. Also, we are exploring the possibility of deriving, for this organizational population, demographic statistics that are normally used for human populations, such as expectancy tables and infant mortality rates. It will also be possible for us to calculate the stability of our population over successively longer periods of time (e.g., over one, two, three, and four quarters).

Because we have a variety of data, in addition to age, on each establishment in the archive, we can develop descriptive profiles of the businesses that enter and exit within any given period. For example, population trends in business type (e.g., clothing stores, home furnishing stores, office equipment stores) can be determined by comparing the type distributions of entering, continuing, and exiting establishments. We will also be able to determine the ages of various types of exiting establishments and to compare them with the ages of continuing establishments. Conceivably some types of businesses may terminate at much younger ages than others, and the age discrepancy between exiting and continuing establishments may be greater for particular business types.

Our planned longitudinal study of a cohort of establishments (cell 5 in Table 9.2) will follow up the 413 new and recently purchased businesses included in the telephone survey. By examining the quarterly archives from the State Board of Equalization, we can determine which sample businesses have exited from the population, and during which quarter. We will be able to compare exiting establishments with continuing establishments on the archival variables and on the variables we measured in the telephone survey. Thus, for example, we will compare continuing and exiting establishments in our cohort in terms of type of business and ownership, initial numbers of workers and paid employees, whether the establishment was newly founded or purchased, and prior entrepreneurial and work experience of owners and employees. Depending on the number of establishments that exit, we also may be able to compare businesses that exit relatively early—say in the first six months of operation—with those that exit later.

The last type of study that we will describe is represented by cell 6 in Table 9.2. Our goal is to explore over time the psychological and social processes associated with the founding of a behavior setting. The present conceptual framework is the starting point for the research: the analysis will begin by examining the various resources, internal dynamics, and contextual factors identified in the framework. In accordance with the "grounded theorizing" approach that we intend to follow (see Glaser, 1978; Glaser & Strauss, 1967), we expect that what we learn will lead to refinement and elaboration of some aspects of the framework and possibly to the formulation of new concepts and hypotheses.

In this research, we plan to work with owners of new establishments to trace the founding of settings from the planning (preconvergence) stage through the time that the establishment has opened (convergence) and operated for several months (continued existence). Prospective founders will be contacted before they have made many of the decisions that are necessary to converge a new setting. A variety of methods and sources of data will be used, including interviews with founders, direct observation, examination of guidelines of regulating agencies, and the like.

Thus far, efforts have been limited to selecting restaurants as one type of business to be studied, and to making initial contacts with prospective new restaurateurs. We have chosen restaurants because they are among the most numerous types of retail/service establishments, and because their typical size, internal differentiation, and complexity of external contingencies seem appropriate for our purposes. Restaurants generally have some paid employees but often fewer than ten of them. The spatial configurations, behavior objects, and staff roles in restaurants are typically rather differentiated. Moreover, the range of activities is sufficiently varied and work loads are sufficiently unpredictable that there is room for a great deal of negotiating among staff members (see Whyte, 1948). Restaurants typically depend upon several different suppliers of food, goods, and equipment, and upon several kinds of repair services, and they are regulated by various taxing, licensing, and health agencies.

Concluding Remarks

Through this series of studies and others yet to be formulated, we hope to refine and extend the present conceptual framework to be more formally adequate and more powerful in capturing significant aspects of everyday events. In fact, our findings to date already have suggested a possible elaboration of the setting life cycle concept.

Changes in a target of study over time may be viewed in numerous ways. One straightforward conception, which is implicit in our analyses, is a start-to-finish or linear progression that does not allow for reversals: Establishments come into existence (enter the population), continue their existence over some period of time, and then die out (exit from the population). In another conception, stages may change in an iterative fashion. We have learned that such changes occur in our population, for example, when a business is sold to a new owner or when a business temporarily closes, reorganizes, and then "reopens."

In the future, it may be useful to refine the conceptual framework to distinguish aspects of settings that are newly converging from aspects of settings that are experiencing major developmental changes but are continuing their life cycles. Unfortunately we are unable to identify accurately all reorganizing settings due to the nature of the State Board of Equalization registration records. In the archives, ownership changes are treated as terminations followed by new openings, but reorganizations that do not involve ownership changes generally are not registered at all. Consequently, an adequate investigation of these "iterative" cases is not possible for our population-level studies.

We concur with the theme of this book that there is much to be learned about groups by considering how they change with time. Moreover, we have argued that people's everyday environments—the many different behavior settings that they encounter daily—are continually changing. Two important patterns of temporal change are incorporated into the conceptual framework reviewed in this chapter: setting-level life cycle transitions, and day-to-day changes in setting elements resulting from negotiations among participants. We are examining these processes using study objects and methods compatible with a temporal approach. As formulated, the current work represents a revitalizing perspective on behavior settings that should stimulate greater interest in the time and place context of social behavior.

REFERENCES

Barker, R. G. (1968). *Ecological psychology: Concepts and methods for studying the environment of human behavior.* Stanford, CA: Stanford University Press.

Barker, R. G., Dembo, T., & Lewin, K. (1941). Frustration and regression: An experiment with young children. *University of Iowa Studies in Child Welfare, 18*(1).

Berger, P. L., & Luckmann, T. (1967). *The social construction of reality.* Garden City, NY: Anchor.

Gerson, E. M. (1976). On "Quality of Life." *American Sociological Review, 41,* 793-806.

Glaser, B. G. (1978). *Theoretical sensitivity: Advances in the methodology of grounded theory.* Mill Valley, CA: Sociology Press.

Glaser, B. G., & Strauss, A. L. (1967). *The discovery of grounded theory: Strategies for qualitative research.* New York: Aldine.

Katz, D., & Kahn, R. L. (1978). *The social psychology of organizations* (2nd ed.). New York: John Wiley.

McGrath, J. E. (1984). *Groups: Interaction and performance.* Englewood Cliffs, NJ: Prentice-Hall.

McGrath, J. E., & Altman, I. (1966). *Small group research: A synthesis and critique of the field.* New York: Holt, Rinehart & Winston.

Miller, J. G. (1971). Living systems: The group. *Behavioral Science, 16,* 302-398.

Rosenblatt, P. C., de Mik, L., Anderson, R. M., & Johnson, P. A. (1985). *The family in business: Understanding and dealing with the challenges entrepreneurial families face.* San Francisco: Jossey-Bass.

Smith, I. (1982). *Diary of a small business.* New York: Scribner.

Stinchcombe, A. L. (1965). Social structure and organizations. In J. G. March (Ed.), *Handbook of organizations* (pp. 142-193). Chicago: Rand McNally.

Strauss, A. (1978). *Negotiations: Varieties, contexts, processes, and social order.* San Francisco: Jossey-Bass.

Weick, K. E. (1979). *The social psychology of organizing* (2nd ed.). Reading, MA: Addison-Wesley.

Whyte, W. F. (1948). *Human relations in the restaurant industry.* New York: McGraw-Hill.

Wicker, A. W. (1983). *An introduction to ecological psychology.* New York: Cambridge University Press. (Original work published 1979)

Wicker, A. W. (1985). Getting out of our conceptual ruts. *American Psychologist, 40,* 1094-1103.

Wicker, A. W. (1987). Behavior settings reconsidered: Temporal stages, resources, internal dynamics, context. In D. Stokols & I. Altman (Eds.), *Handbook of environmental psychology* (Vol. 1, pp. 613-653). New York: John Wiley.

Wicker, A. W., & King, J. C. (1986). A profile of the retail and service establishments in five Southern California counties (Manuscript No. 2755). *Social and Behavioral Sciences Documents, 16*(1), 18.

PART V

Continuity and Change

10

Temporal Qualities of Rituals and Celebrations

A Comparison of Christmas Street and Zuni Shalako

CAROL M. WERNER
LOIS M. HAGGARD
IRWIN ALTMAN
DIANA OXLEY

Cultural rituals, ceremonies, and celebrations are diverse and often complex events that can serve a variety of functions in societies. Our thesis is that no matter what their function, what objects or places are used, or how many people are involved, these events contain inherent temporal qualities that define and lend meaning to them. The purpose of the present chapter is to propose a framework of temporal qualities in the context of a broader philosophical orientation, and to demonstrate through examples and a comparative analysis that these temporal qualities are an integral and essential part of rituals and ceremonies. The chapter has four main sections: (a) a description of the transactional worldview and of rituals as transactional unities; (b) a discussion of the

---

AUTHORS' NOTE: We thank Ronald C. Werner for preparing the figures, and Martin M. Chemers, Seymour Parker, Barbara Rogoff, and Daniel Stokols for commenting on an earlier draft. Request reprints from the authors at the Psychology Department, University of Utah, Salt Lake City, UT 84112.

proposed temporal framework bolstered by examples from a variety of societies; (c) a description and comparison of two annual ceremonies illustrating the framework's utility at highlighting similarities and differences; and (d) a brief discussion of implications for theory and research.

Transactional Worldview

Our theoretical and methodological strategy for studying rituals is based on a transactional worldview (Altman & Rogoff, 1987; Werner, Altman, & Oxley, 1985; Werner, Altman, Oxley, & Haggard, in press). A central feature of this worldview is that phenomena are holistic events, comprised simultaneously of people/psychological processes, their physical and social environment, and a variety of temporal qualities. Thus one cannot understand events by considering only the people, or only the physical environment: Instead, people, place, and time are so interrelated that they can only be understood holistically. Psychological processes link these aspects together in varied patterns, and the relative salience of and interrelationships among the aspects can shift and change with changing circumstances. Thus transactional unities are dynamic, changing processes that unfold over time.

Rituals and other ceremonies and ritualized activities can readily be seen as transactional unities. They involve particular people in particular roles, with particular environmental features such as objects, places, settings, and the like. In addition, rituals are explicitly temporal in that they involve a past and a likely future, as well as the present enactment; they often occur with particular frequency and regularity, for particular lengths of time, and so on. More important, no aspect of the ritual can be understood independent of the others. Thus, for example, an individual's activities at the wailing wall in Jerusalem have full meaning only when we know that they represent religious rituals that link orthodox Jews to past and future generations of Jews, and that the wall, as the center of activities, has come to represent the tradition and the people who celebrate it (see Jacobi & Stokols, 1983).

Some Social and Psychological Functions of Rituals

Before proceeding, a few caveats are in order. First, we follow Child and Child (1983) in defining rituals as "stylized or formalized behavior whose rigidity of form is related to beliefs in supernatural efficacy" (p. 1; see also Hammond, 1975; Lessa & Vogt, 1972; Malinowski, 1931/1972). Thus in traditional societies, rituals are practices having a specific form, undertaken in order to avoid or assure some degree of supernatural intervention. There are several terms that refer to recurrent practices (e.g. rituals, ceremonials, celebrations). In the present manuscript, *tradition* refers to the complex of values, norms, and beliefs that are transmitted through ritualized practices; *ritual* refers to the most stylized and supernaturally oriented kind of practice, *celebration* to the least; and *ceremonial* and *ceremony* to practices intermediate in formality and supernatural orientation.

Second, in focusing on traditional activities, we do not mean to imply that these are the only behaviors that bind people together and to their physical environment. Many other everyday aspects of societies serve similar functions. Ceremonies and rituals do highlight the unity of people, place, and time, however, and provide useful opportunities for a transactional analysis. Third, the following is not meant to represent either a systematically sampled or exhaustive review of the literature on cultural practices, but is only provided to suggest some of the rituals and celebrations that have been described, and to illustrate how they fit into our holistic framework.

Rituals contain a multiplicity of social and psychological processes that serve a variety of societal and individual functions (see, for example, Child & Child, 1983; Hammond, 1975; Kottak, 1975; Lessa & Vogt, 1972; LeVine, 1982; Malinowski, 1931/1972; Radcliffe-Brown, 1939/1972). In previous work, we found it useful to identify three broad categories of processes that seemed to link people and place together in transactional unities. That category system will also be used in the present analysis, although it differs somewhat from other analyses of the functions of rituals.

Many rituals define or reaffirm *social relationships*, such as those establishing geographic/political systems, status relationships and dominance hierarchies (including redistributive systems in which such distinctions are blurred), or those that reflect the social/economic system (e.g., marriage rituals). Some rituals link people to their physical and temporal milieus through *affordance* processes, such as planting, harvesting, hunting, and medicinal rituals that reflect the idea that people are interdependent with nature and need the commodities and protections that it affords, now and in the future. Most rituals involve *appropriation of and attachment to places*, such as decorating for holidays, use of sacramental objects, preparation of a ceremonial site:

All involve an integration of individuals with their environment, and reflect the idea that when people attach psychological, social, and cultural significance to objects, spaces, and activities, and transform them into "places" and "symbols," they bond themselves, the physical environment, and time to a unity. And finally, rituals convey a sense of *identity*, whether the individual's distinctive personal identity (e.g., birthdays, Catholic "name" days), or his or her identity as a member of a family, clan, or larger cultural group. (For longer explications of *social relationships, affordances, appropriation/attachment*, and *identity,* see Werner, Altman, & Oxley, 1985.) Naturally, any single ritual can contain a complex combination of these processes.

Our thesis, and a primary focus of our analyses of the case studies to follow, is that all ceremonies serve the identity function, and in fact are mechanisms that contribute to a dialectic interplay between the individual and community.

The Individuality/Communality Dialectic

In a variety of contexts, Altman and his colleagues have examined the dialectic qualities of individuals and group identities (Altman & Chemers, 1980; Altman & Gauvain, 1981; Gauvain, Altman, & Fahim, 1983). These authors suggest that people have a need to be distinctive and unique, as well as to be a part of a larger group. They suggest that individual/community processes co-occur and are in constant conflict, with personal identity dominant sometimes, group identity dominant at other times, with a continual ebbing and flowing between the two.

This conflict between the individual and society has been addressed by anthropologists, though not necessarily from a dialectic perspective. LeVine's (1982) discussion of socialization indicates that the individual's personal desires are often in conflict with social values or customs, and that religious beliefs and rituals sometimes enforce social values, but can also permit expression of individual desires. Similarly, Child and Child (1983) noted that rituals often suppress individual motives, but that in most societies, other festivals give open expression to these same motives. Altman and Chemers (1980) also reviewed the role of festivals in regulating interactions between people so as to provide a balance between individuality and communality.

Rituals, ceremonies, and celebrations can contribute to this dialectic interplay in a number of ways. For example, in most societies, rituals can be celebrated so as to emphasize either the individual's personal or collective identity; thus particular rituals are associated with different levels of social scale. In most societies, birthdays are celebrated as individual events, away from larger groups, and the individual is highlighted while the other participants are relatively unimportant (and even interchangeable). Similar focus on the individual occurs in many societies with puberty rites and other rites of passage, including death. Although the individual's membership in a society is apparent in these ceremonies, the focus on the individual highlights the individuality side of the dialectic. (Indeed, several religious groups explicitly prohibit individualized celebration of birthdays; some offer instead a single collective birthday party to reaffirm the social identity.)

Other rituals celebrate a variety of collective identities, such as couple, family, clan, village, and so forth. Freeman (1970) described three kinds of recurrent fiestas in a Castilian hamlet, each of which drew together different social units and highlighted unity and identity with that unit. And Orenstein (1965), in his description of an Indian village, described a series of villagewide celebrations, arguing that their primary functions were to instill and to celebrate a sense of group cohesiveness. Consistent with this idea of varying scale, some of the ceremonies highlighted intravillage caste distinctions, whereas at least one highlighted village identity without regard for caste.

Similarly, Kottak (1980) described ceremonies among the Betsileo in Highland Madagascar as involving a "gradual increase in participation from familial through village through neighborhood through regional" levels of scale (p. 222). In fact, some Betsileo identity groups exist only in the context of ceremonies, such as "descent groups" (so-called because of their use of a common tomb for several generations), that are only brought together on an irregular basis for elaborate reburial ceremonies (see also Caplan, 1975; Donoghue, 1977). Thus different rituals make salient different aspects of the individual's personal/group identity.

Anthropologists have discussed the role of ceremonies and celebrations in drawing the individuals into the group, describing participation as both a privilege and an obligation (Freeman, 1970; Kottak, 1980). For example, in describing the religious fiestas in a small village in Spain, Freeman (1970) noted the tension between autonomy and collective interdependence, and held that many religious communal activities were strategically designed to offset tendencies for individuality (e.g., selfishness, competitiveness) at times when cooperativeness and sharing were needed. Large communal feasts, in which food and wealth are systematically redistributed from rich to poor, have also been described in these terms, as have weddings and other smaller scale (i.e., more individualistic) rituals in which the wealthy are encouraged to invite large numbers of people to feast and celebrate (Kottak, 1980; Orenstein, 1965; Wolf, 1959/1971).

Even within these predominantly collective events, individuals can maintain their distinctiveness. For example, the role one assumes can reflect individual identity, as can the manner in which one conducts oneself in that role. Similarly, many people don't participate, or participate peripherally (Press, 1975), or only participate during certain phases of the collective event (Freeman, 1970). Furthermore, participants may vary in the extent to which they respond affectively and feel linked to the group during collective ceremonies (Jacobi & Stokols, 1983). Thus, in many ways, rituals can be viewed as contributors to the dialectic interplay between the individual and community.

In this section, we described rituals as transactional unities in which people were linked to their physical and temporal milieus through social relationships, affordances, appropriation/attachment, and identity processes. We emphasized, in particular, the identity function of rituals, arguing that rituals play an essential role in the dialectic interplay between individual and society. In the next section, we turn to an analysis of the temporal qualities of rituals, illustrating these with an assortment of examples from many societies.

Temporal Qualities of Rituals[1]

In previous analyses, we have found it useful to distinguish between the two overarching dimensions of linear and cyclical time (Werner, Altman, & Oxley, 1985; Werner & Haggard, 1985). Linear time, with its notions of past/present/future, conveys the idea that events unfold over time, and can vary in the extent to which the past is carried forward into the present and on into the future. In contrast, cyclical time refers to repetitive and recurring activities, events, and meanings. For some societies, recurrent events are thought to be identical from one enactment to another, whereas for others, there is a blending of linear and cyclical time, such that what occurred before does not ever occur again in identical fashion. We will use the term *spiraling cyclicity* or simply *spiraling* time to capture the idea that rituals are recurrent events that can contain both continuity and change (see Sorokin, 1957/1985).

The concept of linear time is useful in considering one individual's developing experience with cultural rituals, such as the first time she or he attends a traditional fiesta, his or her own one-time-only rites of passage, and the like. From a broader perspective, however, the individual's experiences are simply part of a longer-term cyclical/spiraling process of recurrent enactments, in which the group absorbs newcomers and replaces past members. Thus, with respect to traditional ceremonies, a discussion of linear qualities seems inappropriate, and we will limit our analysis to recurrent events, all the while acknowledging that what contains cyclical/spiraling qualities from the society's perspective may contain predominantly linear qualities from the individual's or subgroup's.

Rituals can be described in terms of five subordinate temporal qualities: *salience; scale; pace; sequences;* and *rhythm.* Our thesis is that these qualities are integral to the activities, and contribute to the phenomenological experience and psychological meaning of the ceremony. That is, we propose that these qualities have evolved over time with the ritual, and represent sometimes deliberate and sometimes nonconscious choices on the group's part to engender different rituals with different psychotemporal experiences.

Temporal Salience

Temporal *salience* refers to the temporal focus of events and activities, such as the extent to which a ritual reminds one of past, present, or future experiences or enactments. The view is not a myopic one, and events rarely contain one focus to the exclusion of the others; often, they contain all three temporal foci with varying degrees of emphasis on each.

Wedding anniversaries, birthday celebrations, and Christmas reunions are examples of celebrations containing all three foci simultaneously. When the history of the couple or individual is reviewed, or when participants reminisce in other ways about the past, the event is past salient; the celebration is in the present, thereby containing present salience; and often participants discuss the celebrant's future, making plans and anticipating upcoming events, rendering the celebration future salient. Funerals are also multisalient, in that the deceased's past life and possible future afterlife are discussed by mourners who are involved in ongoing, present-focused activities. Thus salience is not fixed, but can rise or fall at different times, depending on thoughts, activities and one's role in the proceedings.

Most affordance-related rituals are primarily future salient, in that they are designed to assure a good harvest and the future well-being of the group, but they can also refer to the past. For example, the nomadic tribes of northwest Australia hold annual "freshening" ceremonies during which they repaint pictures depicting species of plants and animals in order to assure the species' viability, and the tribe's future hunting and gathering success (Blundell, 1980). But Blundell described these ceremonies as bonding the people to their clans, to their ancestors, and to their descendants, that is, to social relationships in the present, the past, and the future.

Orenstein (1965) also described an extensive future-salient practice among villagers in rural India who, as part of a larger ceremony, gathered at the temple of Mariai, the smallpox goddess. During the ceremony, some individuals became possessed and were able to answer questions about the future, such as when it would rain, whether the crops would be plentiful, and so on. Orenstein suggested that this ceremony represented "a symbolic effort of the village as a whole to stave off disease, crop failure, and other disasters" (p. 200).

Temporal Scale

Scale refers to the temporal size or scope of phenomena, and in the cyclical/spiraling sphere refers to the length of a recurrent cycle, or more precisely, the *interval* between the recurrence of an event, coupled with the *duration* of the event. There is considerable variability in intervals and durations of rituals, with some occurring on an annual basis and lasting for moderate periods of time, others recurring more frequently (e.g., daily, weekly, monthly) and being of shorter duration, and so on. Some ceremonies are scheduled on a rigid cycle, with equal intervals between recurrences, and others are on religious or solar calendars with irregular but predictable intervals (e.g., Easter Sunday in the Christian calendar). Other ceremonies are scheduled regularly, not on a predetermined date, but rather "when the time is right," or when a person can afford to sponsor it (Kottak, 1980; Press, 1975). Still other rituals are only used in response to crises, and both the interval and the duration depend on the severity of events (see, for example, Titiev's,

1960, distinction between calendrical and critical rites.)

In summary, cyclical scale refers to the frequency and duration of ceremonies, and thus to the regularity of the cycle; many varieties of scale are reflected in rituals and ceremonies. Ceremonials involving life changes often have the most variable intervals, because life changes such as birth, marriage, and death occur at irregular intervals. They also can be most variable in duration, because that depends on individual finances and motivation. Caplan (1975), in her study of a small village on the Island of Mafia off the East African coast, remarked that a wedding was particularly special because the feasting and dancing "lasted for several days instead of the usual twenty-four hours" (p. 35). Caplan also noted a number of optional ceremonies, held only as desired (death anniversaries, female puberty rites).

Researchers have used changes in either the frequency or duration of ceremonies as indices of commitment to traditional values and/or the coherence of the society. Jaspan (1953/1971) noted that when the Ekunene culture was disrupted after two invasions, the planting and harvesting rituals were held only sporadically rather than on a regular schedule. Press (1975) noted that small villages in the Yucatan subsidized religious festivals with tax funds, but changed from annual to biannual celebrations to save money for the community's economic development. Press suggested that this reflected an effort to maintain the old but still to embrace the new. And Connor (1977), studying Japanese Americans, used participation in and the meaning of festivals as indices of the degree of loss of traditional Japanese values and acculturation into U.S. society. For example, he noted that third-generation Japanese Americans were not only less likely to participate in some religious festivals, but that if they did participate (such as in the O-Bon festival), it tended to be for social rather than religious reasons.

"Entrainment" is the process of fitting two cycles together, and the cycles of holidays in many societies fit into larger seasonal and weather cycles, or religious calendars (McGrath & Kelly, 1986). For example, many rituals serve as temporal boundaries to the harvest season, and are initiated when appropriate to weather and ground conditions. Kottak (1980) documented that most celebrations among the Betsileo of Madagascar were held after the harvest, when people relax from the pressures of farming; it was not uncommon for a funeral (a main Betsileo festival event) to be delayed for several months so that it could be held during the festival season. Other ceremonies are part of a larger festival cycle, and must fit together within the constrains of that cycle; many Catholic and Hindu festivals have this character (Freeman, 1970; Orenstein, 1965).

Temporal Pace

Temporal *pace* refers to the density of events per unit time, or how quickly events unfold during a traditional event or series of events. Cyclical events can be slow or fast paced, setting a somber or more festive mood; traditional settings can become associated with slow- or fast-paced events; and the pace of activities can vary during different parts of the ceremony. In detailed descriptions of ceremonies, it is often possible to discern considerable variability in pace. Preparations for feasts begin well before the event, usually at a moderate pace, and then build to a quicker tempo just prior to and during the festivities themselves, and then the pace slows as events wind down and the celebration ends. Kottak (1980) described Betsileo reburial ceremonies in great detail, and considerable changes in tempo were evident; at some times during the ceremony there was frenzied dancing, and relatives of the deceased even threw the bundled remains up into the air until the bones cracked; at other times there were quieter moments when the ceremonial leader spoke to the ancestors; these were interspersed with moderate-paced activities; and so forth.

Temporal Sequencing

Sequencing refers to the idea that behaviors often unfold in a particular order, and that, furthermore, the particular order is important to the integrity of the phenomenon (see Turner, 1969). Sequences are like scripts (Schank & Abelson, 1977) or behavior setting programs (Barker, 1968; Wicker, 1979), in that there is a known order to events, and this sequence is congruent with the physical and social context. In most ritualized practices, the order of events is clearly specified, both at a broad and general level and at tiny micro-levels of behavior; often a leader specifies the proper sequence of events so that the correct order is maintained. Sometimes the sequences in rituals seem to have a pragmatic basis, such as when a wedding ceremony is performed prior to any celebrating and dancing. Sometimes the sequence seems to serve the function of controlling participants' phenomenological experience, such as when events are designed to build toward a climax or frenzied finale. The sequence of events in Betsileo reburial ceremonies seems to have this character, and Kottak (1980) suggested that relatives of recently deceased individuals needed such a building up to be able to handle and desecrate the corpses.

Similarly, the Ambil Ghugriya ceremony in India builds up toward a climactic finish in which some participants become "possessed" (Orenstein, 1965). Presumably, the procession and singing and dancing that precede this contribute to the frenzy of their possession.

Temporal Rhythm

Rhythm is related to sequencing, but incorporates the idea of patterns, such as repeated combinations of pace and emphasis that can punctuate and lend particular ambience to events. Any recurrent ceremony with recurrent pace and patterns can have a rhythmic quality. Daily prayer rituals among traditional Muslims lend a rhythmic quality to their lives, and even within a single enactment, repetitions and patterns provide rhythm. Similarly, Wolf (1959/1971) noted the rhythmic flow to life among Mexican and Central American Indians:

> The Indian scheme of life moves in an endless round, in which everyday labor issues into the magic moment of religious ritual, only to have the ritual dissolve again into the everyday labor that began the cycle. The Indian community has now forgotten its pre-Hispanic past; its past and its future have merged in a timeless rhythm of alternating mundane and holy days. (p. 248)

Thus the endless flow between work and ceremony becomes a rhythmic aspect of life in the Indian village.

In this section we have provided a brief overview of several temporal qualities, and illustrated how they are manifested in a variety of traditional practices and events. We attempted to demonstrate how the mood and the meaning of the events were integrally linked to their temporal qualities. Next, we turn to a more detailed analysis of two rituals, one of recent vintage, the other more ancient in origin. The two cases are similar in that both represent rituals involving homes, neighborhood, and the broader social/physical milieu. Each of them has distinctive temporal qualities and psychological processes, and can be fruitfully compared according to the dimensions outlined in our framework. Information about Christmas Street was gained through interviews, questionnaires, and rating of the decorations (Oxley, Haggard, Werner, & Altman, 1986; Werner, Altman, Oxley, & Haggard, in press), whereas information about Shalako was obtained from attendance at a Shalako ceremony and from monographs (Bunzel, 1932; Cushing, 1974; Parsons, 1939; Saile, 1977; Stevenson, 1904).

Christmas Street

As its name suggests, "Christmas Street" is more than a physical location: It is a transactional event of social, physical, and temporal dimensions. For almost 40 years, residents have marked the Christmas season with both physical and social activities containing a complex set of temporal elements (much of the following is gleaned from Oxley et al., 1986, and Werner, Altman, Oxley, & Haggard, in press).

Christmas Street is a cul de sac, located well within the perimeter of a metropolitan area of over half a million people in the western United States. At the time of our interviews, the residents were of widely varied ages, middle class in education and occupation, primarily home owners, approximately equally distributed between short- and long-term residents, and from varied Christian backgrounds (although half were members of a single, locally dominant religion). With its modest homes, tree-lined sidewalks, and evidence of children, the street strikes the passerby as an ordinary, tidy residential area.

At Christmastime, the street is transformed into a fairyland, full of lights, decorative objects, and Christmas activities. A large red and green neon sign that reads "Christmas Street" arches over the entrance to the street, and a large, decorated Christmas tree stands in the middle of the circle at the opposite end. Combinations of windows, doorways, porches, eaves, house edges, and front yard bushes are decorated with lights, wreaths, and bows. Occasionally, reindeer, an angel, a star, or other objects having a Christmas motif are placed on the house facade or front lawn. A few of the houses are linked to one another with strings of Christmas lights.

The annual event officially begins with a meeting during Thanksgiving weekend. The meeting is called by the current year's chair, who served as the assistant chair during the previous year, and whose own assistant will take over the following year. This meeting is generally not well-attended, but enough people participate to get things started. Decisions are made regarding the time of the children's party, the date and time that the Christmas lights must be up, the date and time they may be taken down, and the amount of the "assessment" (the tax that pays for electricity for the tree lights and Christmas Street sign, liability insurance, and treats for the children's party).

In addition, people confirm their traditional roles (e.g., Santa Claus; repairman and technician; and so on) and/or volunteer for one of four committees. The tree committee is responsible for obtaining and erecting the large tree in the middle of the circle. The sign committee is responsible for retrieving the "Christmas Street" sign from a resident's garage, and putting it up on the white posts at the entrance to the street. The stocking committee provides stockings, and a fourth committee procures refreshments for the annual children's party.

Serving in special roles and on committees involves people in activities, and binds them psychologically to the events. And because roles and committee membership are fairly constant from year to year, it also gives people a special identity within the Christmas Street period. By giving people clearly defined responsibilities and well-developed expertise, such constancy may also serve to assure that the traditional events will be carried forward into the future.

Each of the committees works within the time frame established by convention and by the annual meeting, thus both the tree and the sign committees must proceed quickly in order to install their decorations on time. Although working on a somewhat longer scale, the stocking and refreshment committees must also set a faster pace as the party approaches.

The pace quickens for all residents as the deadline for decorating approaches. Most residents use the same or similar decorations year after year, so decorating has both a past- and present-salient focus to it. Once the block is decorated, a daily cycle becomes apparent within the larger, annual one; a regular rhythm begins, in which the street is relatively quiet during the day, but activity becomes intense in the evenings as literally hundreds of visitors drive up and down the street admiring the decorations.

The pace quickens again the Sunday before Christmas with the annual children's party. The party has a well-known sequence, and begins with a procession of caroling youngsters, led from the open end of the street to the circle, where they continue singing in front of the communal tree. The singing makes salient the past history of Christmas Street, the historical significance of Christmas itself, and the residents' unity with the larger culture. After the caroling, the children are greeted by Santa Claus who gives each of them a Christmas stocking, after which the entire group enjoys the party refreshments.

On Christmas Eve, the number of visitors' cars is particularly intense, but after Christmas, the pace slows again, with fewer and fewer vehicles visiting the street. The event comes to a close two weeks after Christmas when most residents remove their decorations.

This series of events is illustrated in a general way in Figure 10.1, in which the circle represents a full calendar year, heavy lines mark the first day of each month, and lighter lines represent thoughts and activities about the Christmas Street ceremonies. The most significant annual events are labeled. Interviews indicated that during most of the year, the salience of the Christmas activities occurs sporadically; this varying salience is indicated by widely scattered and irregularly placed lines. During the Christmas season, the series of circles represents the diurnal cycle of relative quiet during the day, and intense activity wrought by visitors during the evenings; their irregular pattern is suggestive of the variability in pace and intensity from day to day. As described below, the circle itself is drawn in different thicknesses to illustrate the ebbing and flowing of communal activities and spirit that we observed during a year's cycle.

Individuality/communality is evident in many aspects of Christmas Street activities, as the community is brought together through a variety of appropriation practices, social relationships, and affordances. First, the fact that almost all of the houses are decorated every year indicates a degree of communal appropriation, effort, and spirit by every household. Furthermore, several residents reported that they occasionally helped others with their decorations, and a few of the houses are linked together with strings of connecting lights, suggesting a symbolic unity through decorating.

Second, the Christmas tree and Christmas Street sign belong to the whole block, and bring people together physically through their work on the decorations, and symbolically through shared ownership, aesthetic appreciation, and the like. Third, the block acts in unison to coordinate the timing of decorating, setting up and removing decorations on the same date, and illuminating and darkening them in unison. Residents stressed this uniformity, and many spoke of rushing home in the evenings to turn on their lights, or giving this responsibility to a neighbor so that their home could fit in with the others. Finally, the season culminates with the communal party, an important part of which is the ceremonious walk—from the Christmas Street sign to the communal tree—that symbolically and physically unifies the block.

Several comments by residents suggest that individuality may be actively discouraged at this time of year. Some residents criticized any trends toward competitiveness, and we noted that they did not offer individual prizes for residents with the nicest decorations, but the block did enjoy winning occasional citywide recognition. And finally, all of the stockings presented at the children's party were identical in an explicit effort to assure similarity.

Still, all was not entirely communal. Every home was distinctively decorated, providing considerable individuality to the decorating. Furthermore, there was variability in Christmas spirit, with some residents extremely positive and others more neutral about the practices: Some residents hardly participated in committee work and other activities, whereas others participated extensively; some residents socialized with their neighbors, and others hardly saw them at all. Even residents who were quite favorable about the activities were ambivalent, expressing criticisms and complaints about some of its aspects. Some residents complained about the cost of decorating, and the occasional vandalization of decorations. In addition, residents complained about traffic congestion, saying that they had to wait in line with the visiting cars just to get into their driveways during peak times. Thus, although the bulk of activities and spirit are communal during Christmas season, individuality is evident in decorations as well as in social contacts, participation, and attitudes.

In addition to collecting information about the Christmas Street event, we were able to measure social relationships and decorating activities during the summer. The results, while much too complex to be presented in this brief description, generally show the block to be more diffuse during the summer, and more cohesive in the winter. At both times of year, the block could be divided into two general groups, one expressing considerable cohesiveness with neighbors and attachment to the block, and the other being more individualistic and detached. During the annual Christmas festivities, the block was not a single tightly knit group, but there was a shift toward more openness and contact, especially by a central core of residents.

In particular, whereas during the summer, care and decorating of the front yard and house facade were related to individual factors (e.g., being retired, having few children, owning the home), during the Christmas season, extensiveness of decorating was related to communal factors (e.g., having the "Christmas Spirit," spending time outside on the block, knowing and interacting with neighbors). Thus within this single annual cycle, we observed what appeared to be a shift from a predominantly individual/family orientation to a more communal orientation, that is, a shift in salience from the individualistic to the communal side of the identity dialectic.

At a broader level of scale, we noticed what appeared to be a generational shift in communal spirit and commitment to the annual events. Older residents thought back with fondness on times when their own children had participated in the event. Many of these same individuals were the most negative about the present state of traffic congestion and decorating competition, and least active during block-wide activities. These contrasting attitudes suggest that these individuals were more communal in the past, and more individualistic in the present, suggesting that the individuality/communality dialectic can wax and wane across decades as well as within a single year.

Christmas Street is an event that binds together a small neighborhood for a brief period of time each year. Collective appropriation of the environment is evident in communal decorating and social activities, and the block appears to be unified both physically and psychologically at Christmas. Cyclical scale is evident in the regularity of the annual meeting; the regularity with which decorations are set up, used, and removed; and the regularity of the annual party. And a regular rhythm is established by the daily influx of visitors in the evenings. This period contrasts with the remainder of the year in which decorating is done more individually, and residents are involved in more exclusive social relationships.

House-Blessing Ceremonies: Pueblo of Zuni

The Pueblo Indians live in tightly knit and compact communities in the southwestern United States. Because of a unique opportunity to visit a Shalako ceremony, and because of the availability of extensive literature on the subject, we will focus on the Zuni people, one of several Pueblo Indian societies. The central place of the home in Zuni culture is made salient through an elaborate annual ceremony that has been practiced for as long as people can remember. This ceremony, the Shalako, is part of a larger winter solstice observance (Shalako is actually the culmination of yearlong events) and is highlighted by a

24-hour period of religious activities associated with the blessing of as many as eight new homes. The ceremonies involve special dances, prayers, and activities throughout the community and in the homes being blessed. Central to the 24-hour ceremonies are the Shalako figures. These elaborately decorated 10-feet-tall masked figures are manned by carefully selected members of the community who train for a year to assume their religious roles.

The various ceremonies and prayers during the Shalako ceremony involve social relationships, affordances, appropriation, and identity. Zuni values emphasize communality over individuality, and the processes of social relationships, attachment, identity, and appropriation reflect this communal tone. Rituals, prayers, and activities simultaneously bond people to the home itself, the clan (familial subdivisions within the tribe), community, ancestors, spirits, and gods. For example, the coming together of relatives, friends, community members, and strangers in the Shalako House symbolizes the social relationships and bonding of people with one another; further, residents and the house are attached to the clan by virtue of the fact that the home is built cooperatively with clan members. In addition, it is richly decorated for the Shalako ceremony with rugs, jewelry, shawls, and other materials given by the clan members. The community is entertained and fed in the house, symbolizing that the home, its residents, and the clan are linked to the larger society. In addition, identical events occur simultaneously in several new homes during Shalako, yielding a broad bond to the community and the religious value system. Finally, the Shalako ceremony occurs throughout the village as well as in particular homes, thereby further bonding the community together.

Affordances, or utilitarian aspects of the home, are displayed throughout the Shalako house-blessing ceremonies, particularly in relation to food production and preparation. For example, the symbol of corn is prevalent, and dancers and ceremonial figures are sprinkled with cornmeal or corn pollen, prayers are made with corn kernels, and seeds are planted in the floor of the home. Food appears in other rituals associated with health and well-being, and in prayers for rain and other aspects of agricultural productivity.

The annual cycle begins with the naming of the households that will be blessed at the next Shalako observance and the appointment of the "impersonators" or Shalako dancers who will be central to the ceremonies a year hence and who will impersonate or represent the rain god. Soon after their appointment, the impersonators begin a lengthy period of learning prayers, chants, rituals, and dances under the tutelage of the elders and religious leaders of their clans. Throughout the year they participate in daily, monthly, and other recurrent and cyclical religious activities associated with their special roles—daily offerings of prayer to the rising sun, evening prayers at the river, monthly prayer activities at holy places in the surrounding countryside, and the like. The impersonators also work throughout the year for the household who will entertain them at the time of the Shalako ceremonies—bringing in wood, working in the fields, building the house to be blessed, and the like.

Over a long time scale, therefore, a variety of smaller-scale cycles of activity come to be associated with the Shalako ceremony. These sacred and mundane activities make salient the past history and culture of the tribe, as well as its long-term future prosperity, embedding impersonators and those around them simultaneously in a blend of past-, present-, and future-salient cyclical events.

The exact date on which the 24-hour ceremony will occur is decided upon by the holy men of the tribe, depends on a complex set of factors, and varies from year to year. After its announcement, and several weeks before the Shalako ceremony, two of the impersonators begin a complex period of counting down toward the main ceremony. Their activities involve daily rituals and prayers, again weaving a number of small-scale, recurring cycles into the yearlong cycle. These events and the durations between them are short, thereby giving the process a quickening pace. Eight days before Shalako, sacred clown figures appear in the evening, visit throughout the community, announce the coming of Shalako, and begin a retreat. Four days before the ceremony, another group of sacred figures appears. They signal the impending events and engage in various ritual activities. In the intervening days, more and more activities, rituals, and religious events occur, thereby quickening the pace, telescoping the temporal scale, and creating an atmosphere of excitement.

The 24-hour Shalako ceremony begins in the late afternoon, when the Shalako figures appear in the distance on the south bank of the Zuni River. For the next few hours, various figures, including the impersonators, leave the Shalako masks at the riverfront and go to all parts of the village to announce the impending arrival of the figures, plant prayer sticks under the thresholds of the homes to be blessed, and sprinkle cornmeal or corn pollen, seeds, and other materials at the threshold and around the home.

In the next phase of the ceremony, when it becomes dark, the Shalako figures are led by their clan members, who chant and sing along the way, to the homes to which they have been assigned. When they reach a home, the clan members surround the Shalako figure and sing and pray at the threshold, following which the figure enters the home. Clan members, villagers, and visitors are assembled in the home to watch the next phases of the ceremony. There is then a period during which a group of male singers chants and prays, which is followed by a lengthy ceremony in which the impersonators, who have temporarily emerged from the Shalako masks, chant from memory the history of the Zuni people from their origin to the present time. In this historical recounting, the past is salient, but is linked to the present as the history of the people is updated, made a continuous and unending stream, and taught anew to the assemblage. The oral recitation also includes future-oriented prayers for the health of the residents of the home, for many children who will live to old age, for rain and good crops, and so forth. Simultaneously, there are repeated references to spirits and gods of the past, ancestors, and important historical events.

The linking of past and present occurs in a variety of other forms throughout the Shalako ceremonies. For example, following the oral history recitation, women bring large tubs of food into the house. The Shalako impersonators take a sample from each tub and carry the food to the Zuni River, where they feed the spirits of the ancestors who have come up the river from a distant place to participate in the Shalako ceremony. Thus past and present are salient and fuse in this part of the celebration.

The Shalako ceremony is punctuated near midnight by a meal to which all are invited. Members of the community, Indians from other tribes, and non-Indians, many of whom are strangers, are entertained with politeness and grace. The mealtime event alters the pace and rhythm of the ceremonies by demarcating sharply the earlier events from the forthcoming dramatic dance of the Shalako figures.

After midnight, the people reassemble in the house to be blessed, and the Shalako dance begins. Following a period of chanting by the men's group and additional prayers and rituals, the 10-foot Shalako figures dance for several hours until morning. The dance is stylized and repetitive and follows a certain pattern and pace. Sometimes a second impersonator joins the dance. Periodically, the Shalako dancer returns to a corner of the room and is surrounded by assistants who hold up blankets to hide the fact that the impersonators are changing places in the mask. This recurring cycle of dancing and switching of dancers occurs until dawn. The repetitive dance process, like the preceding and remaining chants, creates a sense of fusion of past, present, and future in a way that defies total description. Attention by observers appears to be unswerving. One is completely caught up in the event, and one suspects that participation on several occasions produces a phenomenological blending of past, present, and future, or a form of timelessness that has often been used to describe Zuni and other Pueblo cultures (e.g., the Hopi; Tuan, 1977).

On the following day, the Shalako figures participate in a new cycle of events—the race of the Shalakos. The figures reassemble at the river, thereby completing the cycle from the time of their first appearance in the village. They then participate in a complicated series of events, such as racing to the river one by one, burying prayer sticks in designated holes in the ground, and other activities. This part of the ceremony, although the culmination of the 24-hour period, is not the end of the yearlong celebration. For several days thereafter, the sacred clowns and other figures continue the celebration, dancing and playing in the plaza throughout the community and engaging in ritual activities in the designated house.

Thus the Shalako ceremony and the temporally larger events within which it is embedded unify psychological and social processes and homes in a transactional whole. Although the main Shalako ceremony occurs in a 24-hour period, it is embedded in a longer time frame that extends several days after and several weeks before the 24-hour ceremonies. Moreover, even these events are part of a yearlong series of activities that are initiated almost immediately following the completion of the Shalako activities. Thus events surrounding Shalako occur from one winter solstice to another, although the scale, pace, and rhythm of events change throughout the year. The yearlong events are very complex and involve cycles of activities within larger cycles, rituals, and practices that vary in their temporal scale, pace, and rhythm. As the year progresses, the activities become telescoped and accelerated in pace as they lead up to the 24-hour period. Following the 24-hour ceremonies, the scale lengthens for several days and the pace slows, signifying the ending of one cycle of events and the beginning of another.

Comparison of Christmas Street with Shalako

The information that we have about each of these events is quite different, and therefore it is not entirely appropriate to make specific comparisons, or to draw sweeping generalizations about them. A comparison, however, can suggest similarities and differences, as well as opportunities for future examination.

The function and psychological processes in each event appear to be quite different. The Shalako ceremony appears to be more integral to the religion and cosmology of the Zuni people, and to be more essential to beliefs about the viability of the people. Shalako incorporates all of the psychological processes and functions detailed in our framework. The religious details are much more explicit, affordance aspects are much clearer, linkages to the history of the tribe and to ancestors are much more prominent, and so forth.

Christmas Street has its basis in religious beliefs, but religion is a much less salient part of this event. Few of the decorations have any religious motif (two stylized angels and a star were the only visible religious decorations at the time of our observations), and Christmas Eve and Day are not highlighted by group activities. Appropriation, social relationships, and individual and community identity are the dominant psychological processes, and affordances are not salient at all. Residents are not bound to neighbors through lineage in the way that the Zuni are, so although social relationships are an important part of Christmas Street, they are not the same kinds of relationships as are reaffirmed during Shalako. Although religion was not highly visible, interviews suggested that this aspect was not ignored on Christmas Street, but was practiced outside of the block in various churches, or more individualistically in the privacy of residents' homes.

Figures 10.1 through 10.3 provide overviews of one annual cycle for both Christmas Street and Shalako. Figure 10.1 indicates that the Christmas season (from Thanksgiving to New Year's Day) is the primary core of activities on Christmas Street. As is indicated by the thickness of the line, attitudes of block members are primarily communal during that brief period, and more individualistic during the rest of the year. Intermittent slashes around the edge of the circle indicate that thoughts, recollections, and activities around the ritual are irregular during most of the year, but increase in frequency and pace as

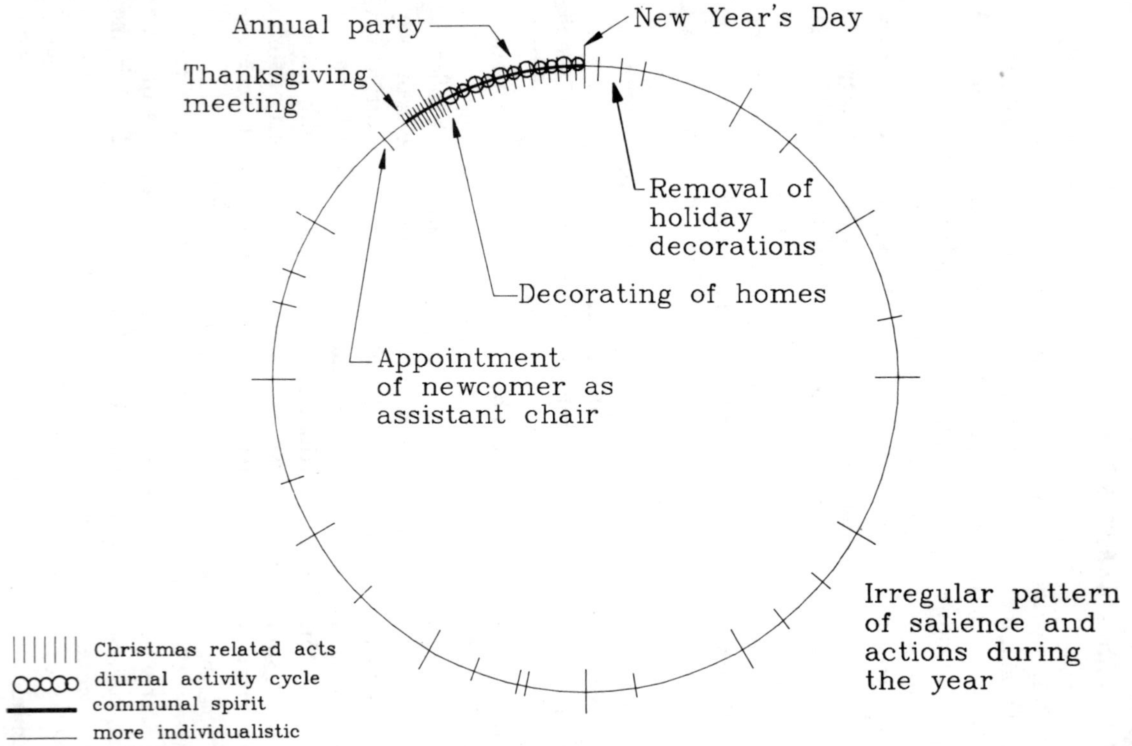

Figure 10.1. Annual Cycle on Christmas Street

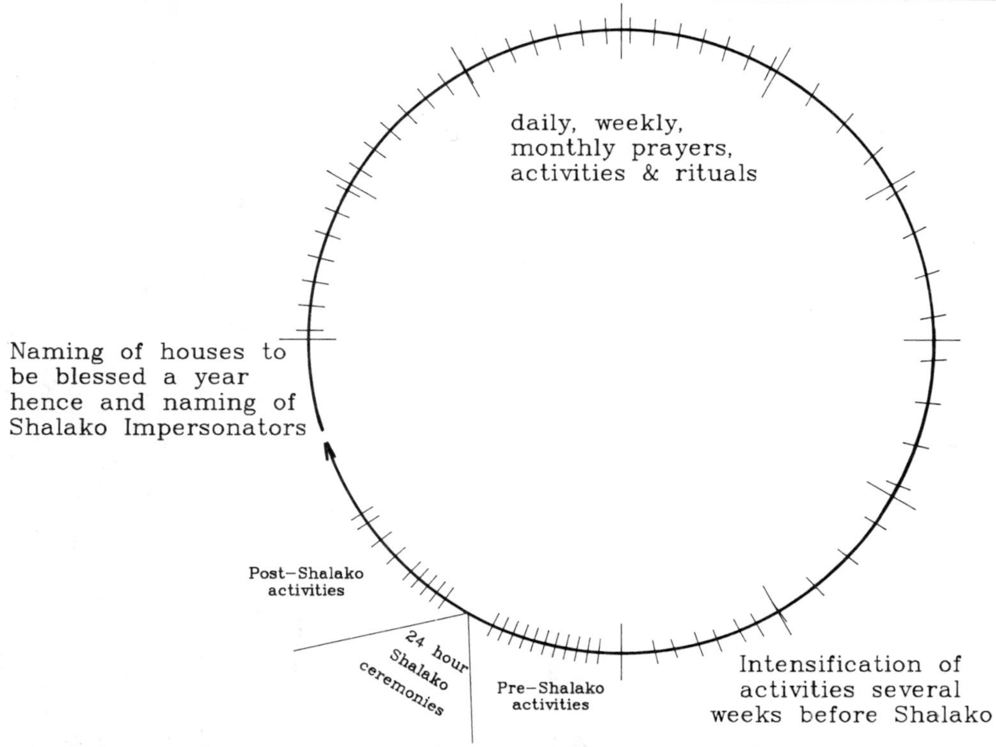

Figure 10.2. Annual Cycle of Shalako

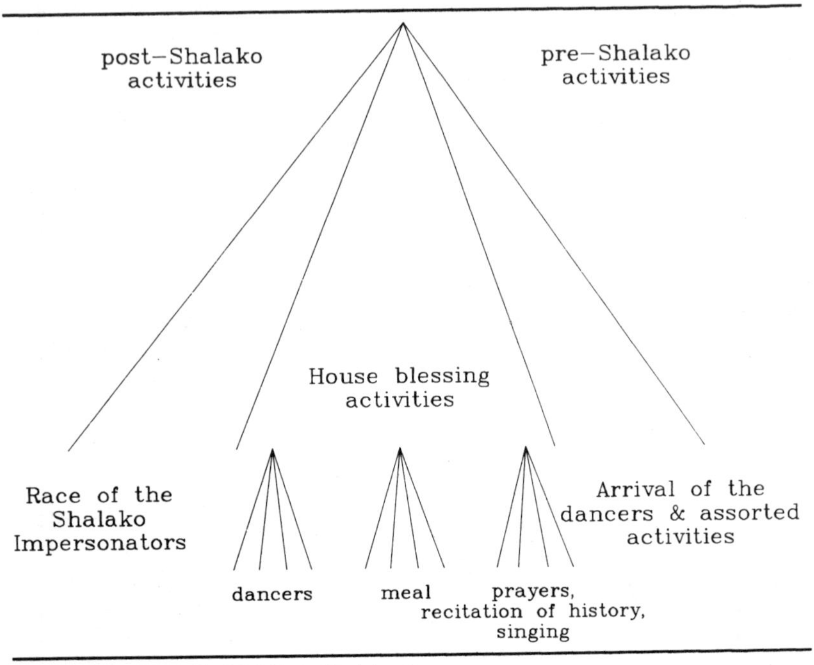

Figure 10.3. Detail of 24-Hour Shalako Ceremony

the decorating season approaches, and as committees meet and social activities are held.

In contrast, the figures dealing with Shalako show that this event is always salient and in many ways is an ongoing aspect of daily life. It is difficult to point to a single point in time when the ceremony begins, for the cycles flow into each other. The impersonators for the following year are specified during the Shalako ceremony itself, as are the homes to be blessed during the following year. Immediately after the main Shalako ceremony, there is a period of slowed activity, but this interval is brief, and activities begin again soon thereafter. Dashed lines around the edge of the circle indicate continual involvement in various stages of Shalako-related activities, with a quickening of the pace of activities as the house-blessing ceremony approaches; the continuous heavy line on the circle reinforces the idea that the Zuni are a predominantly communal people, and Shalako a communal event.

In sum, the two rituals differ in many of their temporal qualities: They differ in terms of scale, with Christmas Street activities being more regular in both interval and duration than Shalako. They differ in the salience of the event during the year and the temporal saliences during the events themselves. Although the two rituals unfold with different paces, they share in having variable pace throughout the year, with pace most rapid just prior to and during the culminating events. Similarly, both show variations in pace during peak celebrations, such as Christmas Street's diurnal cycle of heavy activity in the evenings when the street is flooded with visitors and light activity during the day, and the Shalako ceremony's variously fast- and slow-paced activities. It is difficult to compare them on the dimension of sequencing; each group follows a specified sequence of events, and in that respect the two events are similar. Christmas Street's seems to be primarily a practical sequence (organizational meetings must precede organized activities; the children's party is scheduled so as to fit other religious requirements); there is likely a similar practicality to many aspects of the Shalako sequence (e.g., the spirits arrive, then go to the homes), but many activities are more symbolic and abstract, and their positions in the ceremony may reflect more complex origins (Turner, 1969).

Summary and Discussion

At the outset, we proposed that rituals could fruitfully be understood as transactional unities, comprised simultaneously of people/psychological processes, temporal qualities, and the physical and social environment. We developed a framework comprised of psychological processes and temporal factors that could be used to analyze a broad variety of rituals and ceremonial activities. First, we suggested that rituals linked people to each other and their environments through affordances, social relationships, and appropriation and attachment, and especially through *personal and group identity* processes. We argued that, in many ways, individual and communal identity could be seen as dialectic opposites, and that ritualized practices were processes that contributed to a dialectic ebbing and flowing between the two. We showed how different rituals highlighted social identities at many levels of scale (individual, couple, clan, village, and so on), and how they could be seen as mechanisms that encouraged individuality when individuality was appropriate and that offset selfishness when cooperation and sharing were needed. The second major part of our framework was an examination of the temporal qualities of *salience, scale, pace, sequences,* and *rhythm.* We illustrated these qualities in a number of rituals, and argued that they were an integral and essential part of the activities. And finally, we used this framework to compare and contrast two annual ceremonies.

A critical feature of this model is that temporal qualities are thought to be integral to events, and cannot be separated from them. This concept has several parts to it. One meaning is that the very nature of ritual practices is in part defined by their temporal features. The frequency and duration of a ritual, its rhythm, and pace are as much defining features of it as are the event that is celebrated, the physical artifacts that are used, and the people who are involved. Simply knowing that one is celebrating a daily, brief ritual as opposed to an annual, lengthy one conveys considerable information to the celebrants, and has implications for expected outcomes, effort expended, and activities of the celebrants.

Second, time is integral to events in that it contributes to the actual phenomenological experience of participants. As noted earlier, pace and rhythm relate to the mood and spirit of events, creating a totally festive or somber ritual, or varying the moods within a single ritual. Pace and rhythm can even be manipulated in particular sequences during rituals so that certain climactic events will occur that otherwise might be difficult to achieve. Insofar as rituals are integral to the total culture, it is quite likely that the mood and spirit of ceremonial events reflect and contribute to a society's general tenor. (It should not be forgotten, however, that many groups have at least one annual ceremony that stands in sharp contrast to their general level of more modest decorum.)

A third way in which these temporal qualities inhere in traditional practices concerns continuity and change. Continuity refers to the perpetuation of a ceremony, how its meaning is carried forward from enactment to enactment, and how the group is moved to celebrate it time after time. The residents on Christmas Street held to an almost identical schedule year after year, and during the three weeks of decorating, kept the same regular schedule for turning on and off their Christmas lights. It appeared to us that this temporal regularity contributed to the predictability of the event (people could anticipate and plan for involvement), and therefore contributed to its perpetuation year after year. Change can occur in any of the aspects of a ritual, and these changes can lend novelty and unpredictability to the event. A change in any of the temporal qualities changes the phenomenological and experiential feelings associated with the activities.

In previous work, Altman and his colleagues have discussed the dialectic qualities of continuity and change (Altman & Chemers, 1980; Altman, Vinsel, & Brown, 1981). They suggested that too much stability can lead to stagnation, whereas too much change can lead to chaos, but that a dialectic ebbing and flowing between the two poles can create excitement, maintain involvement, and lead to more viable and effective functioning, whether in interpersonal relationships or in collective settings such as cities and communities. Without invoking a dialectic analysis, Sorokin (1957/1985) also argued that change is inherent in phenomena, but that change to the exclusion of continuity is impossible or leads to self-destruction. We believe that it would be fruitful to consider how both contribute to the viability of recurrent events. That is, it would be useful to know how similar rituals are from enactment to enactment, in what aspects—if any—change is most common, what degree of change is absorbed most readily, and what degree or kind of change leads to chaos.

Beyond the stated theme of this chapter and volume—the intrinsic relevance of and need to understand temporal qualities of social psychological phenomena—we leave the reader with some concluding thoughts. First, a transactionally oriented approach, with its holistic perspective, may open up new and potentially valuable directions for study of traditional social psychological phenomena. Second, any systematic attention to transactional processes may require adoption of a broad range of methodological strategies—experimental, observational, field, archival, ethnographic, and the like. Third, as illustrated in this chapter, the focus on transactional and temporally oriented approaches may necessitate the search for a variety of forms of "data" and information in our own and in other disciplines, including anthropology, history, literature, and elsewhere. There are challenging and provocative possibilities, indeed, but simultaneously fraught with uncertainty and potential error. We think that the opportunities and necessities warrant the gamble and look forward to further work by others in these directions.

NOTE

1. In a book that we just discovered, Robert H. Lauer (1981) presented a broad-ranging analysis of "social time." This volume examined individual, interactional, and

societal processes in relation to temporal issues. In the section on interaction processes, Lauer proposed a framework of temporal qualities that predated and almost perfectly matched our taxonomy. Although he focused on general features of social interaction and we addressed temporal qualities of transactional unities, the similarity in our approaches is striking.

REFERENCES

Altman, I., & Chemers, M. M. (1980). *Culture and environment.* Monterey, CA: Brooks/Cole.

Altman, I., & Gauvain, M. (1981). A cross-cultural and dialectic analysis of homes. In L. Liben, A. Patterson, & N. Newcombe (Eds.), *Spatial representation and behavior across the life span (pp. 283-319).* New York: Academic Press.

Altman, I., & Rogoff, B. (1987). World views in psychology: Trait, interactionist, organismic, and transactionalist approaches. In D. Stokols & I. Altman (Eds.), *Handbook of environmental psychology.* New York: John Wiley.

Altman, I., Vinsel, A., & Brown, B. B. (1981). Dialectic conceptions in social psychology: An application to social penetration and privacy regulation. In L. Berkowitz (Ed.), *Advances in experimental social psychology* (Vol. 14, pp. 107-160). New York: Academic Press.

Barker, R. G. (1968). *Ecological psychology: Concepts and methods for studying the environment of human behavior.* Stanford, CA: Stanford University Press.

Blundell, V. (1980). Hunter-gatherer territoriality: Ideology and behavior in northwest Australia. *Ethnohistory, 27*(2), 103-117.

Bunzel, R. L. (1932). Zuni katcinas. In *Bureau of American Ethnology, 47th Annual Report* (pp. 837-959). Washington, DC: Government Printing Office.

Caplan, A. P. (1975). *Choice and constraint in a Swahili community.* London: Oxford University Press.

Child, A. B., & Child, I. L. (1983, February). *Functional values of ritual.* Paper presented at the 12th Annual Meeting of the Society for Cross-Cultural Research, Washington, DC.

Connor, J. W. (1977). *Tradition and change in three generations of Japanese Americans.* Chicago: Nelson-Hall.

Cushing, F. H. (1974). *Zuni breadstuff.* New York: Museum of the American Indian, Heye Foundation.

Donoghue, J. D. (1977). *Pariah persistence in changing Japan: A case study.* Washington, DC: University Press of America.

Freeman, S. T. (1970). *Neighbors: The social contract in a Castilian hamlet.* Chicago: University of Chicago Press.

Gauvain, M., Altman, I., & Fahim, H. (1983). Homes and social change: A cross-cultural analysis. In N. R. Feimer & E. S. Geller (Eds.), *Environmental psychology: Directions and perspectives* (pp. 180-218). New York: Praeger.

Hammond, P. B. (1975). *Cultural and social anthropology: Introductory readings in ethnology.* New York: Macmillan.

Jacobi, M., & Stokols, D. (1983). The role of tradition in group-environmental relations.

In N. R. Feimer & E. S. Geller (Eds.), *Environmental psychology: Directions and perspectives* (pp. 157-179). New York: Praeger.

Jaspan, M. A. (1971). Communal hostility to imposed social change in South Africa. In G. Dalton (Ed.), *Economic development and social change* (pp. 283-303). Garden City, NY: Natural History Press. (Original work published 1953)

Kottak, C. P. (1975). *Cultural anthropology.* New York: Random House.

Kottak, C. P. (1980). *The past in the present: History, ecology, and cultural variation in highland Madagascar.* Ann Arbor: University of Michigan Press.

Lauer, R. H. (1981). *Temporal Man: The meaning and uses of social time.* New York: Praeger.

Lessa, W. A., & Vogt, E. Z. (Eds.) (1972). *Reader in comparative religion: An anthropological approach.* New York: Harper & Row.

LeVine, R. (1982). *Culture, behavior, and personality.* Chicago: Aldine.

Malinowski, B. (1972). The role of magic and religion. In W. A. Lessa & E. Z. Vogt (Eds.), *Reader in comparative religion: An anthropological approach.* New York: Harper & Row. (Original work published 1931)

McGrath, J. E., & Kelly, J. R. (1986). *Time in human interaction: Toward a social psychology of time.* New York: Guilford.

Orenstein, H. (1965). *Gaon: Conflict and cohesion in an Indian village.* Princeton, NJ: Princeton University Press.

Oxley, D., Haggard, L. M., Werner, C. M., & Altman, I. (1986) Transactional qualities of neighborhood social networks: A case study of "Christmas Street." *Environment and Behavior, 18,* 640-677.

Parsons, E. C. (1939). *Pueblo Indian religion* (Vol. 2). Chicago: University of Chicago Press.

Press, I. (1975). *Tradition and adaptation: Life in a modern Yucatan Maya village.* Westport, CT: Greenwood Press.

Radcliffe-Brown, A. R. (1939, 1972). Taboo. In W. A. Lessa & E. Z. Vogt (Eds.), *Reader in comparative religion: An anthropological approach.* New York: Harper & Row.

Saile, D. G. (1977). Building rituals and spatial concepts in the Pueblo Indian world: Making a house. *Architectural Association Quarterly, 9*(2), 72-81.

Schank, R. C., & Abelson, R. P. (1977). Scripts, plans, and knowledge. In P. N. Johnson-Laird & P. C. Wason (Eds.), *Thinking: Readings in cognitive science* (pp. 421-432). London: Cambridge University Press.

Sorokin, P. (1985). *Social and cultural dynamics: A study of change in major systems of art, truth, ethics, law, and social relationships.* New Brunswick, NJ: Transaction Books. (Original work published 1957)

Stevenson, M. C. (1904). The Zuni Indians: Their mythology, esoteric societies, and ceremonies. In *Bureau of American Ethnology, 23rd Annual Report, 1901-1902* (pp. 1-608). Washington, DC: Smithsonian Institution.

Titiev, M. (1960). A fresh approach to the problem of magic and religion. *Southwestern Journal of Anthropology, 16,* 292-298.

Tuan, Y. F. (1977). *Space and place: The perspective of experience.* Minneapolis: University of Minnesota Press.

Turner, V. W. (1969). *The ritual process.* Chicago: Aldine.

Werner, C. M., Altman, I., & Oxley, D. (1985). Temporal aspects of homes: A transactional perspective. In I. Altman & C. M. Werner (Eds.), *Home environments:*

Vol. 8. Human behavior and environment: Advances in theory and research (pp. 1-32). New York: Plenum.

Werner, C. M., Altman, I., Oxley, D., & Haggard, L. M. (in press). People, place and time: A transactional analysis of neighborhood social networks. In W. Jones & D. Perlman (Eds.), *Advances in interpersonal relationships.* New York: JAI Press.

Werner, C. M., & Haggard, L. M. (1985) Temporal qualities of interpersonal relationships. In M. L. Knapp & G. R. Miller (Eds.), *Handbook of interpersonal communication* (pp. 59-99). Newbury Park, CA: Sage.

Wicker, A. W. (1979). *An introduction to ecological psychology.* Monterey, CA: Brooks/Cole.

Wolf, E. (1971). The Spanish in Mexico and Central America. In G. Dalton (Ed.), *Economic development and social change: The modernization of village communities* (pp. 228-256). Garden City, NY: Natural History Press. (Original work published 1959)

11

Transformational Processes in People-Environment Relations

DANIEL STOKOLS

The past two decades of psychological research have witnessed a growing interest in ecological and contextual influences on human behavior and well-being. This trend is reflected in the conceptual and empirical contributions of environmental, population, and community psychology, all of which are part of a growing interdisciplinary field of environment-behavior research. The environment-behavior field also encompasses several other disciplinary paradigms such as environmental sociology, behavioral geography, natural resources management, and environmental design research, which share a common interest in the relationships between people and their everyday environments.

The rapid growth of the environment-behavior field during the late 1960s and early 1970s was precipitated not only by global environmental problems (e.g., depletion of natural resources, overcrowding, urban violence), but also by the neglect of important theoretical concerns within more traditional areas of the behavioral and environmental sciences. For instance, earlier psychological research had neglected the molar environmental contexts of everyday behavior (e.g., schools,

---

AUTHOR'S NOTE: Adapted from a paper presented at the U.S.-Japan Seminar on Environment-Behavior Research, University of Arizona, Tucson, October 1985. The helpful comments of Irwin Altman, David Canter, and Joseph McGrath on earlier versions of the chapter are appreciated.

homes, work settings, neighborhoods) and, instead, had construed the environment in more "micro" terms as an array of isolated, diverse stimuli. Also, much of that research had been dominated by linear, stimulus-response models of environment and behavior that virtually ignored the geographical, historical, and sociocultural contexts of people's daily activities (see Gergen, 1973; Michelson, 1976).

By contrast, the newly emerging field of environmental psychology signaled a surge of scientific interest in more complex and molar patterns of people-environment transaction (see Ittelson, 1973; Wapner, Kaplan, & Cohen, 1973). From the late 1960s onward, research attention began to shift away from discrete stimuli within the physical environment toward more highly structured units of analysis such as behavior settings, neighborhoods, and activity systems (see Barker, 1968; Chapin, 1974; Michelson, 1977). The social and physical facets of behavior settings were viewed as highly interdependent rather than as independent of each other. Also, the occupants of organized settings were portrayed as actively involved in the design and management of their surroundings rather than as passively responding to immediate environmental constraints (see Ittelson, Proshansky, Rivlin, & Winkel, 1974). All of these developments were part of a broad-based effort within the environment-behavior field to establish a more transactional and contextually oriented view of human behavior than had been evident in earlier research (see Lazarus & Launier, 1978; Little, 1987; Stokols & Shumaker, 1981).

The philosophical perspective of transactionalism encompasses certain key assumptions about the relationships between people and their environments (see Altman & Rogoff, 1987; Dewey & Bentley, 1949; Ittelson, 1973; Wapner, 1987). First, rather than simply construing environment and behavior in terms of independent and dependent variables, transactional analyses are concerned with more enduring qualities of interdependence that can arise between people and places. Second, human behavior is assumed to be embedded in and markedly influenced by the environmental contexts or settings in which it occurs. Thus the interrelations between specific environmental conditions (e.g., noise, high density, architectural enclosure) and behavior are understood to be highly dependent on the types of situations and settings (e.g., formal versus informal, primary versus secondary, public versus private) in which they are observed. Third, the relationships between people and environments are viewed as reciprocal rather than unidirectional. People not only react to existing environmental conditions—

they also take an active role in shaping and modifying their surroundings. Fourth, people-environment relations are assumed to be inherently dynamic rather than static: They are characterized as much by departures from equilibrium as by equilibrium maintenance.

To date, much progress has been made in translating the first two assumptions of transactionalism into operational strategies for theorizing and research. Several new concepts have been developed for representing the complex and varied forms of interdependence that can exist among particular people and places. For example, the concepts of undermanning (Barker, 1968), sociofugal setting (Osmond, 1957; Sommer, 1983), defensible space (Newman, 1973), place identity (Proshansky, 1978), and life situation (Magnusson, 1981) all highlight emotionally significant and enduring qualities of people-environment relations, rather than more circumscribed links between immediate environmental conditions and behavioral responses. Also, strategies for mapping spatially and temporally extended patterns of behavior across multiple settings have been proposed (see Barker & Schoggen, 1973; Ittelson, Rivlin, & Proshansky, 1976; Lenntorp, 1978; Stokols, 1982; Wicker, 1979). These approaches have broadened the geographic, temporal, and cultural scope of behavioral research and have encouraged the development of "contextual theories," or those that explain cross-setting variations in the relationships between particular facets of environment and behavior (see Stokols, 1987).

At the same time, however, the third and fourth assumptions of transactionalism noted earlier—that people and their environments mutually influence each other, and that these reciprocal patterns of influence are continuously changing rather than static—have received considerably less emphasis in environment-behavior research. For instance, the majority of research on behavior settings has taken the existence of these settings as a "given," and has emphasized their stability rather than their inherent changeability. Only recently has research attention shifted to the processes by which settings are established, imbued with social meaning and a "sense of place," structurally modified, or disbanded (see Barker, 1987; Canter, 1984; Relph, 1981; Rowles, 1983; Seamon, 1982; Sime, 1986; Wicker, 1987). Also, efforts to develop contextual theories often assume that the situational moderators of environment-behavior phenomena, once identified, can be reliably detected across different programs of research. Yet, the key sources of contextual influence on environment-behavior relationships may shift dramatically especially during periods of rapid social, cultural, geographic, and technological change (see Archea & Kobayashi, 1985; Saegert, 1987). Moreover, these social and environmental transformations may be triggered by fortuitous and unpredictable events and, therefore, are not readily accommodated by existing models of environment and behavior that presume the stability of environmental settings and the links between contextual factors and target phenomena.

Thus although much progress has been made over the past two decades in achieving a more contextually oriented approach to the study of environment and behavior, an important challenge for future work in this field is to give greater expression to the reciprocal, dynamic, and fortuitous aspects of people-environment transaction than has been evident in prior research.

The Two Streams of Environment-Behavior Research

At present, there appear to be two broadly discernible streams of environment-behavior research, each of which emphasizes different aspects of transactionalism. I shall refer to the first stream as the *nontransformational perspective*. This perspective emphasizes the study of relatively stable patterns of person-environment transaction, and has been the predominant conceptual orientation within environmental psychology and related areas of environment-behavior research. The nontransformational perspective assumes that the relationships between people and their sociophysical surroundings are largely predictable and relatively unaffected by chance. Also, nontransformational analyses emphasize processes of adaptation, normalization, and equilibrium maintenance in people's encounters with their milieus, and view the geographic and sociocultural context of human behavior as stable rather than unstable.

The second stream of environment-behavior research I shall refer to as the *transformational perspective*. Transformational analyses of environment and behavior have been relatively sparse to date, but they are likely to exert a strong influence on the future directions of the field as researchers become increasingly aware of the limitations of relying exclusively on nontransformational models. In contrast to nontransformational approaches, the transformational perspective assumes that fortuitous events play an important role in shaping the patterns of people's transactions with their everyday environments. Also, transformational analyses give explicit attention to deviation-amplification and optimization processes in people-environment transaction, as well as those of equilibrium maintenance and normalization (see Maruyama, 1963; Sampson, 1985; Stokols, 1977). Finally, the transformational perspective assumes that certain forms and phases of people-environment transaction are highly prone to rapid change and extreme instability. Thus transformational analyses are explicitly concerned with the myriad factors that influence the relative stability or instability of people's relationships with their sociophysical milieu.

For the most part, the nontransformational and transformational perspectives have developed independently and have remained relatively separate from each other, as they emphasize rather different assumptions about the nature of people's relationships with their surroundings. The continued separation of these perspectives in future research could promote an unfortunate polarization and reification of our assumptions about the stability or instability of environment-behavior relations. On the other hand, efforts to integrate these perspectives would be valuable to the extent that they differentiate between those facets of people-environment transaction that are most consistent with nontransformational models, and those that can be better understood from a transformational perspective.

Before we can effectively integrate nontransformational and transformational models and develop strategies for selectively applying these approaches to environment-behavior phenomena, it is necessary to give more detailed attention to the unique research questions raised by the transformational perspective. Thus the ensuing discussion offers a preliminary agenda of research issues concerning processes of change in people-environment relations. This discussion may provide a preliminary basis for linking the transformational and nontransformational perspectives in future research.

Developing Transformational Theories of Environment and Behavior

Transactional analyses of environment and behavior, while emphasizing the dynamic quality of people's relationships with their surroundings, have generally stopped short of addressing a whole series of crucial questions about the nature of change in those relationships. For instance, are all forms and phases of people-environment transaction equally susceptible to change? If not, what situational and personal factors account for the variable rates of change or stability associated with different aspects of people-environment relations? Also, to what extent are changes in environment-behavior relations predictable or, instead, attributable to chance? In what ways might future theories better accommodate the role of chance events in altering patterns of people-environment transaction?

The preceding questions suggest an important direction for future research on environment and behavior: namely, the development of *transformational theories*, or those that explain the circumstances under which people-environment transactions are likely to undergo fundamental and demonstrable change. Examples of transformational analyses are Archea and Kobayashi's (1985) research on the behavior of household members during emergency situations such as earthquakes and fires; Wapner's (1981) analysis of the processes by which people prepare for and cope with "environmental transitions" such as residential relocation; Wicker's (1987) discussion of the social, psychological, and locational factors that encourage the formation, modification, or termination of behavior settings; and Saegert's (1987) analysis of the ways in which researchers promote social change through the very process of studying the relations between people and their environments. Each of these analyses focuses directly on different sources and rates of change in people-environment transaction.

To be useful for research purposes, several key terms in the proposed definition of transformational theories must be clarified. Each of these terms raises a host of complex issues concerning the description, measurement, prediction, management, and outcomes of change processes in people-environment relations. For instance, what distinguishes changes in people-environment transactions from nontransactional forms of change? Also, can "fundamental and demonstrable" changes in people's relations with their environments be reliably measured and differentiated from those that are routine and inconsequential? We begin below by addressing some of the descriptive tasks associated with the development of transformational theories.

Describing Patterns of Transactional Change

The concept of change as it applies to patterns of people-environment transaction must first be distinguished from changes that occur within individuals as the result of physiological or developmental processes, and from those that occur in the physical structure of environments as a result of erosion or routine wear and tear. Such changes reflect purely intrapersonal or environmental processes and do not necessarily promote a restructuring of the relationships between people and their surroundings. On the other hand, developmental transitions such as graduation from college, marriage, or retirement, that substantially alter earlier patterns of people-environment transaction (e.g., through changes in one's residence or social networks) would be relevant to transformational theories as they are defined above. Similarly, transformations of the physical environment that are triggered by purely geographic factors (e.g., natural disasters), but which subsequently promote fundamental and persisting changes in people's relationships with their surroundings, would be encompassed by the proposed definition. Thus the basic units of analysis in transformational theories are those qualities and patterns of people's relationships with their environments that undergo fundamental and demonstrable change during a particular period.

The focus of transformational theories on changes in people's relationships with their surroundings requires a rather different descriptive approach than is typical of most behavioral theories. The traditional focus of nontransformational theories is on *behavioral change* rather than *transactional change*, as shown in Figure 11.1. Four categories of nontransformational theories are depicted, namely: trait, environmental, interactionist, and contextual theories (see Endler & Magnusson, 1976; Altman & Rogoff, 1987; and Stokols, 1987; for further discussions of these theories). *Trait models* portray behavioral change as an outcome of intrapersonal processes such as personality, physiology, and life-span development. *Environmental theories* account for behavioral change entirely in terms of specific stimuli and events occurring within the individual's social or physical environment. *Interactionist theories* explain behavioral change in terms of the interplay between intrapersonal and environmental factors. And *contextual theories* focus on behavioral variations that are attributable not only to the interactions between intrapersonal and "target" environmental ("E_T") events, but also to the influence of contextual qualities of a particular situation or setting ("P-E_C"). By incorporating terms to represent these structural qualities of settings, contextual theories give greater expression to the transactional view of environment and behavior than do trait, environmental, and interactionist models. Like these other models, however, contextual analyses generally focus on

1. Trait Theory:

$$\text{Trait} \rightarrow \text{Behavior}$$

2. Environmental Theory:

$$\text{Environment} \rightarrow \text{Behavior}$$

3. Interactionist Theory:

$$\text{Environment} \times \text{Trait} \rightarrow \text{Behavior}$$

4. Contextual Theory:

$$\{\text{People-Environment}_C\} \times \text{Environment}_T \times \text{Trait} \rightarrow \text{Behavior}$$

Figure 11.1. Nontransformational Theories

changes in individual behavior as the central phenomenon to be explained, rather than on fundamental changes in the transactional qualities of situations and settings.

By contrast, the unique focus of *transformational theories* is on properties of a situation at time_1, $[\text{P-E}]_1$, that prompt intrapersonal processes, (P), and individual (or collective) behavior, B, yielding a modified situation at time_2, $[\text{P-E}]_2$:

$$[\text{P-E}]_1 \rightarrow (\text{P}) \rightarrow \text{B} \rightarrow [\text{P-E}]_2$$

(The inclusion of "P" within parentheses denotes cognitive processes, rather than overt behavior as represented by "B".) In transformational theories, the key phenomena to be explained are the structural changes that occur in particular situations between two or more points in time ($[\text{P-E}]_1 \rightarrow [\text{P-E}]_2$), rather than individual or group behaviors, B, that mediate these altered patterns of transaction. Thus behavioral change is viewed as an intermediate step that accompanies certain processes of situational transformation rather than as the "endpoint" of theoretical analysis.

Four descriptive categories of situational change are depicted in Figure 11.2. Each category represents a different pattern of change processes. The first category describes a sequence whereby events within a situation at time_1, or $[\text{P-E}]_1$, stimulate new insights (P) about possible changes in that setting at time_2, or $(\text{P-E})_2$. The enclosure of "P-E_2" within parentheses rather than brackets denotes a "cognitive transformation" of the existing setting through one's imagination of an alternative situation (see Kelley & Thibaut, 1978; Mischel, 1973).

1. Cognitive Transformation of Situations:

$$\{P-E\}_1 \rightarrow (P) \rightarrow (P-E)_2$$

2. Enactment of Intended Situational Change:

$$\{P-E\}_1 \rightarrow (P) \rightarrow B \rightarrow \{P-E\}_2$$

3. Serendipitous Changes in Situations (behaviorally mediated):

$$\{P-E\}_1 \rightarrow B \rightarrow \{P-E\}_2$$

4. Serendipitous Changes in Situations (environmentally induced):

$$\{P-E\}_1 \rightarrow \{P-E\}_2$$

Figure 11.2. Descriptive Categories of Transactional Change

Examples of cognitive transformations include the processes by which architects design new buildings, entrepreneurs formulate plans for establishing a new business, and homeowners develop contingency plans for dealing with impending emergencies such as earthquakes.

The actual implementation of planned changes within settings involves a more elaborated sequence of events, whereby mental images of an alternative situation are translated into intentional actions that lead to observable changes in the setting at $time_2$. In this instance, overt patterns of behavior are instrumental in altering the structure of the situation. Examples of planned situational changes include voluntary residential moves, the development of new technologies that fundamentally restructure people's work environments, the design and construction of "planned communities," and efforts among household members to reduce their consumption of electrical energy.

The third pattern of change shown in Figure 11.2 involves unplanned or serendipitous alterations of people's relationships within their environments. In these instances, an initial situation affords opportunities for novel and spontaneous behavior that eventually alters the original pattern of transaction among individuals and their surroundings. The "Commons Dilemma" (Hardin, 1968) exemplifies this transformational sequence. The ready availability of natural resources at $time_1$ encourages excessive consumption of those resources, resulting in unanticipated shortages at a later time. Also, exposure to stressful situations and life events may prompt new patterns of behavior that eventually bring about noticeable improvements in one's overall life situation.

Figure 11.2 depicts one other sequence of serendipitous change that is instigated by environmental forces, rather than mediated by individual or group behavior. Environmental transformations such as earthquakes, volcanic eruptions, and floods occur quite independently of cognitive, behavioral, and social processes. Yet, these massive and sudden events impose long-standing and pervasive changes in people's transactions with their social and physical milieus.

The above-noted categories of transactional change are useful in suggesting several directions for future research on the measurement, prediction, management, and outcomes of transformation processes. Some of these avenues for future study are outlined below.

Measuring Transactional Change

The basic units of measurement in transformational research are changes in the qualities of people's relationships with their surroundings. These transactional qualities of situations and settings (e.g., "person-environment fit," "defensible space," "public territory," "restorative environment") are generally more subtle and difficult to observe than the overt behavior of individuals or the physical conditions of environments. A prerequisite for measuring patterns of transactional change is a clear conceptualization of the dimensions on which change is expected to occur during a particular time interval. Yet, relatively little attention has been given in prior environment-behavior research to the development of theoretical constructs for representing the transactional or "composite" qualities of situations (see Stokols, 1987). Thus an important direction for future work is to develop taxonomic frameworks for describing and comparing situations and settings in terms of their distinctive transactional properties.

Once the key transactional dimensions of a situation have been identified, criteria for detecting quantitative and qualitative change along those dimensions can be derived. Quantitative aspects of change include the magnitude, scope, suddenness, and duration of transformational events. These parameters of transactional change can be used to describe a variety of events ranging from relatively modest and gradual changes to those that are quite massive and abrupt. In the definition of transformational theories proposed earlier, the phrase "fundamental and demonstrable change" is used to shift the focus of analysis away from the routine (and inconsequential) fluctuations that occur during people's day-to-day encounters with their environments, toward those that entail significant and noticeable departures from previous transactional patterns. At the same time, however, it is important that future transactional research address a broad spectrum of change processes (some of which occur more slowly than others), rather than focusing only on the most extreme and clear-cut instances of change.

Certain qualitative aspects of change also warrant attention in future research. These qualitative dimensions include the source (internal/external), level (individual/aggregate), and focus (social/physical) of transactional change. For instance, some change processes originate internally whereas others arise from sources outside the target situation (e.g., voluntary organizational changes enacted by the members of a setting versus those imposed by external constraints). Some are manifested through altered patterns of individual-environment relations while others occur at the level of group-environment transaction. Furthermore, situational changes can be differentiated in terms of their focus on interpersonal processes or, alternatively, on people's transactions with nonsocial aspects of their milieus. Taken together, these dimensions illustrate the diverse types of measurement criteria that can be used to detect patterns of transactional change.

Predicting and Explaining Transactional Change

Transformational theories, as defined above, seek to explain important sources of change in environment-behavior phenomena. Considering the alternative categories of transactional change summarized in Figure 11.2, it appears that certain patterns of change may be considerably more difficult to model and explain than others. For example, although it may be possible to predict the timing and direction of planned changes in people's relations with their surroundings, serendipitous changes occur in a much more spontaneous or random fashion. The occurrence of fortuitous changes within situations raises some intriguing questions for future research: First, are certain facets of people-environment transaction more susceptible to the influence of chance events than others? If so, what circumstances increase or reduce the likelihood that chance events will significantly alter existing patterns of environment-behavior transaction within a particular spatial, temporal, and cultural context?

Although the exact nature and timing of fortuitous events cannot be reliably modeled, it may be possible to identify certain forms or phases of people-environment transaction that are especially susceptible to influence by such events. As noted earlier, the impact of chance factors on environment and behavior may be particularly great during periods of environmental upheaval and developmental transition (see Wapner, 1981). Also, acutely stressful events that restructure a person's life situation (e.g., death of spouse and subsequent residential and employment change) may instigate unanticipated encounters with new settings and people that profoundly affect the future course of the individual's life (see Aldwin & Stokols, in press). Thus an important direction for transformational research is to assess the varying influence of chance factors across different forms, phases, and contexts of environment and behavior, and to identify those situations in which chance factors are likely to play a major or minor role in shifting the course of people's relationships with their surroundings.

Additional questions for future study relate to the processes by which people cognitively transform their environments and actually modify those settings through intentional behavior. For example, what situational circumstances prompt individuals to visualize and prepare for potential environmental crises (see Edney, 1980; Kaplan, 1972)? Also, are some environments more conducive to creative thinking and innovation than others (see Hamblin, Jacobsen, & Miller, 1973)? Along these lines, situations can be characterized as "generative" to the extent that they promote insight and functional environmental change, and "degenerative" to the degree that they discourage creativity and/or promote dysfunctional environmental change (see Stokols, 1981).

The notion that some environments are more conducive to transactional change than others suggests the possibility of modeling the "transformational potential" of settings—that is, the extent to which group members are motivated to modify the physical or social structure of a setting in accord with their environmental preferences. The degree of transformational potential reflects the discrepancy between existing and potential levels of environmental quality. To the degree that group members possess clear images of preferred future environments, the current quality of their situation may be judged as inferior to its potential quality. But high levels of transformational potential do not necessarily result in actual modifications of the setting. The accomplishment of environmental change requires not only salient images of the future but also sufficient levels of environmental flexibility and behavioral competence among group members. Thus assuming that group members are motivated to improve their environment, the greatest amount of change would be initiated by imaginative groups within flexible settings whereas the lowest levels of change would be achieved by unimaginative groups within rigid settings.

The change-promotive circumstances noted above hardly constitute a predictive theory of transactional change; but they do illustrate some of the conceptual issues that remain to be addressed by future transformational models.

Managing the Occurrence and Outcomes of Transactional Change

A final set of research questions pertains to the management of transactional change and its outcomes. The management of change refers to the application of strategies to prevent or facilitate the occurrence of transformational events, and to reverse, ameliorate, or amplify the outcomes of such events. Opportunities for managing and coping with transactional change are greatest when the processes of change are planned and/or predictable, and when the positive or negative consequences of those events can be clearly specified.

In some instances, individuals have a clear image of the type of change they would like to achieve, and an action plan for implementing that change. Yet, the effectiveness of efforts to promote intentional change is often thwarted by an incomplete conceptualization of situational structure. Consider, for example, an organization that is committed to promoting higher levels of health or energy conservation among its members. All too often, health-promotive interventions or those to encourage resource conservation focus narrowly on changing individuals' life-styles and habitual patterns of behavior, while ignoring other aspects of settings that may be relevant to achieving the desired outcomes (see Figures 11.3 and 11.4). In this regard, the physical design of facilities is a pivotal element that is often overlooked in behavioral change programs. Yet, the ergonomic design of work areas and the installation of high-quality acoustical, lighting, and ventilation systems may be as important in promoting employees' health as those interventions that focus solely on changing individual's health habits (e.g., smoking, alcohol consumption, dietary and exercise regimens; see

Behavior Setting Components		Temporal Focus of Health Promotion Strategies: Preoccupancy Affordances for Health Promotion	Temporal Focus of Health Promotion Strategies: Postoccupancy Interventions to Promote Health
	Physical Milieu	* installation of appropriate HVAC, air purification systems * installation of appropriate lighting systems * installation of noise reduction devices * space planning to reduce visual and auditory distractions * ergonomic design of work areas * installation of envornmental monitoring devices	* regular assessments of environmental quality data (air quality, noise levels, ventiliation, lighting quality, and illumination) * regular assessments of individual and aggregated health data * retrofit to replace faulty HVAC, lighting, seating, and related equipment * development of restorative settings
	Organizational Program	* organizational size, structure, management style as sources of stress * financial status of the firm * commitment of the firm to health promotion * employee health benefits * clear versus vague health planning goals	* smoking cessation programs * hypertension reduction * alcohol intake reduction * nutrition, weight management * fitness, exercise * stress management * job redesign * ride-sharing programs

Figure 11.3. A Summary of Health Promotion Strategies in Relation to the Physical Milieu and Organizational Program of Work Environments

		Temporal Focus of Resource Conservation Strategies	
		Preoccupancy Affordances	Postoccupancy Interventions
Behavior Setting Components	Physical Milieu	* geography, climate, size of setting * energy efficient architecture (e.g., solar-oriented site plans, thermal insulation) * energy-efficient appliances and labeling of appliances according to their efficiency (e.g., solar water heaters, refrigerators, air conditioners) * household-specific metering devices * availability of fuel-efficient automobiles	* energy audits to establish energy-efficient levels within the dwelling * retrofit to replace inefficient appliances and to install energy-saving devices * postoccupancy installation of household-specific metering devices
	Organizational Program	* development of resource-sharing strategies among setting members * social cohesion among setting members * communication and modeling among neighbors about energy conservation and consumer preferences * availability of community recycling programs * availability of neighborhood ride-sharing programs	* cash rebates on utility bills for reduction of consumption * feedback about consumption patterns to setting members * social praise of setting members for reduced consumption * prizes, rewards for outstanding conservation efforts * community cable TV programs to provide information and modeling about resource conservation strategies

Figure 11.4. A Summary of Resource Conservation Strategies in Relation to the Physical Milieu and Organizational Program of Behavior Settings

Stokols, 1985). Similarly, the installation of household appliances that conserve electrical energy and metering devices that provide feedback to family members about their levels of energy use may, in the long run, have a greater impact on consumption patterns than efforts to modify individuals' daily behavior (e.g., encouraging people to set heating thermostats at lower levels or to turn off all lights when they leave a setting; see Stern & Gardner, 1981). Thus a transactional approach to environmental change emphasizes the interdependencies among the behavioral, social, and physical components of settings and the importance of considering these relationships when attempting to bring about desired patterns of situational change.

Perhaps the most difficult forms of change to manage are those that are undesirable, unpredictable, and unpreventable (e.g., natural disasters). In such instances, management efforts shift from change-promotive or preventative programs toward those involving preparatory coping and cost-containment strategies. For example, community residents may be provided with information about how to prepare for environmental emergencies and where to obtain government aid following such events. Also, strengthening community sources of social support may be an effective strategy for enabling individuals and groups to cope successfully with acutely stressful events (see Cohen & Syme, 1985; Sarason & Sarason, 1985; Shumaker & Brownell, 1985).

The preceding examples of change-management strategies presume that the outcomes of specific changes are clearly positive or negative. Yet, it is often extremely difficult to specify the quality of outcomes associated with certain types of situational change. First, there is the issue of deciding on the most appropriate time interval in which to measure the positive or negative consequences of change. For instance, the short-term gains in productivity resulting from the installation of automated office equipment may be offset by the potential health costs associated with employees' exposure to video display terminals (see Pearce, 1984). In this example, short-term assessments of employee productivity are likely to be insensitive to the longer-term impacts of organizational change.

The above example illustrates a second complexity inherent in the measurement of change outcomes: the fact that many instances of change bring about a mixture of both positive and negative events. In research on environmental stress, for example, there has been a tendency to focus on the negative impacts of environmental constraints and undesirable life events. This emphasis on the negative impacts of stressors tends to obscure some of the more positive consequences of exposure to situational challenges and constraints (e.g., increased levels of immunocompetence, behavioral innovation, self-esteem, virtuosity of performance, and social cohesion that result from coping with certain types of stressors; see Aldwin & Stokols, in press). Also, the multiple impacts of stressful changes in environments may occur at both individual and aggregate levels. For example, although exposure to increased population density sometimes provokes stress and health problems among individuals, the same conditions, when viewed at a sociocultural level and within an expanded time frame, may be found to promote higher levels of technological innovation, resourcefulness, and coordination among group members (see Hawley, 1950; Keyfitz, 1966).

Thus the effective management of transactional change and its outcomes presupposes a conceptual perspective that is sensitive to the structural complexities of situations; and a methodological orientation that encompasses multivariate and cross-level assessments of both the positive and the negative impacts of change.

Summary and Conclusions

The preceding discussion has outlined what appear to be some of the distinctive contours of a transformational perspective on environment and behavior. Several descriptive categories of transactional change were presented, along with an agenda of research questions concerning the measurement, prediction, management, and outcomes of transformation processes in people-environment relations. This discussion has merely "scratched the surface" in considering the range of theoretical and procedural questions that remain to be examined in future transformational research. Also, the relationships between transformational analyses of environment and behavior and related programs of psychological research—for example, on the "chance-dependency" of human development (Gergen, 1982), the nonhomeostatic facets of self-identity and social order (Sampson, 1985), and psychotherapy as a context for promoting interpersonal change (Strupp, 1986)—have not been examined here. A major goal of this chapter has been to delineate several descriptive and taxonomic issues posed by a transformational perspective on environment and behavior. It is hoped that this discussion will serve as a useful, albeit partial, basis for future theoretical and empirical work.

REFERENCES

Aldwin, C., & Stokols, D. (in press). The effects of environmental change on individuals and groups: Some neglected issues in stress research. In D. Jodelet & P. Stringer (Eds.), *Towards a social psychology of the environment*. Cambridge, England: Cambridge University Press.

Altman, I., & Rogoff, B. (1987). World views in psychology: Trait, interactional, organismic, and transactional perspectives. In D. Stokols & I. Altman (Eds.), *Handbook of environmental psychology*. New York: John Wiley.

Archea, J., & Kobayashi, M. (1985). *Behavior during earthquakes: Coping with the unexpected in destabilizing environments*. Paper presented at the U.S.-Japan Seminar on Environment-Behavior Research, University of Arizona, Tucson.

Barker, R. G. (1968). *Ecological psychology: Concepts and methods for studying the environment of human behavior*. Stanford, CA: Stanford University Press.

Barker, R. G. (1987). Prospecting in environmental psychology: Oskaloosa revisited. In D. Stokols & I. Altman (Eds.), *Handbook of environmental psychology*. New York: John Wiley.

Barker, R. G., & Schoggen, P. (1973). *Qualities of community life*. San Francisco: Jossey-Bass.

Canter, D. (1984, July 16-26). *Action and place: The existential dialectic*. Paper presented to IAPS 8, 8th International Conference on Environment and Human Action, West Berlin.

Chapin, F. S. (1974). *Human activity patterns in the city: Things people do in time and space*. New York: John Wiley.

Cohen, S., & Syme, S. L. (1985). *Social support and health*. New York: Academic Press.

Dewey, J., & Bentley, A. F. (1949). *Knowing and the known*. Boston, MA: Beacon Press.

Edney, J. J. (1980). The commons problem: Alternative perspectives. *American Psychologist, 35*, 131-150.

Endler, N. S., & Magnusson, D. (1976). *Interactional psychology and personality*. New York: John Wiley.

Gergen, K. J. (1973). Social psychology as history. *Journal of Personality and Social Psychology, 26*, 309-320.

Gergen, K. J. (1982). *Toward transformation in social knowledge*. New York: Springer-Verlag.

Hamblin, R. L., Jacobsen, R. B., & Miller, J. L. (1973). *A mathematical theory of social change*. New York: John Wiley.

Hardin, G. (1968). The tragedy of the commons. *Science, 162*, 1243-1248.

Hawley, A. H. (1950). *Human ecology: A theory of community structure*. New York: Ronald Press.

Ittelson, W. H. (1973). Environment perception and contemporary perceptual theory. In W. H. Ittelson (Ed.), *Environment and cognition*. New York: Seminar Press.

Ittelson, W. H., Proshansky, H. M., Rivlin, L. G., & Winkel, G. H. (1974). *An introduction to environmental psychology*. New York: Holt, Rinehart & Winston.

Ittelson., W. H., Rivlin, L. G., & Proshansky, H. M. (1976). The use of behavioral maps in environmental psychology. In H. M. Proshansky, W. H. Ittelson, & L. G. Rivlin (Eds.), *Environmental psychology: People and their physical settings* (pp. 340-350). New York: Holt, Rinehart & Winston.

Kaplan, S. (1972). The challenge of environmental psychology: A proposal for a new functionalism. *American Psychologist, 27*, 140-143.
Kelley, H. H., & Thibaut, J. (1978). *Interpersonal relations: A theory of interdependence.* New York: John Wiley.
Keyfitz, N. (1966). Population density and the style of social life. *Bioscience, 16*, 868-873.
Lazarus, R. S., & Launier, R. (1978). Stress-related transactions between person and environment. In L. A. Pervin & M. Lewis (Eds.), *Perspectives in interactional psychology*. New York: Plenum.
Lenntorp, B. (1978). A time-geographic simulation model of individual activity programmes. In T. Carlstein, D. Parkes, & N. Thrift (Eds.), *Human activity and time geography* (pp. 162-180). New York: John Wiley.
Little, B. (1987). Personality and the environment. In D. Stokols & I. Altman (Eds.), *Handbook of environmental psychology*. New York: John Wiley.
Magnusson, D. (1981). Wanted: A psychology of situations. In D. Magnusson, (Ed.), *Toward a psychology of situations: An interactional perspective* (pp. 9-32). Hillsdale, NJ: Lawrence Erlbaum.
Maruyama, M. (1963). The second cybernetics: Deviation-amplifying mutual causal processes. *American Scientist, 51*, 164-179.
Michelson, W. (1976). *Man and his urban environment: A sociological approach.* Reading, MA: Addison-Wesley.
Michelson, W. (1977). *Environmental choice, human behavior, and residential satisfaction.* New York: Oxford University Press.
Mischel, W. (1973). Toward a cognitive social learning reconceptualization of personality. *Psychological Review, 80*, 252-283.
Newman, O. (1973). *Defensible space.* New York: Macmillan.
Osmond, H. (1957). Function as the basis of psychiatric ward design. *Mental Hospitals, 8*, 23-29.
Pearce, B. (Ed.). (1984). *Health hazards of VDTs?* New York: John Wiley.
Proshansky, H. M. (1978). The city and self-identity. *Environment and Behavior, 10*, 147-169.
Relph, E. (1981). *Rational landscapes and humanistic geography*. London: Croom Helm.
Rowles, G. D. (1983). Place and personal identity in old age: Observations from Appalachia. *Journal of Environmental Psychology, 3*, 299-313.
Saegert, S. (1987). Environmental psychology and social change. In D. Stokols & I. Altman (Eds.), *Handbook of environmental psychology*. New York: John Wiley.
Sampson, E. E. (1985). The decentralization of identity: Toward a revised concept of personal and social order. *American Psychologist, 40*, 1203-1211.
Sarason, I. G., & Sarason, B. R. (Eds.). (1985). *Social support: Theory, research and applications*. Boston: Martinus Nijhoff.
Seamon, D. (1982). The phenomenological contribution to environmental psychology. *Journal of Environmental Psychology, 2*, 119-140.
Shumaker, S. A., & Brownell, A. (Eds.). (1985). Social support: New perspectives in theory, research, and intervention. Part II. Interventions and policy. *Journal of Social Issues, 41*.
Sime, J. D. (1986). Creating places or designing spaces? *Journal of Environmental Psychology, 6*, 49-63.
Sommer, R. (1983). *Social design: Creating buildings with people in mind.* Englewood Cliffs, NJ: Prentice-Hall.

Stern, P. C., & Gardner, G. T. (1981). Psychological research and energy policy. *American Psychologist, 36*, 329-342.

Stokols, D. (1977). Origins and directions of environment-behavioral research. In D. Stokols (Ed.), *Perspectives on environment and behavior: Theory, research, and applications* (pp. 5-36). New York: Plenum.

Stokols, D. (1981). Group x place transactions: Some neglected issues in psychological research on settings. In D. Magnusson (Ed.), *Toward a psychology of situations: An interactional perspective* (pp. 393-415). Hillsdale, NJ: Lawrence Erlbaum.

Stokols D. (1982). Environmental psychology: A coming of age. In A. G. Kraut (Ed.), *The G. Stanley Hall Lecture Series* (Vol. 2, pp. 155-205). Washington, DC: American Psychological Association.

Stokols, D. (1985). Developing contextual theories of environment and behavior: Implications for work environment research. In R. Ward (Ed.), *Proceedings of the workshop on the impact of work environments on productivity*. Washington, DC: Architectural Research Centers Consortium.

Stokols, D. (1987). Conceptual strategies of environmental psychology. In D. Stokols & I. Altman (Eds.), *Handbook of environmental psychology*. New York: John Wiley.

Stokols, D., & Shumaker, S. A. (1981). People in places: A transactional view of settings. In J. Harvey (Ed.), *Cognition, social behavior and the environment* (pp. 441-488). Hillsdale, NJ: Lawrence Erlbaum.

Strupp, H. H. (1986). Psychotherapy: Research and practice, and public policy (how to avoid dead ends). *American Psychologist, 41*, 120-130.

Wapner, S. (1981). Transactions of persons-in-environments: Some critical transitions. *Journal of Environmental Psychology, 1*, 223-240.

Wapner, S. (1987). A holistic, developmental, systems-oriented environmental psychology: Some beginnings. In D. Stokols & I. Altman (Eds.), *Handbook of environmental psychology*. New York: John Wiley.

Wapner, S., Kaplan, B., & Cohen, S. B. (1973). An organismic-developmental perspective for understanding transactions of men in environments. *Environment and Behavior, 5*, 255-289.

Wicker, A. W. (1979). *An introduction to ecological psychology*. New York: Cambridge University Press.

Wicker, A. W. (1987). Behavior settings reconsidered: Temporal stages, internal dynamics, context. In D. Stokols & I. Altman (Eds.), *Handbook of environmental psychology*. New York: John Wiley.

PART VI

Conclusion

12

Time and Social Psychology

JOSEPH E. McGRATH

I noted in the first chapter of this book that time is ubiquitous but understudied within the field of social psychology. There and elsewhere (e.g., McGrath & Kelly, 1986) I have argued that we need a "full-fledged" social psychology of time. In this final chapter I will try to do three things that may help us toward that goal:

(1) to examine some alternative conceptions of time, by introducing some of the major unresolved philosophical issues involving time, deriving from them the main features of our culture's dominant conception of time and several alternative conceptions of time, and noting some of the consequences that can ensue when such multiple conceptions of time are juxtaposed in the individual's experience;
(2) to reexamine the six temporal facets, discussed in the introductory chapter and used in organization of the book, as the basis for a temporal framework that can help structure a social psychology of time; and
(3) to list some research areas, including many not covered in the chapters of this volume, in which we will need further research if we are to develop a social psychology of time.

Conceptions of Time

People have multiple conceptions of time, and these sometimes conflict. A central idea in several chapters of this book is that, in spite of our culture's fascination with clocks and calendars, people experience time in their everyday lives in ways that go far beyond a simple Newtonian conception. Our lives unfold in cycles and phases and other complex temporal patterns, not just in linear ordered sequences of events. The "meaning" of time in everyday experience is not nearly as clear-cut as one would expect given our culture's extreme commitment to a Newtonian conception and our longtime fascination with temporal accuracy, promptness, and a conception of time that treats it almost literally as a form of money.

McGrath and Kelly (1986) have discussed a number of these ideas in the context of a set of unresolved philosophical issues regarding time. They laid out eight major unresolved philosophical issues about time, in four major clusters, and derived from them several major alternative conceptions of time that represent different cultural or subcultural preferences on those issues. The four clusters and their underlying issues are:

The structure of time:

Is time to be regarded as *holistic* or *divisible* (atomistic)? Is time to be regarded as *homogeneous* (every part of it is like every other part) or as *epochal* (some moments in time are different, special)?

The flow of time:

Does time flow *uniformly*, or in a nonuniform or *phasic* manner? Is the flow of time *directional* or *bidirectional* (i.e., reversible)?

The reality of time:

Is time to be regarded as merely an *abstraction* or as having *concrete* effects? Is time to be regarded as *absolute*, existing without reference to objects/observers, or as *relational*, with its meaning being relative to objects, observers, and events?

The validity of concepts and measures of time:

Is time *singular* or can there be *more than one* "valid" time? Is time an *independent, measurable construct* (independent of space, motion, and change), or is it *inherently confounded* with both concepts and measures of space, motion, and change?

McGrath & Kelly (1986) derive four main conceptions of time from choices on the eight issues underlying these four clusters. The dominant conception of time in western culture is a (modified) Newtonian conception in which time is regarded as if it were *structured as succession* (divisible and homogeneous); *linear* (uniform and unidirectional) in its flow; *abstract and absolute*; and in principle, *singular* and *independently measurable*. This is a *modified* Newtonian conception because Newtonian physics had a reversible or bidirectional time. The irreversibility of time is the one feature in which the currently dominant cultural conception of time departs from the classical Newtonian conception, an aftermath of the development of thermodynamics and its law of entropy.

McGrath and Kelly (1986) contrast this modified Newtonian time with several other conceptions of time. One of those is the time conception of the "new physics"—time as transposable, linear irreversible, relational, and an inseparable part of a space-time continuum. Another is the time conception characteristic of some parts of the life sciences, and also of some views of social behavior. McGrath and Kelly call that latter conception a *transactional* conception of time, to indicate that it is close kin to the transactional views expressed by Altman and colleagues (e.g., Altman & Rogoff, 1987; Altman, Vinsel, & Brown, 1981) and others. This transactional conception of time regards time as duration rather than succession, as flowing in spiral or cyclical rather than linear fashion, as potentially multiple, and as concrete and relational rather than abstract and absolute. Several chapters of this book present conceptions of time similar to this transactional view (see Jones's Chapter 2, Werner et al.'s Chapter 10, and Stokols's Chapter 11).

McGrath and Kelly (1986) argue, and I would argue here, that much of our day-to-day experience does not map directly to the kind of linear, directional, equiunit, absolute, and abstract dimension by which time is represented in the culturally dominant Newtonian conception. Rather, much of our routine experience resembles more nearly the conceptions embedded in the transactional view. Human life involves rhythmic oscillations, with periodicities all the way from seconds and microseconds to major stages of a life span and even over generations. It involves patterns that are cyclical, epochal, and relational, and that seem to involve multiple time streams that do not necessarily correspond closely to one another.

Sometimes these different time conceptions and modes of time experience are in conflict with one another. Some of these conflicts involve individual experiences and judgments of time. Some involve potential conflicts between two or more individuals, or between individuals and the organizations and communities in which they are embedded. In organizations, such conflicting temporal conceptions get entangled in temporal issues such as scheduling, synchronization, and allocation (McGrath & Rotchford, 1983). R. Levine implies that such differences in implicit conceptions of time underlie the adjustments that must be made when a person moves from one culture to another. Jones treats such differences in conceptions and experience of time as central to his conceptualization of TRIOS, and therefore as central to the conflicts faced by Afro-Americans operating within mainstream Euro-American culture. Such multiple and potentially conflicting temporal perspectives are implicit in other chapters of this book as well: In the Werner, Haggard, Altman, and Oxley comparison of rituals and celebrations; in Moreland and J. Levine's juxtaposition of group development and member socialization; and in Stokols's consideration of multiple transformational processes in person-environment relations. Such conflicting temporal perspectives are central to many other areas that were not considered in the materials of this volume, some of which are noted in the discussion of research needs later in this chapter.

A Temporal Framework

Both the introductory chapter and many of the 10 main chapters of this book make the fundamental point that time plays a major and pervasive role in human life and experience. Temporal considerations permeate our everyday lives, whether or not social psychologists include them in their studies. Therefore, a social psychology that seriously purports to provide an analysis and understanding of everyday human life must take some of those temporal factors into account.

Temporal matters affect our lives at several different system levels—individual, interpersonal, organizational, and cultural. All of these levels are touched upon in some of the chapters of this book. The chapters by R. Levine, Jones, Freedman and Edwards, and Robinson dealt primarily with individual-level behavior. The chapters by Warner, Kelly, Moreland and J. Levine, and, in a sense, Wicker and King, focused primarily on an interpersonal or small group level. The chapters by Werner, Haggard, Altman and Oxley, the chapter by Stokols, and, in a sense, the chapters by Wicker and King, Jones, and R. Levine, focused on more macro-system levels—the organization or the community or the broad environmental-cultural context.

Furthermore, there are different temporal issues or facets at these different system levels. There are at least six aspects of time that have been given some attention, both in the field and in the chapters of this volume. Five of them have been used to demarcate the parts of this book: pace, rhythm, allocation, developmental cycles, and continuity and change processes. These aspects are distinct enough so that they could be used to organize the parts of this book; but there are many interconnections among them, both at the general conceptual level and in the concrete instances of the chapters in this volume.

Each of those five parts of the book reflects not only different temporal facets (pace, rhythm, and so on) but also different system levels (individual, small social systems, and so on). Moreover, as suggested in Chapter 1, the five subsections involving different temporal facets and different system levels also involve different levels of a very important sixth temporal facet: temporal scale. But that representation oversimplifies the relations among these temporal facets considerably. Although temporal scale varies systematically across those different system levels as reflected in the chapters of this book, each of those temporal facets operates at other system levels as well.

Thus issues involved in temporal pace, as here considered in the chapters by Jones and by R. Levine, have to do with behavior sequences occupying very short intervals of time—seconds and microseconds. But Werner et al. and Stokols talk about pace in large temporal scales as well. Similarly, the behaviors involved in the kinds of behavioral rhythms considered by Warner and by Kelly subsume temporal intervals in the range of seconds and minutes; but there are potentially important oscillations all the way down to the microsecond level, and there are important rhythms in human life at the level of hours, days, months, years, and even larger temporal scales. Some of those are reflected in the chapters by R. Levine, by Freedman and Edwards, and by Werner et al. The temporal facet of time allocation and use, especially as discussed here in Robinson's chapter, refers to activities subsuming minutes, hours, perhaps days. But time allocation operates at other temporal scales, larger and smaller, as well—down to the allocation of attention and effort at the level of seconds and microseconds (as in the Freedman & Edwards chapter) and up to the level of years and decades as reflected in the long-range planning of many institutions. Phases of developmental cycles, as discussed here by Moreland and J. Levine in the context of the development of groups, and by Wicker and King in the context of the life cycles of behavior settings, are matters of hours, days, and months. But developmental stages and cycles operate at the level of a social unit's lifetime for individuals, groups, and organizations, and even for the evolutionary cycle of a species. Finally, the system continuity and change processes discussed here by Werner et al. and by Stokols are ones that operate over days, months, and years. But issues of continuity and change processes are vital at even larger temporal scales, and at many smaller ones as well.

These temporal facets involve *different temporal parameters* as well. Pace has to do with *rates* of some kinds of recurrent behaviors. Rhythm refers to the *periodicity* of those recurrences. The allocation issues treated here involve not rates or periodicities but *durations*. Questions of developmental cycles deal with *ordered sequences*. System continuity and change processes refer to multiple-featured *temporal patterns of system states* over some specifiable *interval* of time. Temporal scale—a kind of sixth superfacet—refers to the scope of the *time period* (and along with it, the size of the social unit) that is the focus of any given analysis.

These facets of time, though not exhaustive, together subsume much of the temporal material that gets attention currently within the substantive domain of social psychology. Together, also, they allow room for many different conceptions of time—as linear or cyclic, as holistic or atomistic, as homogeneous or differentiated and epochal, as involving succession or extension/duration, as necessarily singular or potentially multiple, and as abstract and absolute or concrete and relative to the point and processes of observation. Such alternative and multiple conceptions of time, and the conflicts they potentially produce, were discussed briefly in the preceding section of this chapter (and are discussed in more detail in McGrath & Kelly, 1986). I turn now to a brief discussion of some of the areas of research that are not reflected in the chapters of this book and that have received less research attention than their importance merits.

A Research Agenda for Building a Social Psychology of Time

Each of the chapters of this book offers some suggestions for research that would advance our understanding of the role of time in human lives. In each case, those research suggestions extend and expand the topics addressed in that chapter and closely related areas of study. But there are a number of temporal topics that are not addressed in the chapters of this book at all, or are addressed less fully than their importance would warrant. The final section of this concluding chapter is devoted, therefore, to some suggested areas of research that seem fruitful ones to pursue if we are, collectively, to develop a full-fledged "social psychology of time."

Cognitive Processes and the Experience of Time

One very fertile area for research involving temporal matters is on time and cognitive processes. Those temporal issues received far less attention in this book than their importance warrants. The chapters in this book only begin to touch the complexities of temporal perception, and of how people experience time and judge its duration.

One area that has a long history of study within psychology is the "psychophysics of time," or study of judgments of the passage of time. Doob (1971), Ornstein (1969), and McGrath and Kelly (1986), among others, have reviewed some of the classic work on psychophysics of time. Each of those reviews proposes a model for understanding the vast and complex literature on judgments of the duration of time in passing and of past times. The McGrath and Kelly (1986) model combines the long-held idea of a psychological clock (or counter) with some ideas from current models of social cognition (e.g., a work space and long-term storage "bins") (e.g., Wyer & Srull, 1980). But their model of time judgments has not been tested. Experimental research to explore the parameters of that model potentially could shed much light on those long-puzzling issues.

Over and above the question of judgments of passage of time, there are many other issues involving temporal orientations, conceptions, perceptions, and experience that have been paid only limited attention. Two of the chapters in this volume (Jones and R. Levine) deal with some aspects of time perceptions and experience. So does Nuttin (1985), Warner (1979, 1984), and Kelly (Kelly & McGrath, 1985; McGrath & Kelly, 1986). But these contributions also only scratch the surface regarding how multiple time conceptions play a part in day-to-day life, and what conflicts they sometimes pose. Those issues, too, deserve much more research exploration than they have yet received.

Entrainment and Other Rhythmic Processes in Groups

The chapters in this book by Warner and by Kelly bear on the idea of entrainment of rhythms of behavior both within and across individuals. Earlier work by Chapple (1970), Jaffe and Feldman (1970), Dabbs (1983), and others, as well as some earlier work by contributors to this book (Kelly & McGrath, 1985; McGrath & Kelly, 1986; Warner, 1979, 1984) are part of this research effort as well, although not all of those authors made extensive use of the entrainment concept.

The evidence about entrainment thus far suggests that human social behavior, like human physiological behavior, is replete with oscillatory or rhythmic processes; that these do indeed mutually entrain to one another and to certain strong external pacers; and that such entrainment processes play a major role in shaping the when, if not also the what, of human behavior (Chapple, 1970; Dabbs, 1983; Jaffe & Feldstein, 1970; McGrath, Kelly, & Machatka, 1984; Moore-Ede, Sulzman, & Fuller, 1982; Warner, 1979, 1984). We need more research on these issues of rhythms of behavior—even though such research is difficult and costly—because these issues are central to our understanding of the role of time in human experience.

Time, Task Types, and Task Performance

Another set of issues that is given less attention here than befits its logical place in the time domain has to do with how time interacts with features of the task and situation to influence group task performance and member reactions. The Freedman and Edwards chapter, as well as the Kelly chapter, explore temporal factors in task performance. But there is much more to be done than that.

In some of their earlier work, McGrath and Kelly (1986; Kelly & McGrath, 1985) have proposed major interaction effects of time limits and task type, not only for task performance parameters but also for features of the interaction process. Freedman and Edwards suggest such effects as well, as does some prior work by Dabbs (1983). Some research to explore those relations for a systematic set of task types (McGrath, 1984) is already underway (McGrath, Futoran, & Kelly, 1986). This, too, is a very fruitful area for advancing our understanding of temporal factors in human behavior.

Time and Group Development

The chapter in this book by Moreland and J. Levine presents an agenda for two crucial areas of temporal research: temporal factors in group development and temporal factors in member socialization. But even their ambitious agenda leaves many parts of those and related questions untouched. For example, how can we integrate what Wicker and King have to say about temporal features of the life cycles of behavior settings with the Moreland-Levine formulation about group development?

Furthermore, other recent research (Gersick, 1984; McGrath, 1988) raises very interesting questions about the role of time in the ongoing processes—as well as in the developmental patterns—of task groups. Gersick, for example, found that each of a number of natural groups working with a specific preset task and a preset time limit made drastic and dramatic changes *at almost exactly the middle of the group's life span* (even though the different groups had quite different life spans, varying from a few days to several months). That work and other research suggests that events within the first few minutes of the "lifetimes" of some natural groups have rather major effects for group activities and outcomes much later in the groups' lives. McGrath (1988) has proposed a time-based theory of group functioning that tries to take into account the group's simultaneous conduct of task production, group maintenance, and member support functions. These matters need much more research.

Allocation of Time Across Activity Spheres and Other Temporal Interactions Between Work and Nonwork Settings

Another set of important time-based issues is concerned with how people allocate their time over activities and activity spheres. Robinson's chapter tackles this problem at a macro-system descriptive level. Wicker and King's chapter touches on these issues at the somewhat less-macro level of behavior settings. Freedman and Edwards, and Kelly, deal with these issues at the still more micro level of individuals and small groups performing specific tasks.

The time-diary method that Robinson champions in Chapter 7 is a fairly well established, direct, and systematic way to document such allocation of time. It nevertheless has some problematic features, as he points out. For example, in some uses, it has been assumed that self-reported time allocation represents an index of *activity preference*. But this connection is apparently less straightforward than we might have assumed, as indicated, for example, by Robinson's findings that people increased their allocation of time to TV watching but did not increase their preference for or enjoyment of that activity. Furthermore, while such time-diary data can track patterns and changes in allocations of time between work and nonwork spheres, such patterns are much more complex than they seem. We can get much better "conceptual leverage" on them by using time diaries in combination with other methods—depth interviews, observations, and even experiments (see Freedman & Edwards).

The whole question of allocation of time across life spheres raises a number of other topical areas. There are potentially crucial temporal issues in such topics as absence from (or participation in) some behavior settings of special interest (e.g., the workplace); role conflict, stress, and work overload associated with dual-career couples or with individuals who have heavy responsibilities in both work and family roles; and questions of contributions to household and child care tasks by various members of families. Along similar lines, McGrath, Kelly, and Machatka (1984) have studied some questions regarding effects of unusual work shifts on the nonwork lives of workers and their families. More is needed along those lines as well.

Temporal Issues in Organizations

Of the chapters in this book, only the Moreland and J. Levine treatments of group development and the Wicker and King treatment of behavior settings address temporal issues relevant to behavior in organizations. Elsewhere (McGrath & Kelly, 1986; McGrath & Rotchford, 1983), I have identified three key temporal issues in organizations (temporal uncertainty, temporal conflict, and time scarcity), and three major organizational responses to them (synchronization, scheduling, and allocation). Those responses pose problems for individuals within such organizations (role ambiguity, role conflict, and role overload), and those individuals' responses may pose further problems for the organization (McGrath & Kelly, 1986; McGrath & Rotchford, 1983).

Other recent research (e.g., Gersick, 1984) also deals with some of these issues, but that, too, only begins to scratch the surface of this problem area. These issues deserve much more research consideration than they have yet been given.

Studies of Time in Relation to Our Methods

Perhaps the most important temporal issues that are given little or no treatment—in this book and in the field—are issues involving the crucial role of time in our research methodology. One crucial temporal relation (that cause precedes effect) is essential to the Humean causal logic that underlies our experimental methodology; and another—a temporal interval of more or less specified duration—is crucial to our positivistic concepts of causal processes. Furthermore, time factors play a very important role in the procedures by which we explore the validity of our research strategies and study designs. Time orders and intervals play a central role in virtually all of the major research strategies (laboratory experiments, field studies, surveys, and the like), and a known time relation between variables of interest is essential to the interpretive logic of all of our study designs.

At another level of consideration, time factors are central in our quest for reliable and valid measures. Temporal simultaneity and succession is at the heart of virtually all definitions of reliability-testing operations; and techniques for assessing the validity of instruments also hinge on time orders and intervals. Finally, time plays a key role in our notions of the flow of events and the operation of the systems that are the subjects of our study.

There is virtually no consideration of these methodological issues anywhere in this volume. That is the case, also, for almost all other volumes in social psychology—including textbooks on research methods. Gergen (1973) raised some of these issues, and various contributions in the Gergen and Gergen (1984) volume touch upon some of them. McGrath and Kelly (1986) devote one chapter of their book to temporal issues in research methodology. A book now in press by those authors (Kelly & McGrath, 1988) is devoted wholly to the systematic exploration of these temporal issues within our methodology and some ways we can try to cope with them. But there is little else currently available on the topic, and much more is surely needed. This is perhaps the biggest single deficiency of the social psychological literature in relation to temporal matters, and it is a deficiency that constrains research in that discipline in the most pervasive ways. Therefore, one essential feature in the development of a meaningful social psychology of time is the clarification, if not the resolution, of many of these methodological issues.

Concluding Comments

I have tried, in this final chapter, to describe some major conceptual themes within a social psychology of time, and then to sketch out some of the main areas in which research on time is much needed and could profitably be pursued. All of this chapter—and for that matter, all the chapters of this book and the research programs upon which they are based—presuppose *that time is important in human life, and, therefore, that time is important in social psychology*. In large part, these materials also are built on the premise that a concerted effort to develop a "social psychology of time" is both feasible and desirable.

I hope the preceding material in this book has made the case for the importance of time in our lives, for the negative consequences of past neglect of temporal matters in our field, and for the consequent need for increased attention to the myriad temporal factors that inhabit the social psychology of everyday life. I hope, too, that the preceding material has conveyed some of the excitement and fun that all of the contributors have experienced in their research on these issues. To some degree, their work is at an intellectual frontier, and we are all convinced that this "new territory" will prove to be both exciting and rewarding to explore much more fully than has been done to date. I hope, too, that this material has helped fulfill one final purpose of this book: to induce many other social psychological researchers to join us in our explorations of the fascinating topic of time.

REFERENCES

Altman, I., & Rogoff, B. (1987) World views in psychology: Trait, interactionist, organismic, and transactionalist approaches. In D. Stokols & I. Altman (Eds.), *Handbook of environmental psychology*. New York: John Wiley.

Altman, I., Vinsel, A. M., & Brown, B. B. (1981). Dialectic conceptions in social psychology: An application to social penetration and privacy regulation. In L. Berkowitz (Ed.), *Advances in experimental social psychology* (Vol. 14). New York: Academic Press.

Chapple, E. D. (1970). *Culture and biological man: Explorations in behavioral anthropology*. New York: Holt, Rinehart & Winston.

Dabbs, J. (1985) *Fourier analysis and the rhythm of conversation*. (ERIC Document Reproduction Service No. ED 222 959)

Doob, L. W. (1971). *Patterning of time*. New Haven, CT: Yale University Press.

Gergen, K. (1973). Social psychology as history. *Journal of Personality and Social Psychology, 26,* 509-520.

Gergen, K., & Gergen, M. (Eds.). (1984). *Historical social psychology*. Hillsdale, NJ: Erlbaum.

Gersick, C. G. (1984). *The life cycles of ad hoc groups: Time, transitions, and learning in teams*. Unpublished dissertation, Yale University, New Haven, CT.

Jaffe, J., & Feldstein, S. (1970). *Rhythms of dialogue*. New York: Academic Press.

Kelly, J. R., & McGrath, J. E. (1985). Effects of time limits and task types on task performance and interaction of four-person groups. *Journal of Personality and Social Psychology, 49,* 395-407.

Kelly, J. R., & McGrath, J. E. (1988). *On time and method*. Newbury Park, CA: Sage.

McGrath, J. E. (1984). *Groups: Interaction and performance*. Englewood Cliffs, NJ: Prentice-Hall.

McGrath, J. E. (1988). Toward a time based theory of functional groups. In R. McGlynn (Ed.), *Groups and organizations* [Conference]. Texas Tech University, Lubbock.

McGrath, J. E., Futoran, G. C., & Kelly, J. R. (1986) *Complex temporal patterning in interaction and task performance: A report of progress in a program of research on the social psychology of time* (Technical Report 86-1). Urbana: University of Illinois, Research Program on Social Psychology of Time.

McGrath, J. E., & Kelly, J. R. (1986). *Time and human interaction: Toward a social psychology of time*. New York: Guilford.

McGrath, J. E., Kelly, J. R., & Machatka, D. E. (1984). The social psychology of time: Entrainment of behavior in social and organizational settings. In S. Oskamp (Ed.), *Applied social psychology annual* (Vol. 5). Newbury Park, CA: Sage.

McGrath, J. E., & Rotchford, N. L. (1983). Time and behavior in organizations. In L. Cummings & B. Staw (Eds.), *Research in organizational behavior* (Vol. 5, pp. 57-101). Greenwich, CT: JAI Press.

Moore-Ede, M. C., Sulzman, F. M., & Fuller, C. A. (1982). *The clocks that time us*. Cambridge, MA: Harvard University Press.

Nuttin, J. (1985) *Future time perspective and motivation: Theory and research method*. Hillsdale, NJ: Leuven University Press, Lawrence Erlbaum.

Ornstein, R. E. (1969). *On the experience of time*. Middlesex, England: Penguin.

Warner, R. M. (1979). Periodic rhythms in conversational speech. *Language and Speech, 22,* 381-396.

Warner, R. M. (1984). *Rhythm as an organizing principle in social interaction: Evidence of cycles in behavior and physiology*. Unpublished manuscript, Dover, NH.

Wyer, R. S., Jr., & Srull, T. K. (1980). The processing of social stimulus information: A conceptual integration. In R. Hastie, T. M. Ostrom, E. B. Ebbesen, R. S. Wyer, Jr., D. L. Hamilton, & D. E. Carlston (Eds.), *Person memory: The cognitive basis of social perception* (pp. 227-500). Hillsdale, NJ: Erlbaum.

About the Authors

IRWIN ALTMAN is a Distinguished Professor in the department of psychology at the University of Utah. He received his Ph.D. in social psychology from the University of Maryland in 1957. His areas of interest include study of the temporal and environmental aspects of interpersonal relationships. Recent work has focused on cross-cultural aspects of home environments.

DONALD R. EDWARDS is currently a Ph.D. candidate in psychology at the University of Toronto. His major interests are in the effects of time pressure and psychometrics.

JONATHAN L. FREEDMAN is a professor in the psychology department at the University of Toronto. He received his Ph.D. from Yale, and taught at Stanford and Columbia Universities. His major interests are in the effects of stress, decision making (especially in legal situations), children's conceptions of money, and the reverse incentive effect.

LOIS M. HAGGARD is a Ph.D. candidate in the psychology department at the University of Utah. She has conducted research on privacy regulation and neighborhood social relationships, and is interested in applying models of psychological privacy to wilderness situations.

JAMES M. JONES is Professor of Psychology at the University of Delaware. He earned his Ph.D. from Yale University (1970). His major current interests grow out of his work on the cultural basis of prejudice and racism.

JANICE R. KELLY is an assistant professor in the department of psychological sciences at Purdue University. She received her Ph.D. from the University of Illinois in 1957. She is coauthor of two books with Joseph E. McGrath: *Time and Human Interaction* (1956, Guilford Press) and *On Time and Method* (1988, Sage). Her interests include the social psychology of time, temporal patterns in group performance and interaction, and the effects of mood states on dyadic interaction.

JEANNE C. KING is a Ph.D. candidate in the psychology department at the Claremont Graduate School. Her specialty is organizational psychology. Her research interests include changes in organizational populations, and policy and social psychological aspects of newly established businesses.

JOHN M. LEVINE is Professor of Psychology at the University of Pittsburgh. He received his Ph.D. from the University of Wisconsin at Madison. His current research interests include small group processes, particularly socialization and majority/minority influence; social comparison of abilities and outcomes; and motivational determinants of computer-based skill learning.

ROBERT V. LEVINE is Professor of Psychology at California State University, Fresno, where he was recently awarded a Meritorious Performance and Professional Promise Award. He received his Ph.D. in 1974 from New York University. He has served as a Latin American Teaching Fellow at the Universidade Federal Fluminense in Niteroi, Brazil, and has traveled across four continents to study cross-cultural differences in the pace of life.

JOSEPH E. McGRATH is Professor of Psychology at the University of Illinois, Urbana. He received his Ph.D. in social psychology from the University of Michigan in 1955. His research interests include small group processes, social and psychological factors in stress, research methodology, and the social psychology of time.

RICHARD L. MORELAND is Associate Professor of Psychology at the University of Pittsburgh. He received his Ph.D. in social psychology from the University of Michigan. His general interest in small groups has led him to study some of the inevitable changes that occur in such groups over time. These changes include the formation, development, and termination of small groups, as well as socialization processes within small groups.

DIANA OXLEY is currently a research scientist in the Research, Demonstration and Policy Division of Bank Street College, New York City. She received her Ph.D. in environmental psychology at Arizona State University, and then completed a postdoctoral traineeship in the area of social/environmental psychology at the University of Utah, where she collaborated with Irwin Altman and Carol Werner in the development of transactional approaches to the study of homes and neighborhoods. She conducts action research in educational settings and is primarily interested in the social organizational context of schooling.

JOHN P. ROBINSON is Professor of Sociology and Director of the Survey Research Center at the University of Maryland, College Park. He received his Ph.D. from the University of Michigan. He is the author of several books and journal articles on the public's use of time and leisure, including *How Americans Use Time*, *Public Participation in the Arts*, and *American Recreation Trends*. His other research interests include the effects of mass communication, trends in public opinion, social measurement, and public policy uses of social science data. He is currently directing the Americans' Use of Time Project and other national surveys tracking changes in the public's use of time and leisure.

DANIEL STOKOLS is Professor of Social Ecology at the University of California, Irvine. He received his Ph.D. from the University of North Carolina at Chapel Hill. His research and teaching interests are in the areas of environmental, social and health psychology, community planning, and environmental design. He edited the *Handbook of Environmental Psychology* (with Irwin Altman); he edited a research monograph on environmental psychology titled *Perspectives on Environment and Behavior: Theory, Research, and Applications* (Plenum Press, 1977); and he coauthored *Behavior, Health, and Environmental Stress* with Sheldon Cohen, Gary Evans, and David Krantz (Plenum Press, 1976). His current research focuses on the effects of physical and social conditions within work environments on employees' health, motivation, and performance.

REBECCA WARNER is Associate Professor in the psychology department at the University of New Hampshire. She received her

Ph.D. degree from Harvard University in 1978. Her research interests include the statistical analysis of social interaction rhythms, physiological changes that occur during social interactions, and the effect of expressive behaviors on person perceptions.

CAROL M. WERNER is a professor in the psychology department at the University of Utah. She received her Ph.D. from Ohio State University in 1973. She is interested in privacy regulation, and conducts research on accessibility/inaccessibility mechanisms. She is also interested in environment/behavior relationships and the worldviews and temporal qualities that they reflect.

ALLAN W. WICKER is Professor of Psychology at the Claremont Graduate School, Claremont, California. He received his Ph.D. from the University of Kansas and has held teaching positions at the University of Wisconsin, Milwaukee, and the University of Illinois, Urbana. He has been a visiting professor at Cornell University and at the University of Tuebingen, Federal Republic of Germany. His specialty is ecological psychology, an area to which he has contributed a textbook (*An Introduction to Ecological Psychology*) and a number of journal articles. His current research interest is in how behavior settings come into being, adapt, and terminate.

NOTES